SCARECROW STUDIES IN YOUNG ADULT LITERATURE
Series Editor: Patty Campbell

Scarecrow Studies in Young Adult Literature is intended to continue the body of critical writing established in Twayne's Young Adult Authors Series and to expand it beyond single-author studies to explorations of genres, multicultural writing, and controversial issues in Young Adult (YA) reading. Many of the contributing authors of the series are among the leading scholars and critics of adolescent literature, and some are YA novelists themselves.

The series is shaped by its editor, Patty Campbell, who is a renowned authority in the field, with a thirty-year background as critic, lecturer, librarian, and teacher of YA literature. Patty Campbell was the 2001 winner of the ALAN Award, given by the Assembly on Adolescent Literature of the National Council of Teachers of English for distinguished contribution to YA literature. In 1989 she was the winner of the American Library Association's Grolier Award for distinguished service to young adults and reading.

1. *What's So Scary about R. L. Stine?* by Patrick Jones, 1998.
2. *Ann Rinaldi: Historian and Storyteller*, by Jeanne M. McGlinn, 2000.
3. *Norma Fox Mazer: A Writer's World*, by Arthea J. S. Reed, 2000.
4. *Exploding the Myths: The Truth about Teens and Reading*, by Marc Aronson, 2001.
5. *The Agony and the Eggplant: Daniel Pinkwater's Heroic Struggles in the Name of YA Literature*, by Walter Hogan, 2001.
6. *Caroline Cooney: Faith and Fiction*, by Pamela Sissi Carroll, 2001.
7. *Declarations of Independence: Empowered Girls in Young Adult Literature, 1990–2001*, by Joanne Brown and Nancy St. Clair, 2002.
8. *Lost Masterworks of Young Adult Literature*, by Connie S. Zitlow, 2002.
9. *Beyond the Pale: New Essays for a New Era*, by Marc Aronson, 2003.
10. *Orson Scott Card: Writer of the Terrible Choice*, by Edith S. Tyson, 2003.
11. *Jacqueline Woodson: "The Real Thing,"* by Lois Thomas Stover, 2003.
12. *Virginia Euwer Wolff: Capturing the Music of Young Voices*, by Suzanne Elizabeth Reid, 2003.

Jacqueline Woodson

"The Real Thing"

Lois Thomas Stover

*Scarecrow Studies in
Young Adult Literature, No. 11*

The Scarecrow Press, Inc.
Lanham, Maryland, and Oxford
2003

SCARECROW PRESS, INC.

Published in the United States of America
by Scarecrow Press, Inc.
A wholly owned subsidiary of
The Rowman & Littlefield Publishing Group, Inc.
4501 Forbes Boulevard, Suite 200, Lanham, Maryland 20706
www.scarecrowpress.com

PO Box 317
Oxford
OX2 9RU, UK

British Library Cataloguing in Publication Information Available

Library of Congress Cataloging-in-Publication Data

Stover, Lois T.
 Jacqueline Woodson : "the real thing" / Lois Thomas Stover.
  p. cm. — (Scarecrow studies in young adult literature ; 11)
 Includes bibliographical references and index.
 ISBN 0-8108-4857-0 (alk. paper)
 1. Woodson, Jacqueline—Criticism and interpretation. 2. Young adult
fiction, American—History and criticism. 3. Women and
literature—United States—History—20th century. 4. African Americans
in literature. I. Title. II. Series.
PS3573.O64524 Z87 2003
813'.54—dc21

                                                        2003009881

⊗™ The paper used in this publication meets the minimum requirements of
American National Standard for Information Sciences—Permanence of
Paper for Printed Library Materials, ANSI/NISO Z39.48-1992.
Manufactured in the United States of America.

To Amanda, Karly, and Toshi, and all strong girls everywhere who are growing into courageous young women.

With thanks to David for his support and belief, to Patty Campbell for offering me the incredible opportunity to work on this project, to Jacqueline Woodson for her gracious, open, and welcoming response to the project, and to her editors—Wendy Lamb, Dianne Hess, and Nancy Paulsen—for their contributions, as well as to the Faculty Writing Group for their editorial insights, and to the Faculty Development Committee and the Educational Studies Department at St. Mary's College of Maryland for allowing me the time the project required.

~

Contents

Preface

I was first introduced to Jacqueline Woodson by a student, a twenty-year-old young woman who stumbled onto Woodson's novel *I Hadn't Meant to Tell You This* almost by accident. I had just returned to class after having heard Woodson speak at a conference of ALAN, the Assembly on Literature for Adolescents of the National Council of Teachers of English. I had my huge bag of ALAN free books with me, which I showed off to my children and young adult literature students, inviting them to borrow. I hadn't read the Woodson title at that point, which was one of the titles included in the bag of books publishers prepared for conference attendees, but the next day my student called me and asked for more. As someone who'd experienced the difficulties of growing up biracial in the United States, being a combination of Native American and African-American, she was thrilled to have discovered a work that spoke to her, to her struggles over the years to forge friendships across racial lines, to the guilt she sometimes felt for being, while relatively dark-skinned, from an economically stable and fairly affluent home. I was thrilled with her response, having been impressed at the ALAN conference by Woodson's directness, her articulate and honest ability to discuss her own experiences, and what she tries to accomplish as an author. I sat down and read *I Hadn't Meant to Tell You*

This, about the friendship between Marie, upper middle class and black, and Lena, poor and white, who, it turns out, hides the fact that she has experienced abuse at the hands of her father throughout most of the novel. Hungry for more, I then picked up *From the Notebooks of Melanin Sun*, about an African-American teenaged boy who has to come to terms not only with the fact that his mother is a lesbian, but that she has a white partner—and I was hooked.

My affection for Woodson's work has only deepened as I have plunged into reading her novels for young adults, her children's picture books, her essays and National Public Radio commentaries, her adult novel, and her short stories. Her works often make me cry with their poignant, truthful presentations of many of life's difficult realities, but her characters give me joy and hope because they find strength to face those adversities and to become more true to themselves in the process.

I was fortunate to meet Jacqueline Woodson when she invited me to her home in the Park Slope section of Brooklyn for a morning of conversation on September 27, 2002. Woodson and her dog, a German Shepherd mix named Maus, greeted me at their door and welcomed me into the lower-level apartment of a brownstone house. Woodson was wearing jeans and a turtleneck and she was laughing. As soon as I stepped across the threshold, she told me to follow her into the kitchen where she showed me a picture on the computer that sits in a tiny alcove off the large airy space, its hardwood floors lined with bookshelves. A friend who works for CNN had forwarded the photo to her, and it made me smile too—President Bush was sitting next to a young girl who was reading out loud, promoting literacy, and Bush also held a book, but his was upside down!

After sharing the irony of the photo, Woodson's inherent graciousness became apparent as she fixed me a huge cup of rich coffee and brought out muffins for munching. She curled herself up into an overstuffed armchair in the living room and settled down to talk with me about her life and her work, about her writing process, and about being a new mother. Throughout this book, quotations from the author came from that interview and our subsequent telephone conversation, unless otherwise noted. Over the past few months, Woodson has corresponded with me via e-mail, continuing to answer my questions and to share biographical details. She is a warm, passionate, generous woman who creates characters whom readers know will be successful in their struggles to find themselves and their places in the world because she herself continues on her own journey to do so.

Woodson's seventh grade English teacher returned her first story to her with the comment, "You are the real thing."[1] In this volume I will be exploring how Woodson became "the real thing," why she deserves to be acknowledged as one of the finest writers for young adults today, who her literary mentors have been, and how her family history has helped to shape her as an artist, beginning with the success of her first novel, *Last Summer with Maizon*. Its appearance in 1990 marked Woodson's arrival on the literary scene for young adults. Over the past decade, Woodson has made a steady contribution to the field, providing quality literature for both younger and older adolescents and tackling difficult themes in the process. Additionally, Woodson has published numerous short stories, essays and commentaries, a novel for adults, and children's picture books. In 1994, she compiled *A Way Out of No Way: Writings About Growing Up Black in America*, a collection of excerpts of writers from Baldwin to Bambura. These writers inspired her as a young reader and continue to be role models for her as she herself uses the art of writing to provide a "way out of no way" for other young readers, pointing a "beautiful black finger toward a holy, holy place" (p. 3).

As Woodson has taken an increasing number of risks with her themes, she has also continued to develop as an artist. In *If You Come Softly*, Woodson experiments with alternating narrative voices. In her work in general, Woodson uses the lyrical language of her own childhood, of her grandmother's home in South Carolina. *Locomotion* experiments with the use of poetry by the first-person narrator to unfold the story. Her characters all have distinctive voices, and through these voices they convey to readers that sense of struggle and triumph for which so many young readers are hungry. Her body of work makes a distinctive contribution to the young adult literary world and clearly demonstrates both the writer's commitment to young adults and her ability to continue to grow as a writer; this volume includes a critical analysis of how Woodson's life and work intertwine and of the themes and her own goals as a writer and artist.

Just before I began writing this critical biography, I finished reading a brand new piece titled "Lorena" by Woodson in an anthology of "first love" short stories. In just a few brief pages, Woodson manages to create two characters who now haunt my mind because of the poignancy of the writing and the tragedy they experience. The fact that the story is about two young women didn't really register until after I turned the last page; the tenderness of their love set against the brutality of their world is what affected me as a reader. As Woodson herself notes,

> I feel compelled to write against stereotypes, hoping people will see that some issues know no color, class, sexuality. . . . I write from the very depth of who I am, and in this place there are all of my identities.[2]

I hope to hook others on this outstanding artist who gives us characters and stories that teach us more about how to negotiate the world on our own while reaching out to others in the process. Here, then, is Jacqueline Woodson, "the real thing."

Notes

1. Judith Hayne, "Jacqueline Woodson," in *Writers for Young Adults: Supplement*, ed. Ted Hipple (New York: Charles Scribner's Sons, 2000), 377–386.

2. "Jacqueline Woodson," in *Contemporary Authors: A Biocritical Guide to Current Writers in Fiction, General Non-fiction, Poetry, Journalism, Drama, Motion Pictures, Television and Other Fields—New Revision Series*, Vol. 87, ed. Scott Peacock (Boston: The Gale Group, 2000), 433–437, 441.

~

Chronology

1963 Born February 12, Columbus, Ohio, into extended family of Jehovah's Witnesses. In May, parents, Jack and Mary Ann, separate; Woodson moves to Greenville, South Carolina, with older brother, Hope, and older sister, Odella, to live with her grandparents.

1965 Mother moves to Bushwick section of New York.

1966 Woodson's sister teaches her to write her own name at age three, and she learns the power of putting words on the page. Roman, their biracial brother, is born in New York (January 1966). Mother returns to South Carolina.

1968 In time for Jackie to start kindergarten, Woodson's mother moves family to New York.

1973 In fifth grade, wins poetry contest with "Tribute to Martin Luther King." Serves as literary editor for the school paper. Still spending summers in South Carolina and actively participating in ministry of Jehovah's Witnesses. Woodson's grandfather dies and shortly thereafter grandmother moves into Woodson's mother's house in Bushwick section of Brooklyn.

1974 Woodson feels defeated when Ford takes over after Nixon's resignation of the presidency; begins writing out her feelings in poems and song lyrics.

1975 In seventh grade writes first short story and her teacher comments, "You are the real thing."

1977–1981 Is cheerleader in high school; dates Donald Douglas, the captain of the basketball team. A teacher advises her to choose a career about which she can be passionate, and she begins to recognize that becoming a writer, which she had often considered doing, is a realistic career goal.

1977–1982 Reads important books, *Daddy Was a Numbers Runner* by Louise Merriweather; *The Bluest Eye* by Toni Morrison; *Ruby* by Rosa Guy; various titles by James Baldwin; *Zeely* by Virginia Hamilton.

1981 Starts Adelphi University in Garden City, New York; pledges Alpha Kappa Alpha sorority. In sophomore year, names herself as "gay" after meeting another queer person and recognizing a great deal of herself in the other woman; in her creative writing class, begins to deepen her sense of self as a writer while exploring her identity as a lesbian.

1985 Receives B.A. in English, with a focus on British literature. Works as editorial associate for children's book packaging company, Kirchoff/Wohlberg. Uses section of manuscript of *Last Summer with Maizon* as part of a standardized test in reading she is working to develop. Agent Liza Voges asks Woodson if she can represent the novel.

1987 Takes creative writing class from Bunny Gable on writing children's books at the New School for Social Research. Editor Bebe Willoughby from Delacorte visits class and buys *Last Summer with Maizon*; she leaves Delacorte, and Wendy Lamb takes over as Woodson's editor shortly thereafter. Stops working a 9–5, though continues to work about thirty to forty hours a week doing freelance writing and word processing to pay the rent. Works briefly as a drama therapist for ten-to-seventeen year olds in East Harlem, many of whom are runaways and homeless.

1990 Is awarded fellowship at the MacDowell Colony, Peterborough, New Hampshire. By this time, has sold the Maizon and Margaret trilogy and is under contract to write *The Dear One*. At this point, stops working full time. Publishes *Last Summer with Maizon*, Delacorte; *Martin Luther King, Jr., and His Birthday*, Silver Burdett.

1991 Publishes *The Dear One*, Delacorte; four pieces that ultimately appear in *Autobiography of a Family Photo* published in fall, 1992 *Kenyon Review*; *Among Good Christian People* with Catherine Gund Saalfield (video, later wins award from American Film Institute).

1991–1992 Residency at the Fine Arts Work Center, Provincetown, Massachusetts; lives in Provincetown until 1994.

1992 Publishes *Maizon at Blue Hill*, Delacorte.

1993 Starts training in the martial art Poekoelan, a form of Indonesian street fighting.

1993 Publishes *Between Madison and Palmetto*, Delacorte. "A Stolen Childhood" in *Essence; Maizon at Blue Hill*, listed on Best Books for Young Adults.

1993–1995 Goddard Master of Fine Arts Writing Program, associate faculty member.

1994 Publishes *Book Chase* (based on *Ghostwriter* television series), Bantam; *Autobiography of a Family Photo*, Dutton; *I Hadn't Meant to Tell You This*, Delacorte. Charlotte Sheedy as Woodson's agent negotiates deal with Putnam (after *Autobiography of a Family Photo*) for four young adult novels and one picture book; Woodson begins working with Nancy Paulsen as editor. Eugene Lang College associate faculty member. Receives *Publisher's Weekly* Award for *I Hadn't Meant To Tell You This*; wins another MacDowell Colony Fellowship. Publishes "Slipping Away" in *Am I Blue? Coming Out from the Silence*.

1995 Vermont College at Norwich University—associate faculty in the Master of Fine Arts program in Writing for Children. *I Hadn't Meant to Tell You This* named a Coretta Scott King Honor Book. Publishes *From the Notebooks of Melanin Sun*, Scholastic; "A Sign of Having Been Here," in *Horn Book*.

1995, 1996 Writer in Residence for National Book Foundation.

1996 Lambda Literary Award for Best Fiction—Best Children's Fiction; named one of "Fifty Best American Authors under 40;" *From the Notebooks of Melanin Sun* named Coretta Scott King Honor Book, listed as ALA Best Books for Young Adults, and ALA Notable Books for Social Studies, CBS/NCSS Notable Children's Trade Books in the field of Social Studies and wins Jane Addams Children's Book Award; Compiles *A Way Out of No Way*, Holt. Publishes "What Has Been Done to Me" in *Go the Way Your Blood Beats*.

1997 Publishes *We Had a Picnic This Sunday Past*, Hyperion; *The House You Pass on the Way*, Delacorte.

1998 Goddaughter, Kali, born. Publishes *If You Come Softly*, Putnam; *Lena*, Delacorte; "Thirteen" in *Queer Thirteen*; "Who Can Tell My Story?" in *Horn Book*.

1999 Publishes "The Other Half of Me" in *Tomorrowland*; "July Saturday" in *Places I Never Meant to Be*; "Common Ground" in *Essence*; "Going to My Room and Closing the Door" in *Speaking of Journals*; NPR Commentaries.

2000 Publishes *Miracle's Boys*, Putnam; "On Earth" in *I Believe in Water*; *Sweet, Sweet Memory*, Hyperion.

2001 Wins the Coretta Scott King Award for *Miracle's Boys*. Publishes *The Other Side*, Putnam; "Beanie" in *Girl's Got Game*; "The Rialto" with Christopher Lynch in *The Color of Absence*; Gay Teens—NPR commentary. *Miracle's Boys* wins the Los Angeles Book Prize.

2002 In March, birth of daughter, Toshi Georgianna. Publishes *Our Gracie Aunt*, Hyperion; "Lorena" in *One Hot Second*; *Hush*, Putnam; *Visiting Day*, Scholastic. *Hush* named National Book Award Finalist.

2003 Publishes *Locomotion*, Putnam.

~

CHAPTER ONE

On Becoming—and Staying—
a Writer

Jacqueline Woodson, not yet forty, has in many ways already "arrived" as an author known for her development of character, her poetic and increasingly spare style, her risk-taking approach to her craft, and her willingness to tackle tough issues in realistic ways. She does so in writing that appeals to a wide variety of audiences. She has published books for middle grade readers, novels for high school readers, children's picture books, and an adult novel. She also writes essays and articles for magazines that vary in format from *Hornbook* to *Essence*. Additionally, she is an award-winning filmmaker for the documentary *Among Good Christian Peoples*, and she has done commentary work for National Public Radio. Since the publication of her first novel, *Last Summer with Maizon* in 1990, Woodson's work in all genres has won critical acclaim, culminating in 2001 when her novel *Miracle's Boys*, published in 2000, won the coveted Coretta Scott King Award.

The Early Years

What is the history of this lively, articulate, engaging woman, and how does her writing and the development of her craft over time reflect her personal development? Jacqueline Woodson was born on February 12, 1963—contrary to some published reports of a 1964 birth date—in Columbus, Ohio, to Mary Ann and Jack Woodson, and was named for her father. Approximately two months after her birth, her parents separated, and Woodson's mother moved to South Carolina with the baby Jacqueline and her two older siblings. Hope, the brother, is the oldest, followed by Odella. The three children stayed in Greenville for several years, cared for by their grandparents, Hope and Grace, while their mother moved to Brooklyn, New York. Woodson and her siblings traveled back and forth to New York until Jackie was about to enter school, living primarily in the south. At that point they moved to the Bushwick section of Brooklyn full time to join their mother and their younger half brother, Roman, who is biracial, the son of a white, Jewish father. For several years, the Woodson children continued to go to South Carolina for the summers, but when their grandfather died, their grandmother also moved to New York, into her daughter's home.

The time spent in Greenville shaped Woodson in several important ways. Her grandmother took her faith as a member of the Jehovah's Witnesses very seriously. While her mother was less religious than the grandmother, and was never baptized as a Witness, as Woodson writes in an NPR commentary, her mom nevertheless "enrolled" all the children in "Witnessing the way one enrolls a loved one into boarding school; packing our bags each summer and sending us tearfully to our grandmother's house down south."[1] For many years, Jackie spent significant hours each week, especially during the summers, engaged in Monday night Bible study, in going door to door "spreading the word of God" and distributing the literature of the church and seeking converts to "the truth" on Saturdays, attending church on Sundays and "ministry school" on Thursdays. As she describes this part of her life, "at the end of the summer, we sat the satchels neatly inside our grandmother's closet, packed up our suitcases, and headed back to New York, where we were allowed to exist religion-free for three seasons."[2] As the children became teenagers, able to argue with their mother in a united front, their mom set them free of that particular aspect of their religion and let them stay in New York for the summer.

There are several characters in Woodson's novels who share this aspect of her family's religious orientation. In particular, the mother in *Hush* becomes devoted to her faith and the community of her own

Kingdom Hall when life is falling apart for her and her family in many other ways, and she imposes that belief structure on her daughters. Interestingly, in spite of Woodson's difficulties with the structures of much of organized religion, those characters who have a strong religious or spiritual orientation are portrayed for the most part with dignity and care by Woodson. Although she is no longer an active Jehovah's Witness, a result in part of the tensions between the values of that faith community and her own sexual orientation and beliefs about religion, she credits her upbringing with providing her with the kind of discipline she brings to bear on her writing. As she puts it, "I think one thing the religion gave me was this really strong meditative ethic which is translated into my writing in terms of being able to sit for long hours, plodding over the same material over and over again."

Jackie's grandmother was the primary caretaker of the family while her mother worked, trying to provide food and a roof over their heads. Unfortunately, there were a number of factors, including Jackie's less than ideal relationship with her mother's boyfriend, that made Jackie's home life at this time less than tranquil.[3] When she was fourteen, her parents reunited, though they subsequently divorced. Because of the somewhat unstable conditions under which Woodson lived as a young child, and knowing how hard her mother had to work to take care of the family, she says she has never had a fear of losing everything, remarking, "I think if I woke up tomorrow and didn't have any money, I would fear losing my family but in terms of material things, I don't have this urge to really hoard or hold on or collect. It's not the *stuff* that's important." This belief that in the higher scheme of things material belongings are not all that important also comes from her training as a Jehovah's Witness as Witnesses are taught to be "in the world, but not of the world."

Many characters throughout the body of Woodson's writing find their way through their losses of both family members and material security into a position of inner strength: from Margaret of the Maizon and Margaret trilogy whose father dies, to Lena, from *I Hadn't Meant to Tell You This* and later *Lena* (1999), whose father abuses her after her mother's death, to Lonnie, the eleven-year-old poet-narrator of *Locomotion*, whose parents die in a fire. In *Hush*, an entire family loses not only all their material belongings but also their identities when the father, a police officer, testifies against fellow officers in return for entry into the federal Witness

Protection program. Woodson is able to show how, individually but also as a family, they are able to come to terms with their new circumstances. Even in her picture books, Woodson reflects her spiritual orientation. In *Sweet, Sweet Memory*, a young child is grieving over the loss of a beloved grandfather, but the story is one of joy and hope as the family finds ways to savor his "sweet, sweet" presence in their lives even after his death.

Woodson herself says, "I feel so grateful to have had both worlds. The south was so lush and so slow-moving and so much about community. The city was thriving and fast-moving and electric."[4] She loved the diversity of her Brooklyn neighborhood, inhabited by Germans, Dominican Republicans, Puerto Ricans, individuals from various Caribbean countries, blacks, Asians, whites. Her books often deal with the need for individuals to reach out to each other across cultural and economic boundaries. As Lena says, "Black, white, it shouldn't make no difference. We all just people here."[5] In the recent picture book *The Other Side*, Woodson shows young children finding ways to break through both emotional and physical boundaries separating whites and blacks when their parents cannot seem to see their way clear to do so, and her own upbringing contributes to her belief in the value of diversity.

Becoming a Writer

Odella, Woodson's older sister, taught her to write her own name at age three. From that moment on, Woodson knew the power of print. In an interview with Jennifer Brown, for *Publisher's Weekly*, Woodson claimed, "I loved the power of that . . . of being able to put a letter on the page and that letter meaning something. It was the physical act of writing for me that happened first,"[6] and she spent hours writing out her whole name: Jacqueline Amanda Woodson. She continues by noting she was not so much enthralled by the telling of stories as she was by "actually having the tools with which to create a *landscape* with words."[7] As Brown observes, all of Woodson's characters inhabit "very detailed physical landscapes,"[8] and this is an aspect of writing with which Woodson became intrigued very early on.

Woodson's first literary success came in fifth grade when her teacher asked the students to write a poem about a hero. Woodson, taking her first few lines from a piece her sister had begun, wrote "A Tribute to

Martin Luther King," and was called to the principal's office for plagia-
rizing. Once cleared of that accusation, the poem won an award. Even
in this small piece, Woodson's attention to issues of race and class, and
to physical landscapes—all later hallmarks of her work—are apparent:

> Black brothers
> black sisters
> all of them were great
> no fear,
> no fright
> but a willingness to fight
> In fine big houses lived the whites and in little old shacks lived the blacks.
> One of them as Martin with a heart of gold, not like the white bigots with
> hearts colder than cold. He fought for peace and freedom too. He fought
> for me and probably for you.[9]

Writing this piece also gave Woodson her first inkling of what it is like
to work with an editor. Her teacher suggested she change one line to
read "not like *some* white bigots," and while she did not really approve
of the substitution, she did go on to make it and win a poetry contest.[10]
She also served as the literary editor of the school magazine and spent
many hours writing poetry and song lyrics.

Woodson's poetry took a political turn when, at nine and ten, she experienced a sense that the U.S. government could betray its people. As
an ardent McGovern supporter, she had been devastated when Nixon
won election to the White House in 1972. But that was nothing compared to what she felt when, after the Watergate trials, Nixon left the
oval office—and Ford took over as president. She had expected that
McGovern would then become the country's leader, and that he would
make Martin Luther King's dream a reality. When this did not happen,
Woodson recalls in her essay "A Sign of Having Been Here," that "the
word *democracy* no longer existed for me. I began to challenge teachers,
and when they couldn't give me the answers, I became sullen, a loner."[11]
She became even more depressed and disconnected from others when
she saw her neighborhood increasingly populated by Vietnam veterans
returning from overseas with their bodies destroyed and addicted to
heroin. As a result, she remembers, "I took this in and didn't react. The
world became a place that didn't welcome me and the people I loved

and in response I stepped outside of the world. From this vantage point, I watched and took note."[12] Her frustration at not finding "people like my people"[13] in the books she had available to her, and at seeing only white faces on the television reinforced her developing sense that she was outside the majority. As time went on, Woodson determined she did not really want to belong to the majority, but she also began to wonder why so many people were—and are—invisible in the world. As a result, Woodson feels "a responsibility to write beyond the systems of oppression in all communities. . . . It is our responsibility to refocus. In the course of refocusing, we may help a child who is coming out or struggling with abuse or with a family or with health to acquire a clearer vision of the world and thereby grow stronger."[14]

Many of Woodson's characters, from all different kinds of backgrounds, struggle against the sense of being "other." Her personal experiences growing up in several different worlds make her very empathetic to these outsiders, as she has long felt herself to be a true outsider. She never truly belonged to either her grandmother's slow-moving southern community, nor to her more fast-paced Brooklyn neighborhood. As a Jehovah's Witness, she was outside the mainstream both in and out of school. In her documentary film *Among Good Christian Peoples*,[15] Woodson confesses that she longed to be Catholic, to go to Catholic school and wear the cool ties and little pleated skirts of many of her neighbors, but instead, she and her siblings dressed as little adults, in cotton print dresses, gloves and lacy socks, and spent Saturdays bearing witness. Coming from an unconventional family, which included a biracial brother, she remembers hungering to find some sense of her own lived experience in books and school texts, and was delighted when as an adolescent she finally came across books such as *Zeely* by Virginia Hamilton, Toni Morrison's *The Bluest Eye* and *Sula*, and novels by authors such as Rosa Guy and James Baldwin.[16] Feeling emotional or even physical pain taught her to detach herself from the world; in difficult situations, she would close her eyes and imagine "I was a million miles away,"[17] a process she calls "tripping." This is a tool she provides to Lena to help her cope with the abuse she experiences. Being both black and gay taught her that there are many people who "believe that no part of me should be in this world."[18]

Woodson's sense of being an outsider found expression first in poems, which were anti-American and anti-Vietnam War in their tone.

But in seventh grade, she tried her hand at a short story, an assignment for her English class. The teacher returned her paper with the words, "You are the real thing!" at the top, and Woodson began to realize that she might have a talent that could serve her well in the future.[19] Then, in high school, her English teacher, Mr. Miller, gave his students a bit of advice that Woodson took to heart. She recalls that he said, "When you choose a career, choose something that you feel passionate about, because you're going to be doing it for the rest of your life,"[20] and she began to believe that making her living as a writer, which she had often considered as a career option, might be a realistic goal.

In high school, on the surface, Woodson appeared to fit into the mainstream. She had a group of close friends, and, like them, she was a cheerleader. She began chasing boys in elementary school, had her first kisses in junior high, and in high school, she remembers, "I definitely had my clique of girls, and I was a cheerleader and dated a basketball player—but it always felt like I was outside watching and never quite belonging."[21] Although she was sexually active and had not admitted to herself that she was gay, she had a sense that she was different in some way from the other girls in her clique. She had a major crush in junior high on a girl named Alina, also a Jehovah's Witness, but a member of a different congregation. Woodson wrote passionate love letters to Alina, but when her girlfriends began dating boys, she changed the name on her letters to a masculine one and tried to fit into the mold.[22] She says that, as a writer, her starting point is always that of the outsider, of the individual who feels him or herself to be "other," watching, wanting to belong, but never feeling fully accepted.[23]

Coming of Age as a Writer

Going to college was, for Woodson, a more traumatic experience than it is for many students. As Jehovah's Witnesses did not, at that point in time, value college and were not convinced of the need for education beyond high school except as it relates to the ministry of their faith, Woodson knew she would be on her own in terms of financing her college years. She applied to Vassar, where she was accepted but not offered any money. She says she really wanted to go to Antioch, a college in Yellow Springs, Ohio, known for an unconventional approach to education and for accepting students from many diverse backgrounds and cultures, but that school only offered her a work study package. So, Adelphi College, in Garden City, New York, is where she landed. It offered an academic scholarship, and its location, close to the city, meant she could work if she had to do so.

By her second term, Jackie also had won a track scholarship. Although she liked to run, because she had a heart murmur, her mother had vetoed her desire to go out for the team during her high school years. In college, she ran the quarter mile, the 200, the 800, the four-by-four relay and the four-by-two relay, as well as cross country. She says she still likes to run, and although she does not have time for it much any more, when she does find herself outside, running, she still wants to race—and win! Woodson has also studied Poekoelan, an Indonesian form of street fighting, and she gave several of her characters her enjoyment of physical activity. Margaret, in *Between Madison and Palmetto*, begins running at her mother's suggestion, and Toswiah, as Evie, in *Hush* uses running as a way to escape the difficulties of her family situation, as a way to feel in control of her body, and as a way to free her mind of her troubles, finding, in the process, a community of friends and a sense of her own inner strength. Jeremiah from *If You Come Softly* has a similar kind of passion for basketball.

"I hated it there," says Woodson of her time at Adelphi. When asked why, she again points to all the ways in which she felt herself to be an outsider. She majored in English, with a focus on British literature, and she is grateful for that education. But her perception of the college was that, as an institution, it was not particularly supportive of people of color. She says, in retrospect, that had the college had more black professors and more courses about people of color, she would not have felt so isolated. As it was, she had one black instructor and took all the courses about blacks in film and blacks in literature that he offered, but never felt there was a community of people like her who could really help her in her own quest for identity. As a result, she decided to join a black sorority, Alpha Kappa Alpha, known for "its affection for light-skinned black women and for its devotion to black men."[24] While she did not truly fit into the mold, particularly after she named herself as gay and began talking openly with her sorority sisters about her white lover, she did find, in the sorority, a place where she felt accepted as a black woman. As she recalls, "I pledged because I wanted to spend time with black women, wanted a connection, wanted, again, to belong."[25]

It was in the creative writing class that Woodson began exploring her emerging sense of self as a writer and lesbian. There, she began this part of her life journey by using third-person narratives, which gave her a distance from the subject, to explore the theme of sexuality, remembering that writing in third person gave her a sense of freedom to write about anything she wanted. In that smaller community, which valued the writing and the writer's craft above the content and theme, and where she was accepted for all of herself because of her commitment to writing, she was able to start to work out her feelings and to realize that she did not want to live dishonestly.

Again, the kind of isolation Woodson experienced as a student at Adelphi finds expression in her ability to write poignantly about characters who find themselves in less than welcoming environments. Maizon, in *Maizon at Blue Hill*, is one of only five black women at an exclusive boarding school in Connecticut. Far from her Brooklyn roots, Maizon has to decide whether the education she can receive at that institution is worth losing her sense of self. Later, Staggerlee from *The House You Pass on the Way*, is bothered by her community's lack of acceptance of her biracial family. Ellie and Jeremiah from *If You Come Softly* both find themselves out of place in a new school where they, nevertheless, manage to connect with each other across color lines. And Toswiah/Evie from *Hush*, as well as characters who populate Woodson's body of short stories, and even Lonnie, from *Locomotion* struggle to fit in, to retain a sense of identity in the face of societal realities that can undercut that sense of self.

Finding a Voice as Writer

Woodson began working on the manuscript that later became *Last Summer with Maizon* while at Adelphi, but upon graduation in 1985, she had to go to work to support herself. She took a job with Kirchoff/Wohlberg, a children's book packaging company. Located in Manhatten, Kirchoff/Wohlberg puts together textbooks and textbook series for major publishers, packaging them and then letting the publisher do the publicity and then getting them adopted for school use. Woodson was working on a reading test for the company, part of the California standardized reading assessments, and decided to use a section from *Last Summer with Maizon* as one of the text selections. Liza Pulitzer-Voges saw the passage and asked where it was from. When Woodson explained that she had written it and that it was part of a novel, Liza asked if she could work as Woodson's agent and attempt to find a publisher for the book. It went first to Harper, who kept the book for six months, finally sending back a lengthy editorial letter with many, many revision suggestions that might make it acceptable for publication. But Woodson was impatient and angry with the company for keeping the book so long, and did not agree with many of the suggested changes.

Meanwhile, in 1987, Woodson enrolled in a children's book writing class taught by Bunny Gable at the New School of Social Research.[26] Serendipitously, Bebe Willoughby, an editor at Delacorte, happened to be sitting in on the class on the night that Bunny read from Woodson's work. Willoughby asked to see the whole manuscript, and Woodson had Liza send it to her. Willougby bought it, and Woodson's career was launched.

However, Woodson could not yet afford to write full time, so she continued working for Kirchoff/Wohlberg for a time, moving to California with her housemate, Linda Villarosa. Woodson stayed on the West Coast for about nine months but found it difficult to write there, dislocated from her family, friends, and writing support network. So she returned to Brooklyn and began doing word processing to earn a living, while devoting much of her time to her own writing. As she describes her life at that time, "Mostly I would word process from four to midnight, and write during the day, and you know, mostly I had more than one job to pay the rent."

For one of those other jobs, Woodson worked with homeless and runaway adolescents. A friend of hers had started an umbrella organization for people who are HIV-positive called Iris House, and a part of the organization was designed to serve teens in difficulty. Lois, the friend, asked Woodson if she would want to try her hand at doing drama and art activities with them, and Woodson agreed to get involved. However, she "realized it was so emotionally exhausting that I didn't have any energy for writing." But, her experiences with those young adults influenced her writing in several ways. She says that some of the voices of her characters, the language of young people, comes from listening to them on the job. In particular, Rebecca from *The Dear One*, who is a pregnant fifteen-year-old from an impoverished family derived from Woodson's involvement with troubled teens through drama and art therapy.

The success of the first Maizon book helped Woodson win a place at the prestigious MacDowell Writers' Colony from 1990 to 1991. Writers' colonies, in general, are designed to provide writers with the space and time to write by giving them the freedom from attention to the routines of daily life. At MacDowell, Woodson lived with other writers in a rambling old house where she ate breakfast and dinner, but during the day, she had her own cabin in the woods, complete with fireplace and stained glass windows, where she could write, uninterrupted. Lunch was delivered in a basket to her front door, but the delivery person did not even knock to announce its presence. When she got hungry, Woodson would open the door and find her food waiting for her. She reveled in the solitude by day and the company of other writers by night. While there, Woodson thinks she did some of the writing for *Maizon at Blue Hill*, published in 1992, and she began working on another novel that ultimately did not go anywhere, though parts of it she published as short stories in *The Kenyon Review*, and these later formed the basis for her adult novel, *Autobiography of a Family Photo*.

Bebe Willoughby, the Delacorte editor who had signed Woodson, left the company shortly after negotiating the contract with Woodson, turning the manuscript over to Wendy Lamb for editing. The partnership with Wendy Lamb at Delacorte turned out to be exactly what Woodson needed at that point to help her hone her skills as a writer. Lamb recalls being "thrilled" to take on the manuscript, saying, "I just really liked the friendship between the two girls. That friendship spoke to me because of the honesty of it."[27] Although she no longer works with Lamb, Woodson considers her to be "an amazing editor." One of Lamb's gifts to Woodson was that she freed the author to write about what she knew. Woodson recalls beginning to write the novel that was published in 1991 as *The Dear One*, which is about a pregnant teenager from Harlem who is sent by her mother to stay with old friends from college, in a wealthy Pennsylvania suburb, until the baby arrives. While there, Rebecca is cared for by a lesbian couple, and both Rebecca and Feni, the twelve-year-old who now has to share her room with this impoverished city girl, confront the realities of class distinctions. Woodson was nervous, thinking these issues were too provocative for a young adult novel, but she admitted her fears to Lamb who replied by saying, "You can do anything you want." Woodson felt that Lamb had just "opened up the world of literature for me."

Additionally, Lamb had the ability to help Woodson truly shape a manuscript. According to the author, when she would first give a story to her editor, it was likely to be very "raggedy." Lamb would give very specific comments, such as "Your voice is too adult here" or "You've got this action going on offstage, but you need to move it ONstage"[28] with advice about how to proceed. Woodson reflects that Lamb "had such a way of cleaning it [a manuscript] up, helping me to see how my voice could come through, and I felt like by the end of the process these manuscripts had a lot of integrity and they were mine. It wasn't like Wendy was writing them; she just had a way of putting slits into the manuscript so I could see into it better."

As Woodson's success as a writer grew, she was able to stop taking temporary positions. In 1991, she won a place at another artists' colony, the Fine Arts Work Center, in Provincetown, Massachusetts. That fellowship was only seven months long, but Woodson ended up staying in the town for much longer, finally moving back to the city in 1994. Her time in Massachusetts was productive; while living there, she was writing *The Dear One*, *Maizon at Blue Hill*, *Between Madison and Palmetto*, *The Book Chase*, part of the "Ghostwriter" television series, her adult novel, *Autobiography of a Family Photo*, and *I Hadn't Meant to Tell You This*. The volume of mail going back and forth between the writer and her publisher was such that she became friends with the workers at the post office—in one of her novels, she officially thanked them in the acknowledgments section. When Woodson and her family returned to the town this summer, the first place they visited was the post office to say hello to their friends. Asked why she moved back to New York, Woodson said "I can only do a small town for so long. I had gone there to write, but I feel like my anchor, my community is here [Brooklyn], so I always had one foot in both places." Returning to the city was hard because it meant giving up the ocean, but she got to the point that she disliked the summers in the town because of the influx of tourists and summer people.

Maturing as a Writer

During the early years of the 1990s, Woodson's work began garnering critical acclaim. She published four stories in *The Kenyon Review* that later became part of *Autobiography of a Family Photo* and won The Kenyon Review Award. *Maizon at Blue Hill* was honored as one of the "Best Books for Young Adults" by the American Library Association, and *I Hadn't Meant to Tell You This*, published in 1994, won accolades as a *Publisher's Weekly* "Best Book" and was named a Coretta Scott King Honor Book in 1995. Woodson returned to the MacDowell Colony in 1994. Additionally, she taught creative writing at Goddard College from 1993 to 1995.

Literary agent Charlotte Sheedy signed Woodson as a client to find a publisher for *Autobiography of a Family Photo*. On the basis of Woodson's proven track record, Sheedy was then able to negotiate a deal for four young adult novels and at least one children's picture book with Charles Putnam's Sons Books for Children. Nancy Paulsen, now the president of that part of Penguin/Putnam, had just come to the publishing house and one of her goals was to build a young adult line. She had been following Woodson's career and knew the author was the first one she wanted to sign.[29] Woodson agreed, even though she had no ideas about future plot lines, and so admits she found herself a bit intimidated: "I was writing two and three books a year and all of a sudden I was like, 'Wait a second! Now someone is *expecting* me to write a book a year!' What I had to do was make believe it never happened."[30]

The move to Putnam and the work with Paulsen proved to be, like Woodson's partnership with Wendy Lamb, what she needed at that point to continue growing as a writer. According to the author, Paulsen is a less "hands-on" editor, which Woodson says works because she has grown as a writer. Under Paulsen's editorship, Woodson produced *If You Come Softly*, *Miracle's Boys*, which won the Coretta Scott King Award, *Hush*, and the forthcoming *Locomotion*, as well as the picture book *The Other Side*.

Although she has established herself as a productive and accomplished artist, Woodson still feels that "Even now I feel like I live from book to book. Moving on to the next one is starting from scratch."[31] Therefore, what the writer looks to Paulsen for is a "certain kind of faith." According to Woodson, Paulsen's comments run to "'This is great! Keep going,' or 'You have a wonderful beginning here.' And then I can say for myself, 'I have so much work to do' but I have the confidence to do it without her saying specifically what to do." Paulsen tends to write editorial letters that make generalizations such as "Here is the story you are trying to tell." And invariably Woodson agrees; she has never reacted by feeling Paulsen missed her point. Then Paulsen will say, "Here's what's missing in your story." Woodson takes her manuscript away and returns in short order with what is needed to fill in those gaps. Paulsen finds working with Woodson very easy as she thinks of the writer as the "consummate professional," able to take advice, reflect on it, revise, and work toward completion of the manuscript in an efficient way.[32]

Woodson credits her developing skill as a writer to "growing up," saying her work with her different editors over time parallels in some ways her work with therapists. In the early days of therapy, Woodson felt nervous and was grateful for a therapist who, like Wendy Lamb, would give her concrete suggestions about what to try or what to think about. She reflects, "As I grew up, I needed someone who could do something different for me, and the editorial relationship changed that way too." But Paulsen credits some of Woodson's growth and developing independence from editorial managing to her work as a teacher.[33] In addition to her time at Goddard, Woodson has served as a writer in residence for the National Book Foundation, and as an associate faculty member at Eugene Lang College, and in the Vermont College of Norwich University's Master of Fine Arts in Writing for Children program.[34] She has enjoyed her contact with young writers, commenting, "It's so rewarding for me as a writer to know that there are young voices who have something to say, whose stories are coming from different cultures and whose voices have historically been silenced because they're coming from poor communities. The fact that these words are going to be given to the world in some way, shape, or form is thrilling."[35] As a result of working with less experienced crafters of writing, Woodson finds she can detach herself somewhat from her own manuscripts these days. Thus, where Wendy Lamb would earlier have had to remind her "Show, don't tell," Paulsen now has to write those words much less frequently; Woodson says, "I can catch myself, I can say, 'I need to show more.'"

Woodson does not do much teaching at the present time. Like her work with homeless and runaway teens, Woodson finds teaching can be exhausting. Even teaching at the graduate level, having a class one day a week, the author found that preparing for class and responding to her students' stories took a much larger chunk of time, "and at the end of the day, I could maybe get back to writing, but you have the students' stories in your head and you're thinking about those so it's hard to listen to yourself."

These days Woodson focuses on her own writing, which she does in her kitchen, sitting at a desk with a glass top that reveals the rich, warm tones of the hardwood floor below, observed by family pictures, including one of her grandfather, the only black face in his high school class, and those of herself and her partner as young girls, as well as Maus, the family dog.[36] Sometimes she goes to the Writers' Center in the East Village, a space reminiscent of a library where authors can work in total silence, surrounded by others similarly focused on their craft. Sometimes she manages to get away, with her family, to her house in upstate New York, where she has an actual office. As Jennifer Brown observed, "The author's manner and her surroundings convey a sense of belonging, and the critical acclaim and many awards accorded her children's books have won Woodson a spot as a literary insider."[37] Woodson has arrived as an important writer, and as a result she is asked to contribute short stories to anthologies such as the recent *One Hot Second: Stories about Desire*.[38] She is asked to contribute essays to magazines such as *Essence* and to share her thoughts about our world as a commentator for National Public Radio.

Taking on New Roles—and Staying a Writer

But Woodson balances work with attention to her personal life. She also devotes herself these days to supporting her partner, Juliet, who is about to graduate from medical school and move into the residency

phase of her training, with a focus on family practice. And, she is learning a new role, that of "Mom." Toshi Georgianni was born to Woodson
and Juliet in March 2002. Named for Woodon's friend Toshi Reagon,
a musician and godmother to the baby, and for Woodson's grandmother, Toshi's presence means Woodson is rethinking some of aspects
of her life.

For one, Woodson is no longer as comfortable in her Park Slope
neighborhood as she was even five years ago. Whereas it used to be a
very diverse neighborhood in terms of skin color, economic status, and
the life style choices of the community, it has become more traditional
over the past few years. She still loves the fact that there is a park
nearby, Prospect Park, which figures in several of her novels, and that
she can go around the corner for a cup of coffee, that there are still a
number of writers living there, and that she runs into friends all the
time. However, she is unhappy that many of her friends, longtime residents of the area, feel forced to move as rents rise and more well-to-do
families, attracted by the park and the reputation of the local public
school, take their places. She is saddened by the fact that she and Juliet
used to be comfortable strolling the streets holding hands, but now that
there are more traditional nuclear families in the area, they receive
more wondering glances than in the past. While their particular block
of Second Avenue is still quite diverse, and while their house, which
they share with Woodson's original housemate out of college and her
children, is also a home for individuals with diverse backgrounds—they
celebrate Hanukkah, Christmas, and Kwanza—when she is walking her
baby, Woodson now finds that she is perceived as Toshi's nanny rather
than as her mother.

At the end of *Maizon at Blue Hill*, Maizon, who has grown increasingly
uncomfortable and feels unable to be herself at the prestigious boarding
school she has been attending, longs to go back to Brooklyn. She longs
to be someplace where it is safe to be her total self. Woodson admits that
she, too, is working on finding that safe place for herself. And she says,
"I think I'll always be working on it, because you know, we change and
environs change." She does not want to become complacent with her
life, and being mistaken for her daughter's nanny reminds her that for
many other people, "if you look a certain way, this is who you must be."
She is angered when people ask about Toshi, "Is she yours?" She wonders,

"Why even ask that question? Who else's child would she be?" She ruminates, "It was interesting to have grown up in a neighborhood that was not privileged and to move to a neighborhood that is a pretty well-to-do and to have to deal with the stuff that comes from living as an African-American woman in a predominately white neighborhood where certain assumptions are made, then, about who you are."

Nevertheless, Woodson and her family are rooted in this neighborhood. Needing more space as Toshi grows, Woodson and her partner decided to buy a house of their own, instead of continuing to live in the basement apartment of the home of Woodson's longtime roommate. By March of 2003, Woodson will have a study of her own in a townhouse just about three blocks away from their current abode where she can devote herself to her art while not being too far from her daughter.

Often Woodson's characters have to confront the kind of assumptions Woodson has faced as she has pushed Toshi's stroller through the streets of Park Slope, and, in the process, they determine new ways of being in the world. In *If You Come Softly*, tragedy strikes Jeremiah, a black teenaged boy, when, visiting his white, upper-class girlfriend, others make assumptions about his presence in the neighborhood. Toswiah's life is turned upside down when her father witnesses two white police officers kill a young black man about whom they make assumptions in *Hush*. Woodson uses her writing to work out her concerns, or at least to make them real and visible to her readers.

As a mother, Woodson also has a new set of fears and hopes for her daughter that echo themes in her work. In a short story written for *Tomorrowland*, Woodson explored some of her feelings as she and Juliet were thinking about having a baby. In "The Other Half of Me,"[39] the narrator is a young girl whose mother conceived her with the help of a sperm bank. The particular donor chosen by the mother decided not to reveal much about himself, and not to allow any child conceived from his sperm to locate him upon reaching adulthood. As a result, the daughter has a constant longing to know the "other half" of her; she notices men and wonders if maybe she has their features, wonders what her biological father might be doing in the world at specific points in time. Having grown up for most her life without her own father's presence, Woodson and her partner decided they did not want their child to face that particular kind of struggle; they determined that they didn't "want her not to know her other biological half, to not be able to say 'These are my toes; they're from my mom or dad or whatever,'" which is what Woodson's narrator faces. Therefore, they asked a white male friend to be Toshi's biological father.

Woodson is concerned about other struggles her daughter will face, growing up as the biracial daughter of two moms. She fears the earth's peoples will run out of water; she fears that Toshi will be snatched or otherwise harmed by crazy members of our society. She fears that, in terms of education, Toshi will not have the tools she needs because our country does not give, in Woodson's mind, much support to education. But mostly, the author fears that "her generation will grow up with a sense of helplessness, and become, not complacent, but kind of beaten down, that they'll feel, 'This is not my journey; there's nothing I can do about this.'" She is concerned, in general, that young people will just accept the status quo. She says she has to hope that her daughter, like so many of her characters, will develop a strong sense of self, because Woodson believes this is one of the most powerful tools a young person can have.

During the Clinton/Monica Lewinsky scandals, Woodson was asked by NPR to share her reactions to the political situation. In her commentary, Woodson cited lyrics written by Neil Young: "We are all helpless, helpless."[40] And sometimes, particularly in bleak political moments such as that one, she does feel that way. "You know, we can call our senator or our congressman but the people in power are still going to do what they want to do. I look back at Vietnam, and we STOPPED Vietnam because people were angry and knew that the war was jacked up, but how much power do we really have in the political scheme of things? What is the thing as a citizen I can do? I can go vote. But does that work? I mean look what happened in Florida. Voting doesn't even have the power we think it has. . . . I'm stumped, every day I'm stumped about our political system of things."

Although Woodson has this fear of powerlessness, she argues that she would never send that message in her work for younger readers. Indeed, in the worlds of her books, adults often admonish adolescents who say they feel powerless. Asked what tools, as a mother, she will try to provide for her daughter to give her a sense of strength and sense of self powerful enough to fight off apathy, Woodson replies, "Besides coloring all the characters in the fairy tales? I think one thing is her seeing strong women around her, and making sure she's around other people like her, not only people who are biracial and people who have two moms, but people who are progressive, so she knows she's not alone, that she knows she's not the only one like herself." She continues by noting the value of literature as a tool, and she wants Toshi, who already loves to chew on books as physical objects, to be able to find role models and solace in books as Woodson does herself—and as she shows many of her characters doing. And, she wants to make certain that Toshi not only hears the conversations of the adults in her life, who argue about politics and discuss religion and values, but participates in those conversations.

In her books, Woodson gives her readers the chance to find strong role models. She gives readers opportunities to see characters connecting across all manner of boundaries designed to keep them apart. In her books, Woodson shows her readers, through her characters, the importance of the support of communities of friends and family. Through her work, Woodson asks her readers to challenge their own world views by walking for awhile in the shoes of people from very different backgrounds, and to participate, through the literature, in the kinds of dialogue that may help keep apathy and complacency from doing damage to their hearts and souls. And she does all of this by giving readers, too, good stories about realistic individuals who rattle around in our minds for long after the time we close her books or stories. The rest of this text will explore Woodson's talents as a creator of character, a painter of scenes whose environments often reflect the moods and feelings of her narrators, and as an author able to grapple with serious themes directly, openly, and provocatively, a writer committed to serving her audience, particularly the young adults who have come to respect her work for its inherent honesty and integrity, by continuing to hone her skills, trying new strategies for telling her stories, and by "pushing the boundaries of herself as an artist with each new book."[41]

Notes

1. Jacqueline Woodson, "Witnessing," *National Public Radio Commentary* (November 15, 1999). 1. Retrieved from www.npr.org on 9 September 2002. Keyword: Woodson, Jacqueline.

2. Woodson, "Witnessing," 1.

3. Jacqueline Woodson, "A Stolen Childhood," *Essence* 24, no. 1 (May 1993): 81–85. 2. Academic Search Premier. 8 July 2002. Keyword: Woodson, Jacqueline.

4. Jennifer Brown, "From Outsider to Insider," *Publisher's Weekly* 249, no. 6 (February 11, 2002): 156–157. 2. Academic Search Premier. 8 July 2002. Keyword: Woodson, Jacqueline.

5. Jacqueline Woodson, *I Hadn't Meant to Tell You This*. (New York: Bantam/Doubleday/Dell, 1994). Hereafter cited as *Tell*.

6. Brown, "Outsider," 1.

7. Brown, "Outsider," 1.

8. Brown, "Outsider," 2.

9. Catherine Saalfield, "Jacqueline Woodson," in *Contemporary Gay and Lesbian Writers of the United States: A Biocritical Resource Book*, ed. Sandra Pollack (Westport, CT: Greenwood Press, 1993), 563.

10. Saalfield, "Woodson," 563.

11. Jacqueline Woodson, "A Sign of Having Been Here," *Horn Book Magazine* 71, no. 6 (November/December 1995): 711–715. 1. Academic Search Premier. 8 July 2002. Keyword: Woodson, Jacqueline.

12. Woodson, "A Sign of Having Been Here," 1.

13. Woodson, "A Sign of Having Been Here," 1.

14. Woodson, "A Sign of Having Been Here," 2.

15. Jacqueline Woodson and Catherine Gund Saalfield, *Among Good Christian Peoples*. Frameline Release, 1991. 30 minutes. Retrieved from www.frameline.org/distribution from the Enoch Pratt Free Library, Baltimore, MD, 3-4170-06276-6861.

16. Brown, "From Outsider to Insider," 2.

17. Woodson, "A Stolen Childhood," 2.

18. Woodson, "A Sign of Having Been Here," 2.

19. Judith A. Hayne, "Jacqueline Woodson," in *Writers for Young Adults: Supplement*, ed. Ted Hipple (New York: Charles Scribner's Sons, 2000), 378.

20. Brown, "From Outsider to Insider," 2.

21. Brown, "From Outsider to Insider," 1.

22. Saalfield, "Woodson," 563–564.

23. Brown, "From Outsider to Insider," 1.

24. Woodson and Saalfield, *Among Good Christian Peoples*.

25. Jacqueline Woodson, "Common Ground," *Essence* 30, no. 1 (May 1999): 148–152. 4. Academic Search Premier. 8 July 2002. Keyword: Woodson, Jacqueline.

26. Saalfield, "Woodson," 584.

27. Wendy Lamb, Wendy Lamb Imprints—Random House Books for Children, Telephone interview with the author 9 December 2002. Hereafter cited as Lamb.

28. Lamb.

29. Nancy Paulsen, president, Charles Putnam's Sons Books for Children. Telephone interview with author 16 September 2002. Hereafter cited as Paulsen.

30. Brown, "From Outsider to Insider," 2.

31. Brown, "From Outsider to Insider," 2.

32. Paulsen.

33. Paulsen.

34. "Jacqueline Woodson," *Contemporary Authors: A Bibliographical Guide to Current Writers in Fiction, General Non-fiction, Poetry, Journalism, Drama, Motion Pictures, Television, and Other Fields, New Revision Series, Vol. 87,* ed. Scott Peacock (Boston: Gale Group, 2000), 433.

35. Brown, "From Outsiders to Insider," 4.

36. Brown, "From Outsiders to Insider," 2.

37. Brown, "From Outsiders to Insider," 2.

38. Cathy Young, Ed. *One Hot Second: Short Stories about Desire.* (New York: Alfred Knopf, 2002).

39. Jacqueline Woodson, "The Other Half of Me," *Tomorrowland: Stories about the Future,* ed. Michael Cart (New York: Scholastic, 1999), 143–146.

40. Jacqueline Woodson, "The Last Waltz: Poetry and Politics," in *Analysis: Hour One—Eight Essayists Explain What They Have Learned during the Investigation, Impeachment, and Trial of the President.* Host Robert Siegel (19 February 1999). *National Public Radio.* Retrieved from www.npr.org on 9 September, 2002. Keyword: Woodson, Jacqueline.

41. Brown, "From Outsider to Insider," 3.

CHAPTER TWO

~

On Being Powerless and Invisible: *The Dear One* and *Hush*

Two of the key themes of Woodson's work are the ways in which society often denies certain groups of individuals a place of authority or power within the community, and, as a result, the ways in which society thereby makes those same groups invisible. As she describes her purpose for writing in "A Sign of Having Been Here," "I write about black girls *because the world would like to keep us invisible* (emphasis added). I write about all girls because I know what happens to self-esteem when we turn twelve, and I hope to show readers the number of ways we are strong."[1] Additionally, in her narratives, Woodson often demonstrates positive strategies adults and society at large can use to help young people break through this cloak of invisibility. Her characters, as Woodson has done herself, turn to the arts as a means of expressing self; they find specialized schools that focus on developing strong individuals, participate in social organizations designed to provide a sense of community and communal power, and rely on networks of family and friends to create an alternative reality when that of the larger society seems to marginalize some of its members. The focus in this chapter is on two works, one from the early years of Woodson's career, and one more recent title, both of which explore this topic explicitly.

Combatting Invisibility

The Maizon and Margaret trilogy introduces readers to the power of neighborhood communities. When Margaret's father dies in Woodson's first novel, *Last Summer with Maizon* (1990), the neighbors seem to swarm around her and her mother and younger brother, cooking, taking care of the baby so Margaret's mother can go to work and school, helping out in any way possible. When Maizon feels she is losing her identity at the prestigious Blue Hill private school that she has decided to attend because of its rigorous academic reputation, she needs to be back in Brooklyn surrounded by her friends, neighbors, and familiar surroundings. When their friend Bo begins having difficulty in school, he switches to an alternative setting, a school designed just for young black men as a place where they can explore, together, with caring adults, issues of societal expectations, identity, and strategies for pursuing their goals without getting sidetracked by stereotyping. In *Between Madison and Palmetto* (1993), when Margaret and Maizon struggle in their friendship as it is tested by their individual growth, and by the introduction of a white school mate who wants to be friends with each of them, it is through the arts that they begin to find their way forward—Margaret directs their new friend in a play Maizon has written.

Many of the concerns Woodson introduces in these early works come into sharper focus in the 1991 *The Dear One*, soon to be reissued. This novel is narrated by Feni, short for Afeni, which means, in Swahili, "the dear one." Feni is turning twelve as the novel opens, and on her birthday her mother tells her that they are soon to be hosting the daughter of Mama's college friend Clair. Rebecca, Clair's oldest child, is fifteen—and pregnant. Feni is both horrified and outraged. She likes her upper-middle-class life just the way it is, even though she misses her father, who now lives in Colorado with his new wife and their infant daughter. Rebecca will have to stay in Feni's room, as the guest bedroom is too cold, especially for an expectant teenaged mother, and Feni absolutely refuses to allow anyone to sleep in her grandmother's room. Even though Feni's Grandma died when Feni was much younger, she still considers the room almost sacred, still believes Grandma was the only person who truly saw her for herself and accepted her totally, and still has yet to fully accept her death. Feni actually went mute for a time after her grandmother's death, and she still is pretty much a loner. Her one friend Caesar is uncomfortable coming to Feni's house because Feni's mom has had a serious drinking problem that probably contributed to the break-down of her marriage, and while it's now under control, Caesar remains afraid of Catherine because of nasty comments Feni's mother made about her. Feni spends much time by herself.

Rebecca is, in some ways, repeating her mother's history. Clair, Feni's mom, and another woman, Marion, were best friends at Spellman dur-ing college. But Clair became pregnant while still in school, and later her husband left the family, leaving her with several additional children and a depression so bad that she got fired from her teaching position for taking so much time off. Now Clair and her children live in Harlem, struggling to make ends meet. In some ways Marion, who remains one of Catherine's best friends and who is, therefore, very much a part of Feni's life, would be a better host for Rebecca as she has no children of her own. But Clair has never come to terms with the fact that Marion is gay. Hence, Clair asks Catherine and Feni to take care of Rebecca until the baby arrives, to ensure Rebecca keeps up with her school work, gets proper prenatal care, has peace and quiet, and eats a healthy diet so that the baby will begin life in the best circumstances possible.

Feni's birthday dawns pale pink, with the wings of birds and bare tree trunks standing out, skeletonlike, against patches of pale snow.[2] The world is quiet and rather lifeless as the novel opens, reflecting, to a cer-tain extent, Feni's interior landscape. But immediately upon her ar-rival, Rebecca's presence begins to upset the status quo at Feni's house. Feni realizes quickly that Rebecca and her family truly have no money, that they live an existence Feni finds hard to imagine. Feni attends Roper Academy, a Quaker school, and goes to the Jack and Jill Club af-ter school, a social club for the children of black professionals, which she hates. She has had dance lessons and ski trips, privileges her mother, an attorney, can provide with a degree of ease, all of which she takes for granted. But when Rebecca steps into their home, she lets out a holler and tells Feni that she is rich, saying "I didn't know rich black people existed except on 'The Cosby Show' and that's on television" (DO, 45). As Rebecca unpacks, Feni just stares at the paucity of her possessions. Later, Feni asks her mother why Rebecca does not have nice things. Mama says Rebecca's family just does not have the money to purchase better clothes. Feni blithely remarks that the family should just find some money. Catherine tries to help her daughter understand Rebecca's circumstances by asking from Feni where she proposes Rebecca and her mom could get more cash. Feni, in her twelve-year-old egocentric way, can only say, "From wherever" (*DO*, 56)—but later comes to realize that her mother, and her mother's friends, Marion and partner Bernadette, are Rebecca's "wherever."

The Value of Friendship and One-on-One Connections in Overcoming Invisibility

As Feni and Rebecca, who are antagonistic and often downright nasty to each other in the beginning, work their way toward friendship, their growth is mirrored by the outside world's movement into spring. But the process is not an easy one. Each girl has to learn to accept the other's differences and to trust that, in spite of those differences of circumstance, as young black women they *can* find points of connection. Rebecca describes her Harlem apartment and Harlem neighborhood for Feni, using details that help the reader really see the "the other." For instance, Rebecca sees a slinky that triggers her recollected images of boys from her neighborhood sitting on the stoops of burned-out buildings trying to make a broken green plastic slinky waddle down the steps, and Rebecca uses that image as a metaphor to describe the sense of hopelessness she has about the future, saying "It made me realize something. It made me think that's what everything is all about—things not working out the way they supposed to, the way somebody promised they would. . . . It's always like that. It's always the same" (*DO*, 62). Although Rebecca misses Harlem and her boyfriend, misses even being pressed against the cold cement wall with her boyfriend's body pushed tight against her, she does begin to recognize that if her baby were to be born there, the baby would develop a sense of being invisible, and a resulting sense of powerlessness similar to Rebecca's own. Rebecca knows all too well that "If you ain't got no money, or you have to quit your job like my mother did when she got sick, you got to get money from the city to feed all your babies, and even after that some of your babies will still be hungry" (*DO*, 67). So Rebecca decides to put her baby up for adoption by a couple who will be able to give the child a better life.

The adults in Feni's life actively work against Feni's tendency to feel powerless, which she experiences primarily because she is a child with limited rights. But she also has a sense of reality, knowing even at age twelve that she will always have to cope with people with more power telling her what to do, because she is a child, or if not that, because she is a woman, and if not that, because she is black. She and Caesar, who is part Native American, know better than to challenge the status quo in school, which works, at times, to keep the realities of their heritages invisible. For instance, at Thanksgiving, the teacher read from the history text about the Pilgrims and the Indians being friends, but Feni and Caesar know that the Pilgrims gave the Indians "smallpox—not turkeys" (*DO*, 18), and they have learned already how to play the school game, how to memorize what the teacher wants them to know and think for the test, and then forget it.

But Feni's mother, along with Marion and Bernadette, structure Feni's life so that she will be able to grow into a sense of self-efficacy and power as she moves toward adulthood, and they want to give Rebecca a glimpse, at least, of other possibilities, and to provide her baby with a different starting point. Catherine took control of her drinking problem the day her husband walked out and tries to be a model for her daughter of how, one day at a time, she can make their lives better. Marion also has had difficulties with alcohol, and with Catherine's support, she decided to quit her job as a prosecutor, quit drinking, and take a position as a legal aid attorney, which affords her less of a salary but more opportunity to feel she can help others take control of their lives. Bernadette belongs to a support group for gay and lesbian teachers. Rebecca cannot believe these well-to-do women are taking care of her, and they tell her they are just doing what friends do, showing Rebecca and Feni by their actions the power of circles of strong female friends.

Catherine makes Feni attend the Jack and Jill Club so that she will have opportunities to socialize with other black children who also are from professional families, and so that, together, they will realize how special black professionals are and will develop a pride of accomplishment and hard work (*DO*, 12). Catherine says Jack and Jill is about black people taking care of themselves; the black community established such social clubs as a way to take care of their own when groups such as 4-H or the Boy Scouts and Girl Scouts were not letting black

kids join. Woodson's own view is that Jack and Jill Clubs and other similar organizations are important for the reasons Catherine articulates
and because they provide a space in which black children and young
adults, particularly if they live in communities in which they are not
the majority, can share their experiences. However, as Feni points out,
Woodson also feels that such organizations can be "dangerous" if they
become focused on class issues and fail to include blacks who are not
well-to-do.

Catherine goes on to tell Feni that taking in Rebecca, attending an
all-black chapter of Alcoholics Anonymous, and pledging black soror-
ities and fraternities are part of the same effort, echoing Woodson's own
experiences in college that led her to join her all-black sorority. As a
writer, Woodson gives books to the world at large that provide her
readers with the kinds of role models Catherine and her friends give to
Feni and Rebecca.

Additionally, Feni and Rebecca show readers the importance of connecting across boundaries one on one. As they become more aware of
their fears of each other, and their jealousies of one another, they begin
to provide mirrors to the other in which they can each study themselves.
Rebecca shows Feni how the death of her grandmother caused her to
create a "gigantic wall" between herself and the rest of the world that
has the effect of telling the world to "go away" (DO, 95), and she warns
Feni that if she keeps pushing people away, out of fear of losing someone
who gets close, then "someday nobody'll come back" (DO, 124).

Because of Rebecca's taunting, centering on Rebecca's perceptions
that Catherine is an unloving mother who uses notes on the refrigera-
tor to communicate and seldom gives physical affection, Feni confronts
her mother and learns more about her mom's difficult childhood. It
turns out that Catherine's own mother died when she was thirteen,
leaving her in charge of the family, that included at one point seven
children but no father. So Catherine learned the importance of showing love by providing for her siblings, by taking care of them. After
Feni's accusations of disinterest, Catherine helps Feni see that, in de-
ciding to stop drinking and to seek help for her problems, in working
hard to provide opportunities for Feni as well as material well-being,
she is telling her she loves her (DO, 84). Rebecca also shares her street
wisdom with Feni; when Feni feels the baby move for the first time, she

begins to think, like Rebecca, that people, such as her beloved grandmother die, "to make space for other people to live" (*DO*, 96). Similarly, Feni helps Rebecca come to terms with her decision to put her
baby up for adoption, and eventually Rebecca comes to wish that all
the kids in Harlem and in Feni's Seton could trade places for a month.

Learning from Experience

As the two girls find their own common ground, they also share an experience that is eye-opening for each of them. Feni has never thought
much about the section of town on the other side of the railroad tracks,
a place filled with shacks housing too-large families of poor whites in
raggedy clothes who live from hand to mouth. Rebecca has never
thought much about the fact that whites can be as poor as the people
in her Harlem neighborhood. While taking a walk one day, far into Rebecca's pregnancy, the girls stumble into this section of town and see a
little boy, about four years old, in a ragged coat. Feni's initially remarks,
"Kids here just walk around like that. They look for junk in the
garbage. . . . That is the way people are around here" (*DO*, 109–110).
Her words show how invisible this little boy is to Feni because he lives
on the other side of an economic divide. They show that she feels
something close to disgust for him, indicating, as she used to think of
Rebecca, he should be able to live in some other way. Being there with
Rebecca, Feni realizes she is being a snob, and that she has failed in the
past to recognize that a child is just a child. When the boy's mother appears, Feni DOES realize the hatred toward her is evident in the young
teen mother's eyes, a result of their very different economic situations.
But the mother truly becomes a real person when she talks to Rebecca
about pregnancy and birth, finding a meeting place with the black girl
that overrides their difference in race. Rebecca and Feni both become
more tolerant, more open to others as they work toward finding their
own common ground, to the point that Rebecca says that if she had not
already committed to giving her baby to another couple, she would
have given it to Marion and Bernadette, reminding Feni and the readers of the problems that come from stereotyping; Rebecca says she did
not like Marion at first because "I didn't know her. . . . How you gonna
judge someone you don't know?" (*DO*, 113).

Ironically, the cover artist first chosen to provide the book jacket for *The Dear One* ended up refusing to take the job. While Wendy Lamb found this novel "really rich," valuing the fact that it portrayed a teenaged girl being treated supportively, without judgment, during her pregnancy, and that there was a gay couple, stable and loving, presented as "just part of the landscape," those are characters who might make some readers uncomfortable. But the artist, herself African-American, did not object to the book on grounds of theme. Instead, as Lamb recalls the situation, the artist did not like the way Feni made fun of the Jack and Jill Club, judging without really knowing the book, which ultimately makes a plea for places and spaces of all sorts in which young blacks can find community.[3]

The husband and wife who are adopting Rebecca's baby want her to help them choose a name, want her input on the kind of religious/spiritual training the baby will have, and hope Rebecca will be a part of the baby's life. Rebecca is pleased both that her baby will have such caring parents and such a secure environment—and that she will be able to know her child, whom she names Afeni, "the dear one," for her new friend. She and Feni both realize, in the end, what Feni verbalizes as she concludes the narrative. The new baby is part of a "long line of dear ones"—a line that includes Feni's grandmother, Marion, Bernadette, Clair, Rebecca, the baby's adoptive mother, and herself. Even though nobody can predict that baby's future—nobody can know just yet how the baby will look, where she will make her home, what her values will be—the baby will be all right because "through the darkest, the toughest, the saddest, the hardest and the best of times, all of us would be around somewhere, pulling for her and pulling her through" (*DO*, 145). Feni precedes other Woodson characters who come to know, as she says of the narrator of her short story "Slipping Away," that strength comes from "acknowledging difference and letting it happen."[4] Rebecca's baby, the reader feels, will grow up to feel neither invisible nor powerless.

The Importance of Literature in Combating Invisibility

One of the ways that Feni and Rebecca find to connect with each other and to gain a sense of control is through the sharing of poetry. Daniel, Rebecca's boyfriend and the father of her child, stays with her though he is in Harlem and she is in Seton, because of a poem he recited to her that she repeats when she is feeling down. In a gesture of goodwill, Rebecca shares the poem with Feni, who has kept her grandmother in her heart in similar fashion by repeating a poem passed on through Grandma from Feni's grandfather. Feni's grandmother tells Feni of the importance of hearing stories and words from the past, of the value of learning about the past and family roots.

The use of literature to provide a vicarious kind of support and sense of community to her readers, which Rebecca's baby will have in reality, is something in which Woodson firmly believes. In the article "Who Can Tell My Story," Woodson talks about herself as a reader, describing how she can reread Henry James's *Portrait of a Lady* or Ezra Pound's "The Seafarer" again and again, each time filtering her own experience through them, and, in the process, creating something of her own, saying "And by this means, through the different, complicated elements of language and experience, through being and reading and listening and re-reading, I have come to understand the world around me—and myself as a writer."[5] For Woodson, books such as those by James Baldwin were important because they gave her a sense of connection to her heritage. She notes her delight in finding Baldwin because he wrote about "people in the city" like herself and her friends and family.[6]

Acting on her belief in the need to give young people such resources, in addition to writing her own stories, Woodson published the anthology *A Way Out of No Way* (1996). In it, she gives to a younger generation selections by some of her favorite writers of color, including Ernest Gaines, James Baldwin, Toni Cade Bambura, Rosa Guy, Tim Seibles, Paul Beatty, Jamaica Kincaid, Ntozake Shonge, June Jordan, Langston Hughes, Toni Morrison, Claude McKay, Nikki Giovanni, Gwendolyn Brooks, and Bernice Johnson Reagon. In describing how she chose the selections to be included, Woodson talks about how she found each author and what connecting with their works meant to her, commenting on how their words made her feel less invisible and gave her a sense of power as a result. For example, she was so entranced with Giovanni's *Spin a Soft Black Song* when she stumbled across it in the library at age ten, that she actually stole it from the library—noting that of course her mother found it and made her use her allowance to pay the fine due when she took it back.[7] She remembers reading Langston Hughes's *The*

Ways of White Folks as a teenager and not quite getting all the references, but has fond memories of her sister taking the time to explain them to her.[8] She cried with her grandmother while watching *The Autobiography of Miss Jane Pitman*, by Ernest Gaines, on television, recalling that neither of them knew whether not Miss Jane was real, but knowing that this did not matter to them; they were sure somebody like her had lived and affected the world as Gaines's character affected them.[9]

The sharing of poetry by Feni and Rebecca in this early novel foreshadows a tool Woodson will use more extensively as Marie and Lena share the writings of Audre Lorde in the more recent books about those girls, *I Hadn't Meant to Tell You This* and *Lena*, and in other later novels, such as *If You Come Softly*, in her short stories, and to a lesser extent, in *Locomotion*. By extension, in writing about characters who find their ways out of invisibility and into positions of strength, Woodson is giving her readers a tool similar to the one she found in other writers' works.

Woodson's Own Experiences in Fighting Invisibility

In some ways, the friendships and their ups and downs over time among Catherine, Clair, and Marion, Rebecca and Feni resemble some of those in Woodson's own life. As she entered adolescence, she had a group of three other girls with whom she spent much of her time. One became pregnant at age thirteen; Woodson says that for ten years, she knew "everything" about the son borne by her friend.[10] But as they grew older, they grew apart, and found it harder to connect across the gulfs created by their different economic circumstances and life choices. Like Marion, Woodson also had to struggle for acceptance once her friends knew she was gay. While Catherine managed over time to reconnect with Marion, Rebecca's mother never does reconcile with her former friend. In similar fashion, Woodson lost touch with the friend who bore the son Woodson so enjoyed. That friend married, had a second child, and asked Woodson to be the godmother—but was told by her new husband to retract that invitation once they learned Woodson was gay.[11]

In the essay "Common Ground," Woodson describes the experience of getting ready for, and then attending, the bridal shower of one of her high school friends. She opens with this poignant passage: "I slowly step outside of who I am in this community of women who love women, into the body of a sexless someone, unloved, unable to acquire a man. 'That's why she's that way,' I've heard straight women say of women like me."[12] As she heads off to the shower, she hopes that this day will not be another one "of defending, of explaining, of endeavoring to be heard and seen."[13] But her hopes are dashed as soon as she arrives at the party and realizes that her gift to the bride-to-be is all wrong, wrapped as it is in earth-toned paper with twine, just as she is wrapped all wrong in a navy blue suit, which stands out against the pastels of Valerie and her other friends, just as her hair, in dreadlocks, stands out against the relaxed hair styles of the other women.

Woodson contrasts the conversations flowing around her at the party with those in which she is used to participating; these other women talk about men, marriage, their children, and who is cheating on whom, while Woodson's everyday life is filled with talk of politics, dealing with homophobia, the expense of conception.[14] She finally is able to enter the conversation when talk turns to how to find hired help who can be trusted; in general, all the women present had grandmothers who were domestics, as were their grandmothers, so that Woodson reflects, "Valerie and I sit at opposite ends of living today—our parallel histories connecting us, a canyon of women dividing us."[15] With the other women in the room, they know they have "made it" against the odds; they are upwardly mobile, drive classy cars, take vacations in Europe, and live in relatively safe and privileged neighborhoods.

Both the sense of shared personal history with Valerie—they were cheerleaders together, ran for and won class president and vice president, were their parents' dream children—and the sense that with the others celebrating on this day they share an awareness of being outsiders in their new economic class help Woodson make it through the event.[16] Thus it is no surprise that parents such as the mothers of Feni and Caesar want their children to have the social spaces in which to connect with other children of black professionals. And it is no surprise that Woodson, who notes that she and her girlfriend will never have society's blessings in the way Valerie does,[17] creates strong, believable gay couples such as Marion and Bernadette who show readers positive images of loving, stable gay relationships. Feni's mother tells her that when Marion came out to her, she was scared. "I didn't know anything about lesbians. . . . Back then I didn't know there were so many ways people loved each other" (*DO*, 30). Feni and Rebecca come to value the kind of affection and support these women give each other; perhaps Woodson's readers will come to value the real-life counterparts of Marion and Bernadette.

In her own life, Woodson tries, too, to be a model for young people, tries to give them a sense of how to move beyond labels. Asked how she feels when reviewers name her as a black or lesbian writer, Woodson responds, "I think one of the issues slash problems in our society is that we need to name and label people, and we need to pigeon-hole them. There are times when I am a black writer, like when I walk into a school and it's all black students, and I'm there as a role model, and what they need to see is that someone who is African-American is writing books, that's who I am. And when I walk into a homophobic community, where people think gays are whatever negative thing they think, then that's who I am. But in the broader scheme of things, when everyone else gets to be called just a writer, I don't want to be qualified. I want to be someone who writes books. I am a woman, I am black, I am all these things, but first and foremost, I'm just a writer."

The Author's Developing Craft

In *The Dear One*, Woodson's growing deftness as a writer who is able to create characters such as Feni's mom, who continues to struggle day by day with an alcohol addiction, or Marion and Bernadette, who are presented as fixtures in Feni's life but who just happen to be gay, becomes apparent. Additionally, Woodson's ability to create character through dialogue sharpens throughout the novel. Interestingly, Woodson looks back on this early novel with a certain degree of horror at what she now perceives to be unsophisticated craftsmanship. *The Dear One* is being reissued in the near future, and Woodson was asked if she wanted to make any changes in the text before it hit the presses again. At the time of the interview for this project, Woodson had managed to go through the first thirty pages of the book and found much she wanted to change. In particular, she finds that she used clichés, that "some of the language is just so bad" when she is making comparisons and writing description. Also, as a reader, she says she now stumbles over the conversations and thinks that originally she had characters use each others' names too frequently, "and that was about not trusting my ability to write dialogue that my readers could follow."

However, while it is true that in the beginning of the novel, some of the language is, as Woodson describes it, "just younger," as she moves into her plot and as the characters begin to come alive on the page, readers can sense Woodson honing her craft, getting stronger and trusting herself more. The rhythms of the conversations become increasingly believable and realistic, and as Roger Sutton remarks in his review, "the best scenes are the angry ones, such as Feni's confrontations with Rebecca or when Feni reminds her mother of past alcohol abuses. . . . When it's fierce, it's real."[18] As Saalfield puts it, "The fierce, well-scripted dialogue evolves into a sharing relationship."[19] Feni and Caesar also have the kinds of conversations young women have about sex before their bodies start to mature and they begin to see young men in a different light:

"Afeni, can you imagine? Lying down naked beside somebody?"

"Kill myself!"

"Double kill myself. Not in a trillion years. I don't even think I'll do it with my husband" (DO, 89).

Such conversations show Woodson's ability to convey character through dialogue and descriptions of their interactions with others. From Rebecca, Feni begins to learn about the realities of sex when Rebecca pragmatically shares details such as the fact that "a lot of times the girls don't even take all their clothes off when they're doing it . . . and that sometimes the people doing it are so into listening out, making sure nobody's coming up the stairs, that they miss all the action right there in the bedroom or corner of the kitchen or in the closet" (DO, 1). Rebecca also makes interesting observations, showing her inherent intelligence, about the importance of the names and nicknames that young people are given by the adults in their lives and that, as a result, define an individual's position in the neighborhood. For example, someone will decide that a young male child resembles a favorite older man in the community, and soon that young boy, regardless of his given name, will find himself referred to as "L'il Bud," and will be expected to live up to that name. And Rebecca's own genuine affection for her mother and for Daniel, her baby's father, comes through in the telephone conversations home that are overheard by Feni. Thus it is no wonder that Ellen Fader judges *The Dear One* to be a "strikingly original book," because of its "richly developed characters, a setting unusual in a book for young adults, and a satisfying emotional conclusion."[20]

Invisibility and Powerlessness Revisited

The experience of being powerless and therefore invisible that is important in Woodson's early novels becomes more complexly lived by the family in *Hush*, a finalist for a National Book Award in 2002. In this more recent work, powerlessness and invisibility are explored with more thematic sophistication, and the novel evidences Woodson's increasingly sparse and poetic style. The narrator is Toswiah, younger daughter of the lone black officer on the Denver, Colorado, police force. While the family has achieved a certain degree of visibility and power, they are aware of the tenuousness of their position, and then they are pushed into the experience of absolute and very tangible invisibility and powerlessness by events and decisions over which they have very little control.

As a police officer, Towsiah's father and her family live with the knowledge that every day members of the police are killed. They live with the knowledge that many people dislike and even actively hate the police. And, as one of a very small number of black families in Denver, they know prejudice. Cameron, the older sister, is a cheerleader, and she knows she is called names behind her back, especially when she begins dating a white boy whom all the others on her squad adore. When one of her supposed friends wonders out loud why this boy would pick Cameron over her white squad mates, Cameron wants to fight; she tells her sister that "sometimes I hate being black."[21] But Toswiah's family is grounded in their belief that the police are active agents for the good. When Toswiah watches her father get a medal of honor for rescuing a mother and child from a hostage situation, she is filled with a belief in the "possibility of perfection" within the Denver Police Department (*Hush*, 33). Toswiah has never experienced racial meanness; unlike Cameron, she draws strength from the knowledge that the mayor of the city is black, that her best friend is black, that her father seems to be respected by his white peers. She actively delights in being black, telling her mother, "I could eat you like a chocolate bar, Ma," (*Hush*, 2), which always makes her mother laugh.

Racism and Invisibility

When a crisis occurs, the entire family is forced to confront the racism that apparently has existed just under the surface of their seemingly easy lives. Toswiah's dad is with two white colleagues when, in the darkness, they panic and shoot a fifteen-year-old black male who posed no threat to them, and who turns out to be an honor student with a bright future. As Toswiah hears her father tell the story, she thinks about the implications of white cops shooting a black youth and the implications for her father: "My father turning at the first shot to see the kid standing there, his arms raised above his head. The second and third shots, the kid falling. My father's face, first surprise, then anger, then fear, maybe—that his friends . . . could be so afraid of a black boy" (*Hush*, 37). The rest of the police force, including the inspector, try to persuade Toswiah's father not to testify against his two colleagues, trying to invoke the "blue wall of silence" between the force and those outside, invoking, too, the fact that both Green and Randall, the officers involved, come from long lines of police officers and only know police work. But this horrible event has reminded Toswiah's father that he has to do more than protect his colleagues—he realizes that he has two black daughters and that they, like other young blacks, could get killed "for no reason at all" (*Hush*, 49), and wants to do everything he can to ensure that the police force, indeed the entire judicial system, protect blacks from the dangers inherent in the white community's fear of them. He just will not be "hushed."

And so Toswiah's father goes to court, violating that "blue wall of silence," and testifies as an eye witness against his fellow officers. For their protection against an expected outpouring of outrage against the family, Toswiah, her parents and sister are forced to leave their comfortable Denver home in the middle of the night under police escort. For several unbearably long weeks, they live in real and absolute invisibility in a "safe house"—an abandoned hotel. They are not allowed to leave the one hotel room they must share, are not allowed to see anyone except the guards who deliver their food, are not allowed to watch television, and are not allowed to communicate with family and friends. Their guards even take the videos out of their protective plastic covers so that the family will not see the name of the nearby town from which they have been rented.

Finally they are relocated to a dark, dank apartment in a California town far from their Denver past. There, they continue to be unable to communicate with anyone from their former lives. Instead, each family member is given a new identity. The girls, formerly Cameron and Toswiah, are now Anna and Evie. As Brown writes, "Towsiah transforms from a well-adjusted twelve-year-old into the ultimate outsider, a recurrent theme in Woodson's work."[22] They are drilled in totally new personal biographies, have to memorize the details of different personal histories. They are assigned to a new school and have to enter midyear under their new identities, while at home, their parents struggle to come to grips with the consequences of an action that felt morally right and yet has caused so much trauma for them all. Toswiah/Evie's mother is desperate because she cannot immediately apply for a teacher's license, and teaching has been the heart of who she is. The father is consumed by guilt over the pain his actions have caused so many people. While the girls feel lighter once they learn that the policemen involved have been sentenced to jail, their father feels as though he has sentenced himself to prison as well.

Coping with Loss of Visibility, Loss of Authority

Each family member copes with their invisibility in a different way. For a long while, Daddy just sits in the darkened apartment, deteriorating to the point that he tries to commit suicide as a result of feeling powerless to help his family, and helpless in the loss of his identity as a police officer. He is, in a word, "disappearing" (*Hush*, 117), and it is not until he almost takes his own life by slitting his wrists with a broken pottery bowl that he realizes how glad he is to be alive, to have the promise of the future. Cameron, now Anna, turns to the future. She is determined to leave her new school, her new town behind. Learning about a college called Simon's Rock in Massachusetts, which accepts students with solid academic backgrounds at age sixteen and offers them full scholarships to pursue their studies without the distractions of high school, Anna focuses all her attention and energy on getting into college—and getting out of her family.

Mama turns to religion. The day before the family is to be moved, two Jehovah's Witnesses show up at the door. Mama takes their pamphlets, *The Watchtower* and *Awake!*, and becomes increasingly drawn into the community of Witnesses. She copes with her own loss of identity and power by clinging to the words of her new faith: "Be in the world not of the world." Unfortunately for the girls, she imposes her new beliefs on them. They no longer have Thanksgiving dinners; they no longer string Christmas lights. Mama copes with the transformation of their lives by focusing on life after death. She takes comfort in the thought that after this life, some people go to heaven, some go to a New World God will create after he gets tired of the mess humankind has made of this one, and some just turn to dust, the way their old lives have done (*Hush*, 112). She focuses on being thankful for what they have left, on trying to win back some former happiness by doing everything right, following all the rules so that she will make it to the New World where people will be able to pet snakes, and lions will be friendly. But, Evie thinks something has gone dead in her mother's face, especially when people stare right through her, as though she's "not even there" when she tries to hand them pamphlets and religious tracts (*Hush*, 101).

Because Mama drags the girls along to Kingdom Hall, Bibles in hand, Evie and Anna find themselves outsiders at their new school, taunted for being "Joho heads." Because Witnesses do not celebrate birthdays, Toswiah, who has already lost her identity under that name, feels as though she has lost even more sense of herself when, as she turns fourteen, her family does not even honor her birth. Toswiah, as Evie, tells us that it is hard to capture in language how events have affected her: "Is *sad* the word I'm looking for? No. It's not big enough. . . . It doesn't tell even a little bit of the truth—that this *missing* is like someone peeling my skin back . . . exposing everything underneath to air" (*Hush*, 11).

Evie's journey toward a new sense of self, a new position of visibility, is hindered by the fact that both the boys and the girls in her new school make her the target of their teasing. The boys call her "Neckbone" as she walks past, making her feel as though she has a third leg, causing her to walk strangely, to make her body feel all wrong (*Hush*, 15). The girls tease her about being from San Francisco, which is what

her new biography dictates she say when asked where she is from, calling her "Rice a Roni," and saying she acts as though being from San
Francisco makes her better than they are. She lives in fear of being
found out—and fear of never fitting in, of staying invisible. She writes,
"Most days my fear is as long as my shadow" (*Hush*, 77).

What makes things even worse for Toswiah as Evie is that there is
another Toswiah in her grade. In the past, Evie has reveled in her unusual name, liking its music, its uniqueness. Whenever she hears the
name "Toswiah" on the tongues of her classmates, she is tempted to
turn, wanting to be recognized. "I want to snatch her name away. . . . I
want to hear people calling it—calling out to *me*" (*Hush*, 79). The absence of her best friend Lulu is a constant hole in her life; Evie sometimes thinks that if only she could talk or write to Lulu, nothing would
feel so hopeless.

As was true for Woodson herself at Adelphi, Evie finally finds a way
out of her despair of invisibility through sports. Although her mother's
faith does not approve of participation on athletic teams, Evie is desperate to belong, to be noticed and truly seen. So she tries out for the
track team and when an older girl, Marie, begins calling her "Daddy
Longlegs" and other teammates dub her "Spider" as a compliment, Evie
begins to blossom. She starts to feel a pride in herself that has long been
missing (*Hush*, 133). She loves not only being part of the team but having a way to make her mark on the world. When she feels anger or sadness, she longs to run. "I wanted to feel the wind fighting me the way I
did when we sprinted outside. I wanted to beat it, push against it like
Leigh [their coach] yelled at us to do" (*Hush*, 140). She is upset when
Anna finds out about her running because she wants to keep it for herself, as she explains, "Because it is mine . . . I want to be good at something. I want to be amazing at it. So amazing that nobody is gonna be
able to take it away" (*Hush*, 151).

Anna and Evie learn to be strong, to fight their way into the light.
Anna gets her scholarship to Simon's Rock, and she actually wins her
mother's blessing to go, which she had doubted she would ever have,
given the Jehovah's Witness mistrust of higher education. Once her
mother finally receives her teaching license in their new state, she too
begins to revive, blossoming as she is offered a teaching job so that she
can once again use her talents to help children. Evie wins her spot on

the track team and finds ways to connect with, of all people, the other Toswiah. As Anna puts it, if the family is not just going to shrivel up and die as a result of their experiences, then, "The way I figure it is, I want to live, I mean really live, until the next thing happens" (*Hush*, 145). Evie relies on her new insights as she reaches out to reconnect with her father after his suicide attempt. She reflects that in the quarter mile she has to focus on each increment, on each "split"—getting around the first curve, then the next straightaway, then another curve until, finally, she can stretch toward the finish line. With her father, she uses this experience as a metaphor, focusing on each moment she has with him after his suicide attempt and subsequent hospitalization, knowing each one is "one more that I almost didn't have" (*Hush*, 163).

Running helps Evie blur her identities, blend her past and present into a different kind of future, one in which she is no longer invisible, one in which she can speak about herself with authority: "I am Toswiah Green. I am Evie Thomas. And, some days I like and love either and both of me. . . . I am no longer who I was in Denver, but at least and at most, *I am*" (*Hush*, 171).

Outer and Inner Landscapes— the Author's Developing Craft

In her *Booklist* review of *Hush*, Hazel Rochman describes Woodson's power as a writer as coming from her ability to use language noteworthy for its "beautiful simplicity, confronting the elemental moral issues through the eyes of a young girl who suddenly loses the protection of home and must make herself over."[23] The book opens with a beautifully poetic passage in a prologue that gives a hint of the fragility of the characters to whom we are being introduced. Two girls are hunched over their homework, sitting in a beam of sun that is backlighting a stream of dust. This image causes the younger—who will be the narrator—to recall a time now in the distant past and her sister's voice saying, "*It's made of bits of skin, mostly, I swear*. Skin that is dust, the youngest thinks. Dust that's sun. Sun that's heat that burns the skin. She shakes her head to stop the avalanche of thoughts from coming" (*Hush*, 1). Woodson here evokes the Biblical passage, "Ashes to ashes, dust to dust," and the reader immediately begins to wonder about the ways in which these two sisters have been reduced to dust—to nothingness—and about the nature of the avalanche of thoughts the younger sister wants to ward off.

Throughout the novel, Woodson uses poetic descriptions of the outer landscape as a metaphor for the interior landscapes of her characters, emphasizing in the process the ways in which a sense of place is important in crafting identity and in becoming visible. Before the slaying of the young black boy, when life feels comfortable and right, before Toswiah becomes Evie, she stares out at a perfect night that takes her breath away, and she tells us, "*Some mornings, when the sun is bright and the birds are going wild, she wants to hug something, hard—the whole world of it she wants to put her arms around*" (*Hush*, 4). Later, after the family has moved to the apartment in California, the earlier landscape contrasts with the new, when Toswiah, now Evie, describes her feelings about her new location: "And now this tiny apartment is supposed to be my home. At night, the building echoes with emptiness" (*Hush*, 10). The earlier descriptions are presented to the reader in italics, emphasizing that they describe a landscape no longer real. The italics look flowing and graceful on the page, a contrast to the more harshly printed descriptions of Evie's new reality, where she feels so lost, saying, "If a soul is the way you feel deep inside yourself about a thing, the way you love it, the way it stops your breath, then mine is still in Colorado" (*Hush*, 12–13). Even the cold of California feels different; it settles deep inside her, just like the terrible loneliness she is feeling (Hush, 87). Without the anchor of her home, Evie writes, simply,

> Who
> Am
> I? (*Hush*, 29)

Later, however, when Evie begins to make a fragile connection with the other Toswiah, she feels the wind differently; it begins to warm her on the outside the way becoming visible warms her on the inside (*Hush*, 110). And, as the novel is moving toward closure, the inner and outer worlds blur for Evie as she runs. Surrounded by the other girls, hearing the voice of her track coach, moving in unison with the team members and feeling connected, nevertheless Evie sees, as she runs, the Rocky Mountains, her grandmother, Matt Catt, Lulu, her father in a hospital gown, and two of herself—Toswiah and Evie, "blurring into each other" (*Hush*, 168).

Intersections of Language, Characterization and Theme

Woodson's use of evocative, poetic language is coupled in *Hush* with her strengths as a developer of character to create a novel that emotionally rings true on every page. Interestingly, editor Nancy Paulsen reports that this novel needed the least amount of line editing of any she has worked on with Woodson, but it did require some major revision. At first, Woodson tried to tell the story using alternating narrators, having the two sisters share responsibility for unfolding their tale. But, as the book is about identity on so many levels, and as there are difficulties for the reader, as is true for the characters, in moving between Cameron/Anna and Toswiah/Evie, they decided one voice would give the book more focus.[24] This was a crucial decision. Because readers come to care so much for Evie and her family, the theses Woodson presents, through their lived experiences, hit home; we believe in the truths the novelist gives us because we discover them with Evie and the others as the story unfolds. Evie, longing for her Lulu and her grandmother says, from the depths of her heart, "What I know now is this: Look at your grandmother's face. Remember the lines. Touch her cheekbones. Hold the memory of her in your fingers, in your eyes, in your mind. It may be all you get to keep" (*Hush*, 22). The reader wants to do just as she advises.

With Evie, we question Mama's religious beliefs. It is natural that Evie wonders why Jehovah would have allowed her life to become so chaotic. Evie thinks that if Jehovah's Witnesses have "the truth," somebody should be able to tell her the truth about why so much has happened to her family, about why her father had to be the one to witness the shooting of the boy (*Hush*, 116). But her thoughts take her further. She wants to know what happens to babies who die. They lose their lives before they have a chance to bear witness, to earn a place in the new world. Will they be destroyed? She and Anna want to know why Jehovah did not intervene to prevent Hitler from perpetrating the atrocities he delivered on the Jews, why Jehovah did not prevent Martin Luther King from being shot. Evie most of all wants to know how to bear this world while waiting for the next. Similarly, when Evie reports on Cameron/Anna's initial response to having her life upended, the bitterness is "so bitter it's refreshing" according to reviewer Arlene McKanic.[25]

In her questions, Evie mirrors the younger Woodson, who ultimately broke with the faith in which she was raised. She recalls going out to witness on a Saturday and coming to the home of an elderly woman who truly seemed to want to receive the word Woodson and her sister wanted to share; she wanted to read the pamphlets they were distributing. However, she had no money—not even the dime required in exchange for the materials. And so Woodson could not give them to her. That night, Woodson remembers begging her grandmother to take her back to the woman's home, asking what would happen to the old woman if Armageddon came overnight and she had not had a chance to know the truth. Woodson's grandmother replied, as Evie's mother does, that Jehovah knows our inner hearts and will understand.[26] But that was not a good enough answer for Woodson, nor is it for Evie.

What is most interesting about the scene in which Evie and Anna almost scream their questions at their mother is Mama's reaction. In spite of the challenges they are throwing at her, Mama is proud of their strength. In the moment of their conflict, Evie "saw her again—the lady I used to know in Denver. My mother" (Hush, 117). Mama responds by almost smiling as she remarks on their strength. Thus as readers we get the message that questioning is a sign of integrity and courage. When asked about her own grandmother's response to Woodson's rejection of the Witnesses, Woodson recalls that, until her death, her grandmother hoped she would return to "the truth," but "I think she was also relieved because I was always asking questions, wondering about the validity of stuff." And one of Woodson's biggest fears is that her own daughter and others of her daughter's generation will grow up not asking questions, so she gives her readers role models in characters who do find the courage to question, and who grow in the process.

In "Who Can Tell My Story" Woodson describes her own path toward acceptance of those who have been brave enough to ask her, honestly, genuinely wanting to know, how she feels about whether or not it is hard to use "standard English," or about how she feels when white authors write about people of color. She recalls reading a line by Audre

Lorde, "Your silence will not protect you," and how "As I came to understand what Lorde meant by this, I became grateful to those who
weren't afraid to take the chance and ask this question of me. And I became grateful for the chance to no longer be silent. Their asking af-
forded me the opportunity to have a dialogue and through this dialogue
to learn more about how people were thinking."[27]

With Evie, as was true for many of Woodson's earlier characters,
we come to understand the importance of stories, of the value of writing as a way to stay connected both with others and oneself. Sometimes Evie feels a "need to write" (*Hush*, 77) in order to make sense
of her emotions. Her family eagerly awaits the arrival of the mail,
hoping for messages from those left behind in Denver. However, letters cannot really communicate how life really feels, especially since
the family now has to follow many restrictions in writing them. They
cannot use their new names; they cannot mention the name of their
new school or town; they can only write letters about the most shallow aspects of their lives, holding themselves constantly on guard
against giving too much away. Their letters go to Texas before being
rerouted somehow to Evie's grandmother back in Denver. Nevertheless, they hunger for letters because in spite of everything, the letters
bring "the knowledge that we're all alive. That somewhere beneath
all the stupid shallow stuff, we're surviving. That we still love and are
loved" (*Hush*, 132).

With Evie, we try to focus on letting go of anger so that there is
space for love. In a poignantly realistic scene at the end of the novel,
Evie goes to see her father, hospitalized after his suicide attempt. In
spite of everything, Evie discovers she feels pride in being his daughter
as the nurses ask her father for an introduction; earlier, the respect all
the women in the family have for him is undercut by their perception
that he is weak for letting his doubts make him unable to function.
Evie's father, realizing this, and now very grateful to be alive, tells her
she has every right to be mad at him, to feel anger at the way his
choices affected her, her sister, and their mother, in so many negative
ways. He says she has a right to be mad at him for trying to take his own
life. But by this time, Evie, like Anna, has started to feel that whatever
the reasons for their circumstances, things are all part of a larger plan,
and the important thing is to be open to that plan, to its possibilities.

In this way, Evie is like other Woodson narrators such as the un-named teller of "What Has Been Done to Me" who discovers, "You spend your life waiting for the moment when you are free of the history your life makes for you—the moment you can step outside of who you once were and into the body of the person you have always been be-coming. Then, from that point on, the things that have been done to you no longer matter."[28] In this spirit, Evie just asks her father if he is truly glad that he is still in this world, and she tells him she no longer feels anger, shrugging, "It goes somewhere, Daddy. . . . I used to be mad about everything. I used to hate this place and all the people in it. I'd stand in the middle of the school yard and just . . . just shut every sin-gle part of me off" (*Hush*, 178). But now, she wants understanding. And she wants the chance to see who she can be, thinking "maybe, just maybe, [God] came up with a better idea" (*Hush*, 180) when she and her family were thrust into these new lives. Thus, says McKanic, "Quiet and heartrending, *Hush* . . . is an ultimately hopeful novel."[29]

Putting Books in the Hands of Children— Authors Fight Invisibility

In a review of the novel *Yo! Yes?* by Chris Raschka, Woodson articulates her views on the importance of communication as a way to minimize in-visibility: "I believe people will always be afraid of 'the other.' And be-cause the solution was, is, and will always be about communication, I choose Chris Raschke's *Yo! Yes?* as a book I would want to put into the hands of children today and a hundred years from now. . . . Raschka moves us through the boys'/peoples' doubt and loneliness into a place of hope. . . . I believe books like *Yo! Yes!* push the world toward thought and action and change and this is what art is meant to do. . . . I believe there will always be room in our world for growth and change, and a book in the hands of a child is a beginning."[30] Woodson's work consistently helps her readers truly *see* "the other." She gives us characters who are, in soci-ety at large, often invisible and shows us our common connections, our shared emotions. When Woodson began to write *If You Come Softly*, a love story about a black boy and a white Jewish girl, Woodson wondered what she could possibly bring to such a novel. She finally decided, "like the characters in my story, I have felt a sense of powerlessness in my lifetime. And this is a room into which I can walk and join them. This sense of being on the outside of things, of feeling misunderstood and invisible is the experience I can bring to my story."[31]

As her characters find ways to become more visible to the others populating Woodson's pages, they show us, too, ways that we can all work to maintain our integrity and the authority that comes from feeling ourselves to be worthy of being seen and valued. In the next chapter the specific difficulties that arise in being visible when one is homeless will be explored, and the ways in which Woodson's characters make homes for themselves, thus challenging society's sometimes thinly veiled desire to keep them homeless and invisible.

Notes

1. Woodson, "A Sign of Having Been Here," 2.

2. Jacqueline Woodson, *The Dear One*. (New York: Delacorte, 1991), 3. Hereafter cited as *DO*.

3. Lamb.

4. Woodson, "A Sign of Having Been Here," 2.

5. Jacqueline Woodson, "Who Can Tell My Story?" *Horn Book Magazine* 74, no. 1 (January/February, 1998), 34–39. 2. Academic Search Premier. 8 July 2002. Keyword: Woodson, Jacqueline.

6. Brown, "From Outsider to Insider," 2.

7. Jacqueline Woodson, *A Way Out of No Way*, 167.

8. Woodson, *A Way Out of No Way*, 168.

9. Woodson, *A Way Out of No Way*, 157.

10. Woodson, "Common Ground," 2.

11. Woodson, "Common Ground," 2.

12. Woodson, "Common Ground," 1.

13. Woodson, "Common Ground," 2.

14. Woodson, "Common Ground," 2.

15. Woodson, "Common Ground," 2.

16. Woodson, "Common Ground," 3

17. Woodson, "Common Ground," 4.

18. Roger Sutton, "Review of *The Dear One*," *Bulletin for the Center for Children's Books* 45 (September 1991), 26.

19. Saalfield, "Jacqueline Woodson," 583.

20. Ellen Fader, "Review of *The Dear One*," *Horn Book Magazine* 67, no. 6 (November/December 1991), 746.

21. Jacqueline Woodson, *Hush*. (New York: Penguin/Putnam, 2002), 42. Hereafter cited as *Hush*.

22. Brown, 1.

23. Hazel Rochman, "Review of *Hush*," *Booklist* 98 (January 1 and 15, 2002). Retrieved from www.ala.org/booklist/v98/ja1/61Woodson.html. Keyword: Jacqueline Woodson.

24. Paulsen.

25. Arlene McKanic, "Staying Strong: A Black Family Endures—Review of *Hush*." Retrieved from www.bookpage/com/0204bp/children/hush.html on 10 November 2002.

26. *Among Good Christian Peoples*.

27. Woodson, "Who Can Tell My Story?" 2.

28. Jacqueline Woodson, "What Has Been Done to Me," in *Go the Way Your Blood Beats: An Anthology of Lesbian and Gay Fiction by African-American Writers*, ed. Shawn Stewart Ruff (New York: Henry Holt, 1996), 87.

29. McKanic, "Staying Strong: A Black Family Endures—Review of *Hush*."

30. Jacqueline Woodson, "Review of *Yo! Yes!*" *Horn Book Magazine* 76, no. 6 (November/December 2000), 777.

31. Woodson, "Who Can Tell My Story?" 2.

~

CHAPTER THREE

On Being Homeless:
I Hadn't Meant to Tell You This,
Lena, and *Locomotion*

Hazel Rochman ends her review of *Hush* by remarking, "Woodson shows that while Evie's situation is extreme, everyone has to leave home and come to terms with many shifting identities."[1] In many ways, it is the loss of their home—the loss of their sense of place, both physical and emotional—that causes Evie and her family to feel so invisible. As they begin to cope with their pain, and to make places for themselves in their new town—by running, studying and getting into college, finding a job, making a suicide attempt and finally finding the space and time to talk about their pain—their new town begins to feel more like home. There is a chicken and egg factor at work in the relationship between being homeless and being invisible. Evie shows us how leaving home, dealing with shifting identities, and making connections with others leads to a sense of being "home."

In two earlier, connected works, Woodson explores the ways in which being homeless makes it difficult for people, particularly young adults, to be visible. *I Hadn't Meant to Tell You This* and its sequel, *Lena,* as well as the forthcoming *Locomotion,* give readers differing insights into other specific aspects of homelessness. Evie and her family have to be strong in order to create their new home, which they lost because, ironically, they stood up for justice and their racial community in the process. They, as Rochman puts it, leave home to find themselves. In other Woodson titles, characters cannot truly find themselves until they first feel a sense of home and belonging. Woodson says that the impulse to write about this need for home comes from her awareness that "the essence of childhood does not change. . . . There's always that sense of being an outsider, of feeling like you don't belong, or just feeling like you're not all right. That's where I usually start writing from, that place of needing something, of being a young person who has this feeling of wanting to have something—whether it's a family that's together, or a sense of themselves in the world, . . . or whatever it is."[2]

I Hadn't Meant to Tell You This, Woodson's 1994 Coretta Scott King Honor Book, is narrated by Marie, a twelve-year-old black girl, the daughter of a college professor, who lives in Chauncey, Ohio. She tells us on the opening page that there is a river, the Hocking River, which runs through her town, separating the well-off black community from the white side, the poor side, of town—and she goes on to say there is a third place, a "middle place," where she and Lena come together. Lena is the other main character in the novel, and she comes from that impoverished side of town. As the story unfolds Marie learns more about just how much Lena's poverty has affected her emotionally as well as materialistically.

A Place to Live is Not Necessarily a Home

The sense of place, important in many Woodson titles begins to mature in this novel. Chauncey was once a prosperous coal-mining town, filled with white miners and their families. But when various ordinances kicked in, closing mines, and the workers realized they were sick, with soot covering their lungs after years of digging, the government stepped in and moved most of the coal families to a nearby city, where they took factory jobs. But meanwhile, upwardly mobile black families realized Chauncey is both a pretty setting, and a commutable distance from the city. They begin to move into the town, transforming it into an all-black suburb. Simultaneously, the factories start to fail, and the mining families, never having truly adjusted to city life, start to move back "into the crevices," the uninhabited, undesirable spaces just outside the town.[3] Their children attend Marie's school where they keep to themselves, bringing their greasy lunches in brown bags, wearing stained and worn clothing. Marie's father calls them "trash," but her mother corrects him, saying they are "people . . . poor white people" (*Tell*, 5).

When Marie is young, she tends to side with her mother's way of looking at the world. But her mother is no longer part of Marie's life, and she has become, like her father, more "practical" about matters such as race relations. Mama has an affinity for the poor because, like them, she feels the atmosphere in Chauncey to be suffocating. When Marie was five, her mother—her face as "vague as the swamp behind Randolf Park" (*Tell*, 8)—said to her, as they wandered outside, "Sometimes a person takes off like maybe she's going fly. . . . Air . . . is something there isn't enough of here" (*Tell*, 8). In her quest for air, for a space to be herself, Mama leaves Marie and her father. Throughout the remainder of the book, Mama only exists through the postcards she sends her daughter from various exotic locations around the globe as she searches for a place to call home.

Meanwhile, on the surface Marie and her father seem to have a "home." They live in a comfortable, well-appointed house. They have routines and friends. Marie's father has a secure position, one of respect as a college teacher, and Marie is part of the popular crowd at school, where she does well both academically and socially. But it is through their contact with Lena that they learn more about what makes a place truly "home."

Though Marie is the narrator, it is Lena's story that carries the novel forward. Lena says to Marie, "I hadn't meant to tell you this"—and Marie swears she will not tell, even crosses her heart. As is true for Lena, Marie does not set out to break the silence, she "hasn't meant to tell" the readers Lena's story, but finally does so in the hopes that someday girls with similar experiences "can fly through this stupid world without being afraid" (*Tell*, 13). And that is why Woodson tells this story—to help all young girls find the courage to tell their stories, to become visible, and to make their places, their homes in the world.

Lena Enters Marie's World

Lena enters Marie's world on the third day of school. As Lena walks into Marie's eighth grade classroom, Marie hopes this new girl, whose white face stands out in the crowd of black ones, will not be seated next to her. But the teacher motions Lena toward the empty chair near Marie and Marie notices her oily hair, the ring around her collar, and she is repelled at first. But Marie also notices that while Lena's eyes are full of sadness, they also hold something else, something "like a thin layer of steel" (*Tell*, 13). The steel in Lena's gaze and her perfect posture intrigue Marie right from the start, even though from her father she has learned to be "not keen" on white people. Her father tells Marie that as a child he thought people were just people, but after marching to protest segregation, being hit in the face by a white man, even being arrested once just for being black in a white neighborhood, he has come to advocate separatism, and Marie too sees things in black and white.

Lena announces, "I am Elena Cecilia Bright. Everybody calls me Lena." Marie's friend Sherry replies with, "Who cares?" (*Tell*, 17). At lunch, as she spreads her napkin over her lap, Sherry glares at Lena, who does not seem to know what to do with a napkin. Lena's dialect sounds black to Marie, who asks her if she is black at all, and Sherry immediately cuts in to say of course not, "She's white trash" (*Tell*, 18). Marie notices how a muscle jumps on the side of Lena's throat, the one indication of how Sherry's words have affected her. Lena's eyes go cold and flat as she repeats Sherry's words, labeling herself: "I'm white trash" (*Tell*, 19)—and Marie is moved by Lena's broken look to somehow protect and befriend this unusual new girl. In spite of Sherry's admonition not to be an Uncle Tom, Marie agrees to show Lena around the school. And so begins a friendship between the two young women.

An interesting side note here is that at one point, early in the creative process, Woodson thought Lena was going to turn out to be the raggedy teenage mother encountered by Feni and Rebecca in *The Dear One*. When that character appeared in the earlier narrative, Woodson was intrigued by her, and wanted to tell her story. When Lena first walked onto the page, Woodson recalls that "I didn't know who she was, I didn't know about her father, I didn't know who Marie was." Woodson had heard, in her head, a raspy voice saying "Black, white, it don't make no difference," and she knew that Lena was connected to the voice, and she thought that voice was the same as the voice of the girl with whom Feni and Rebecca had their conversation. Woodson realized fairly quickly that Lena was not that same girl—for one thing, she never saw that teenaged mother as a southern girl and knew she had lived all her life in the Pennsylvania town where she had met Feni. But, Woodson had been thinking about that earlier character and in some ways, Lena is her successor.

Marie herself is a bit nervy. Like Woodson as an adolescent, she is tall and skinny, she is afraid of the larger high school students, and she feels startled by attention, disliking the limelight. Watching her mother become increasingly unhappy in her home has sensitized Marie to the need to look below the surface. She recalls how, when she was ten, "my mother hadn't been happy. Some nights, when my father was late coming home from work, I would hear her in the bathroom crying . . . sobbing, gulping for air, turning the water" on to disguise the fact of her grieving (*Tell*, 23). Later that year, Marie's mother just walks away, walks out into a rainy day with no umbrella but with her back straight and her head high, without looking back. Marie plans to use her inheritance, the same money that funded her mother's break with Chauncey, to search the world for her mother, and to bring her back to Ohio so that they can be a family once more (*Tell*, 24). Without her mother's presence, her father has gone silent. He no longer hugs Marie, and she is lonely in a house that does not feel like home.

The longing for family, for a mother who makes a house into a home, turns out to be a point of connection between Marie and Lena, who reminds Marie of her mother in some ways as she moves through the school hallways "like a steel wall, impenetrable and upright" (*Tell*, 33). As Marie begins to develop a friendship with Lena, she also begins to realize that she has been friends with Sherry primarily out of a fear of *not* being friends. She starts to see how girls flock around Sherry not because they like her, but because she has the power to hurt, with her words and her shunning, those girls who do not dress as she does or wear their hair like her. And so Marie begins to think more for herself, spending time with Lena, with whom she can really talk about important matters, rather than with Sherry. Lena's mother died of breast cancer, and Marie feels that Lena is her soul mate, because she, too, is "floating through the world without a mother" (*Tell*, 57), whereas with Sherry, Marie has felt only loneliness because Sherry never asks Marie about her mother's absence and has little idea of what is going on inside Marie's head and heart.

Connections Help Make a House a Home

In spite of their closeness, Lena has trouble telling Marie about the difficulties she faces at her own house. She tries to explain that she wishes she could love her father, but she cannot because, contradictorily, he loves her "too much" (*Tell*, 42). Marie does not understand what Lena means, saying—as she misses her mother and her father's hugs— "There's no such thing as too much love" (*Tell*, 42). Marie contends we all want more love; Lena is adamant that not everybody does. Gradually, Marie comes to understand from Lena that her mother had to leave home and the people she loved "in order to live" (*Tell*, 46), and it turns out that Lena will also have to make this same choice.

Why? We learn, with Marie, that Lena's father has been sexually abusing his daughter since his wife's death. Lena tries every possible strategy she can imagine in order to keep him at bay. She cuts her hair as short as possible so she will not have to wash it. That way, she can get out of the house more quickly in the mornings, thereby limiting the amount of time her father has to prey on her. Lena tries to make herself look as unappealing as possible, which Marie does not understand. Marie says if Lena does not take care of herself, people will ignore her, give her a wide berth. And Lena says, "I *want* them to. Everybody. Especially . . ." (*Tell*, 54). Lena reveals she cannot lock her bathroom door, that she cannot stand in front of her mirror without "things happening" to her. Lena wants desperately to be invisible, which Marie, missing her father's touch and closeness, cannot understand at first.

But Marie is a genuinely caring person, and as she begins to process Lena's confession, she does the work of friendship, asking questions that allow Lena to analyze and gain perspective on her situation, inviting Lena and her younger sister, Dion, into her own house to spend the night, to drink hot chocolate, and just to goof around, defending her friendship with Lena to her father. As she finds her way into a deeper level of friendship with Lena, Marie gains strength and self-confidence, and as a result, is able to make her house into more of a home for herself and her father. At the same time, knowing the friendship and concern of Marie, knowing what a home should feel like, gives Lena the confidence, ultimately, to leave her father in search of a home of her own.

In this novel, many of the important thematic elements and many aspects of her craft, which Woodson had been developing in the earlier trilogy and in *The Dear One* start to feel more polished, and they foreshadow the directions she takes in her later books. Most significantly, Woodson shows us, through Marie and Lena, the crucial importance for society as a whole of individual, one-on-one connections in overcoming barriers of race, class, and age. As she comes to know and care about Lena, Marie takes stock of her own situation: "For the first time I began to understand the privilege I had" (*Tell*, 96). Marie comes to recognize the shallowness of judging people based on their appearance and the quality of their clothes. As Marie's father gets used to having Lena and Dion in his house, he comes to admit that they are "nice girls" in spite of being both white and poor, and at one point, when Marie challenges her father about the fairness of using the term "white trash" if "nigger" is forbidden, he admits such names, such categorical ways of thinking about others, are counterproductive.

The Importance of Literature, Story, and the Arts

One of the ways the girls come together is through reading and sharing literature that touches them in some way. Together they wade through Audre Lorde's *The Cancer Journals*. Neither has experienced much breast development to date, but they are both fascinated with the book, using it to "get ready for something" (*Tell*, 102). From Lorde, they learn that battling despair means "teaching, surviving, and fighting with the most important resource I have, myself, and taking joy in that battle" (*Tell*, 102). They learn, too, that battling despair is contingent upon "knowing . . . my life and my love and my work has particular power and meaning relative to others" (*Tell*, 103).

Marie and Lena give each other that sense of providing "meaning relative to others." When Lena begins talking with increasing frequency about leaving her father's house, she wants Marie to know how much her friendship has mattered to her. When Marie watches Lena drawing, she wants Lena to know how peaceful Lena's art makes her feel. In the end, in spite of their very different life experiences, in spite of their parents' prejudices, in spite of the ways others around them would like to keep them apart, both girls feel, as Lena puts it, that "Black, white, it shouldn't make no difference. We all just people here" (*Tell*, 59).

The girls help each other better understand others, too. As Marie listens to Lena talk about her mother's battle with cancer, about how they could not afford to get treatment so that the cancer finally exploded inside her, Marie decides that her mother's desire to be elsewhere was like a cancer, just eating her up. Making this realization, Marie begins to come to terms with her mother's abandonment. In doing so, she can then focus on ways to feel at home with her father and in herself, saying, "The place around where my mother once was had begun closing over, a dull scar of a memory taking the place of what had been an out-and-out longing to have her back in our lives" (*Tell*, 93). Through telling her story to Marie, Lena actually is able to arrive at the remarkable conclusion that her father has not been himself; she recognizes that his wife's death changed him, confused him, threw him out of kilter to the point that he sees Lena as his wife and thus tries to take comfort through physical connections with his daughter.

Together, the girls are able to face the world with strength and courage. At one point a young man sees them together and asks to take their picture with a Polaroid camera because he wants to capture their look "that said neither of those girls in the picture trusts the world, but look how they're planning to blast through it" (*Tell*, 91). And so Lena begins to focus on how to grab some of Lorde's "sweet green silence" for herself and her sister, moving out of being just a victim of her family's situation to being in charge of her fate. Thus, when she and Dion finally take off, Marie, while missing her friend, is filled with a joy "that is screaming inside . . . *Yes! Yes!* They got away!" (*Tell*, 113).

Another theme that begins to ripen in *I Hadn't Meant to Tell You This* is the importance of having an artistic outlet as a means of making sense of the world. Woodson began writing at a very young age, and she continues to write not just creative works for publication, but to process her experiences. In "Going to My Room and Closing the Door," Woodson describes why keeping a journal is so important for her: "When I open my journal, it feels like I'm a child going into my room and closing the door. Exaltation. Exhale. Freedom inside my space. It's a place where I can tell the truth, 100 percent, and be who I am."[4] Woodson acknowledges that she cannot give all her characters writing as a creative outlet, so she often provides them with other artistic impulses. For example, Marie enjoys working with her father on home improvement projects; at one point, she describes the closeness she feels to him as they work side by side putting in a new slate floor, with an oak island, a sliding glass door out to their garden, and silver hooks from which to hang copper pots, and in doing so, how they create a feeling more of "home" (*Tell*, 63).

But it is Lena through whom Woodson truly shows her own belief in the importance of the arts. Lena is compelled to draw, to create alternative landscapes. This impulse is so strong that she actually steals drawing supplies—colored pencils—at one point. She creates a drawing for Marie, of weeping willows lining a lake, telling her friend that "When I'm drawing, it's like I go into another world or something. Nobody can't bother me" (*Tell*, 88). Lena *needs* to draw; she draws on any scrap of paper she can find, including brown paper bags, which she sometimes prefers to white paper because of the texture and shading she can achieve on the darker, rougher background. Through drawing, Lena is able to shape for herself another reality, one that, eventually, she has the courage to leave her father's house in order to seek. It is through her art that Lena makes herself visible. When she and Dion finally head out of town on their own, Lena leaves behind a drawing she hopes Marie will find, with the words "Elena Cecilia Bright and her sister Edion Kay Bright lived here once" (*Tell*, 113). Although Woodson says she herself has no artistic talent, she values "making" in all its forms, and she has characters throughout her work who sew, play musical instruments, and write poetry as ways of making order out of the chaos of their worlds, thus providing her readers with models of ways to handle anger, fear, and sadness themselves. She even describes her own writing as "brushstroking" because, as she says, "the page is very visual for me. I see the pictures in the words on the page . . . with each word and line, it becomes more of a visual image, it becomes more clear what is happening on that page."

Dialogue and Character Development

In terms of her craft, Woodson's skill in writing dialogue that reflects the reality of her characters' developmental needs and emotional maturity, which is strong even in her earlier works, also progresses in *I Hadn't Meant to Tell You This*. The scenes in which Lena tries to tell Marie about her father's abusive behavior are particularly good examples of Woodson's ear for dialogue. At one point, Marie is upset with Sherry's attitude toward Lena, and is upset with herself, and, as is often true for adolescents trying to cope with anger, Marie takes out her emotions on Lena, calling her "raggedy," and sniping about Lena's missing buttons, her unwashed hair. As Lena tries to explain why she does not take care of her appearance, Marie, faced with actions by an adult that are just too horrible to imagine, blocks what she is hearing by yelling at Lena that she is lying, that she just wants attention. At one point, Marie sees Lena's father and is consumed by hatred. However, he is too male, too white, too old for her to tackle, and so her hatred comes out at Lena, and she even yells at her friend that she must *like* what her father does (*Tell*, 81).

Gradually, as Marie is able to process what Lena has been saying, she begins to ask questions that allow Lena, for the first time, to put her experiences into words. And, through Lena, the reader then discovers just how insidious abuse is in its destruction of self-esteem. Asked by Marie how she feels when her father touches her, Lena replies, "Like I'm the dirtiest, ugliest thing in the world. . . . Like I'm not worth the water it takes to wash in the morning. Your father isn't like that. You would know. You would know by how sick you felt every time he touched you" (*Tell*, 57).

Woodson draws on her own experiences, such as working with runaway teens who experienced abuse, or dealing with the physical pain and exhaustion involved in running track to describe Lena's coping mechanism, which Woodson calls "tripping," and which involves trying to imagine herself in an alternative reality.[5] Lena tells Marie that when her father is having his way with her, "I go places now. . . . I take off, bam! And I'm gone. Thailand, Colorado, the Blue Ridge Mountains. I think of all the places I've heard of with beautiful names and try to imagine what they look like" (*Tell*, 76).

When Marie wants to know why Lena will not tell the police or some other authority about her father's behavior, Lena replies, again realistically, that she does not want to be separated from Dion, as happened to the sisters after their mother died. Lena hitched and stole her way to getting Dion back. Now her father moves them to a new loca-

tion "every time somebody comes sniffing around" (*Tell*, 77). Marie's reactions to Lena are consistently on target; she is very much a twelve-
year-old girl in her responses to Lena's story. Once she believes what
Lena is telling her, she has a million questions, and actually asks about
the possibility of pregnancy. But she stops herself from asking too many:
"I wanted to ask what he did and how. There were a million questions
pressing against the back of my teeth. But Lena looked as though she
had taken off. She looked hollow and vacant as the sky" (*Tell*, 79). So
Marie lets go and focuses on just being Lena's friend. In general, Woodson is able to let things "hang in the air," writes Roger Sutton, adding,
"All the emotions played out here are rough-edged and ambivalent, as
are the frank discussions about race. . . . The story has an elegiac quality that gets to the hearts of both girls' dilemmas in ways that a more
prescriptive novel could not, and the spare writing generally allows
events to speak for themselves."[6]

One other aspect of the novel deserves particular note. In addition to
the realism of the voices of the girls, Woodson includes postcards from
Marie's mother, which are written in a very different voice, and through
the snippets of poetry and brief descriptions of what her mother is seeing
in the variety of places she visits, a portrait of this unsettled woman
emerges. Woodson uses language like an Impressionist painter uses color;
we get broken bits of images and fragments of thoughts in both Marie's
memories of her mother and in her mother's postcards that, taken together, for the reader as well as for Marie, create a picture of a troubled
woman. Marie recalls one time when she "had seen my mother shake my
daddy's hand off her like it was a snake, . . . then let go and spit and
scream to send tears and snot flying" (*Tell*, 33). Later, her mother writes
from the south of France, "In this world in this age maybe you will have
perfect moments/when you catch the way light grooves across ice/ . . . You
won't remember how the icy air/pierced the tops of your ears/ . . . In this
world in this age/Maybe you will have an hour to grieve" (*Tell*, 65–66).
Later, she writes that she longs to catch life and let herself swing with
what it has to offer before she is too old or too afraid.

The portrait that emerges from these postcard jottings is that of
someone who feels claustrophobic in her own skin, of someone who has
strong emotions, but who cannot let herself make commitments for fear
of feeling strangled by them. As Marie receives these notes, she comes

to accept that she cannot ask too much of her mother; at one point late in the novel she notes how her mom signs her postcards, "Love, me," which has an ambiguous meaning. Marie wonders if her mother is making a statement, or, more likely, if she is asking Marie for her love. We do not have many such poems and observations, but Marie's mother, absent as she is, has a strong presence in the novel and in Marie's life as a result of Woodson's exquisitely chosen language and attention to detail. Woodson's honesty in describing her characters in all their humanness, and her ability to ask hard questions result in a novel of which Carolyn Polese writes, "By skillfully weaving together themes of abandonment, emotional maturation, and friendship across social and economic barriers, the author goes far deeper than the typical 'problem novel.' . . . While there are no easy answers for the girls, there is honesty, growth, and love in their relationship that gives young readers hope for the future."[7]

Lena: The Story Continues

Interestingly, however, not all readers of I Hadn't Meant to Tell You This felt that sense of hope for Lena and Marie upon finishing the novel. As a result, Woodson says she received many, many letters from young readers asking for more clarity about what happened to Lena and Dion. Woodson recalls, "I thought I was finished, and I thought I had told the whole story, but I got so many letters. . . . I thought it was clear—they got away. But the readers were like, 'That's not good enough for us!' and it was the first time that a kind of peer pressure kept me writing the sequel." That sequel is Lena, which she dedicates to, among others, "brave girls everywhere."[8]

Wendy Lamb, Woodson's editor at the time, talked with the author about the project, noting that in general it is hard to write a sequel or companion book because the writer has to figure out how to deal with all the issues that get raised in the first book, and told Woodson to make sure she really wanted to spend more time with the characters. At first, Lamb was not sure how realistic Woodson's concept for the plot was, particularly the ending, but she did feel that I Hadn't Meant to Tell You This led naturally to a sequel. Ultimately, Lamb trusted Woodson to write her book in her own way and now says that "*Lena* contains some of Woodson's most beautiful writing."[9] In this novel, Lena takes center stage, telling her own story of the journey on which she and younger sister Dion embark as they head out of Chauncey and into a very uncertain future, truly homeless. They hit the road armed with a bit of money, all the layers of clothes they can wear at one time, books for Dion, and Lena's absolute certainty that they "got a right to be in this world just like everybody else walking through it" (*Lena*, 1).

Lena tells us about her family's history and we are given more details about the events that led to Lena and Dion's current plight. While the family was never financially secure, in the past Lena's dad had worked when he could, and their mama made sure they ate regularly and stayed clean. But they lacked money to treat Mama's cancer, and she wasted away, leaving Lena's father distraught and displaced, unanchored. Lena describes her own grief in poetic terms, saying "After a while . . . the *knowing* settled down inside of me. Made itself a home there" (*Lena*, 3). In the same way, she realizes that her father has changed permanently; she knows he is going to continue to abuse her and when she discovers that he has started looking at Dion in the same way he looks at her, she knows in that deep-seated way that she has to leave and must take Dion out of harm's way. While it is scary to be on the run, Lena finds it easier to be scared of strangers, which is a natural sort of fear, than constantly to experience being "scared of my daddy. Scared of the morning and nights in our house. Scared for Dion" (*Lena*, 9).

Lena is a strong young woman with a very practical turn of mind who has an instinct for survival. She and Dion disguise themselves as boys so that, when they hitch rides with truck drivers, they will be better able to keep the men in their place. When they see a woman driver, they let themselves become girls again, knowing ladies are more comfortable with young females. Before hitting the road, Lena uses the library to find out the locations of all the hospitals in the states through which they will travel. When they need warmer coats as December turns colder, they know to go to the Salvation Army for coats and gloves. They rehearse the lies they tell their benefactors on the road so that they will be consistent and will be believed. They learn how to become "invisible," hanging out at libraries, which Dion, a precocious and avid reader, loves, and hospital waiting rooms—places where nobody questions seeing two children without adult supervision.

Nevertheless, at times somebody will see through their act. A wait-ress figures out their secret and, having been in similar circumstances herself, treats them to a huge breakfast, and offers words of advice. Lena later invokes the waitress as a role model, telling Dion, "She's been on the road same as us. And look at her. She made it to the other side. Got herself a job and everything" (*Lena*, 26). The girls do not want charity; they want to make their way to their mama's home-stead, and they want the opportunity to make a home for themselves there. Lena's understanding of the world often shows her to be wiser than her years. While she and Dion are visible to the waitress because of their shared experiences, Lena knows that to many people their unkempt state and raggedy clothes make them invisible: "People see somebody poor and they think it's cause the person don't want to work or don't have good sense or something, but that's not always true. People all the time looking to blame a person's troubles on the person" (*Lena*, 50). So, Lena tries to keep herself and Dion as clean as possible, hoping people will really see them—but while some peo-ple look, they do not really see the two girls as real people: "Calls us white trash. White cockroach. Cracker. There's not a name I haven't heard somebody call me" (*Lena*, 51), and in so labeling them, the world makes them invisible, taking away their worth. As Lena puts it, "It's like the names *own* you" (*Lena*, 51).

One of the survival techniques Lena adopts is that of telling stories. They are on their own, on the road, over Christmas, and to ease their loneliness, Lena begins recalling the details of earlier holidays, remind-ing Dion of how she ate and ate cornbread one Christmas, of how their mama would French braid her hair and find candy canes for them to suck. Lena calls up habitual dialogues they had with their mother, in which she would ask them "Who's your favorite Mama?" and they would answer, entwining themselves in her arms, "The one who can hug us tightest!" (*Lena*, 44). And then the girls hug, remembering their mother's affection and love, and drawing strength to head down the road some more from their memories of her bread baking, of sitting by their potbellied stove drinking hot chocolate with her. Through story-telling, the girls keep their sense of self; through story, they create a sense of "home" even though they are on the road, alone, and home-less. And later Lena shares with Dion some of the passages from Lorde's

Cancer Journals that she and Marie found particularly powerful, telling Dion how Lorde's descriptions made her feel quiet and restful.

The girls' conversations are not always so pleasant. Dion, having escaped, through Lena's interventions, the kind of sexual abuse Lena has known, has mostly fond memories of her father. Lena tries to explain the complexities of their situation, telling her sister, "Our daddy—well, he needs somebody to help him learn to treat us right. But he don't know it yet. And when he finds out and gets some help, then maybe we'll see him again" (*Lena*, 46). Dion wants to know, echoing the cry of so many innocent victims, why it has to be *them* whose daddy cannot be a good parent and provider, asking "What'd we do bad?" Lena, showing her how centered she is, replies firmly, "We ain't done nothin' bad. Not me and not you. . . . It ain't our fault, either. You hear me?" (*Lena*, 47).

Finding Home and Becoming Visible

Eventually the girls are picked up by an older black woman, Miz Lily, driving a Lincoln, who asks them all kinds of questions that the male truck drivers with whom they have been riding have not thought to ask. Dion, having been raised by a father who does not like blacks, initially balks at getting into Miz Lily's car, but Lena reminds her that "We all just people here. Me, you, Miz Lily, Larry, that waitress at Berle's. You keep that in your head, you'll be all right" (*Lena*, 65–66). Miz Lily finds the holes in their story, and seems to know, intuitively, that the girls are in trouble. She takes them to her house, which Lena describes as "one of those neat old-lady houses—the kind with tiny crocheted saucer-looking things laying across the back of her couch and over her table" (*Lena*, 62). Miz Lily has an entire mantel filled with pictures of her family. She is a loving, giving woman who tells the girls that while she does not have much, they are welcome to anything in her home. She sends them to take a hot bath, feeds them stew, washes their clothes, and treats them with respect and tenderness. She asks Dion to pray a blessing for their evening meal, and Dion explains her own views about God, saying he is not in Heaven but is rather inside us. So Miz Lily, honoring her beliefs, suggests she just pray to that God inside herself, which she does, poignantly thanking God for "being inside us and showing us the way . . . and thank you for food and poetry, Amen" (*Lena*, 68).

Poetry is important to Dion, as it is for Woodson, who says she reads her favorite authors over and over again, revisiting texts and getting something new from the words each time.[10] Dion hears Chopin on Miz Lily's radio and comments that the music is poetry without words, saying "And if you was reading a poem you could read it the same way. . . . You could read it like it was—like the words was notes floating on paper. Floating all around the paper" (*Lena*, 70). Lena does not fully understand Dion and her thoughts. She fully admits that her younger sister is more book smart than she will ever be, acknowledging that while her own brain sees things in a straight line, Dion's moves all around, examining the world from various angles, making unusual connections (*Lena*, 70). Dion has a hunger for knowledge that fuels her so that sometimes she walks three miles to a library and then sits there all day reading. Lena wants Dion to be able to explode upon the world, to become something amazing, maybe a college professor like Marie's father. And that hunger to support her sister is what fuels Lena as they walk and walk and walk, searching for their mama's homestead.

However, at Miz Lily's, Lena realizes that her quest for Pine Mountain and her mother's family is probably unrealistic. The care they receive from Miz Lily, and the sense of well-being they have under her care show Lena that they cannot stay on the road. She acknowledges that Dion needs school—and that she herself needs, "I don't know . . . a home, I guess" (*Lena*, 75). Because Miz Lily truly sees them, Lena is able to realize, "Me and Dion was like those actors in *The Wizard of Oz*—the thing we'd needed and wanted most was right there inside us all along . . ." (Lena, 81). She reflects that they are like Dorothy, trying to get home and make themselves a place in the world. She also realizes that at Marie's house back in Chauncey, they had truly felt a sense of being "home"—because Marie, and even her father, had seen them as individuals, had treated them kindly (*Lena*, 82).

So Lena calls Marie, who shares the remarkable news that not only is the whole town looking for the girls, but that their father has taken off, leaving town without a trace; the shack they used to call home is now rented to someone else. Marie also reports that her own father wants Lena and Dion to come back to Chauncey and live with them. She tells Lena that her dad is different now, "Now that I told him everything—It is like. . . I think he knew there was no way he could keep my mother from leaving but there was a way he could have kept you and Dion from going. That changed him. He really wants to find you and Dion" (*Lena*, 89). When Lena hears this, she feels like, in a line from a Jimi Hendrix song girls often repeat, she can "kiss the sky." To Marie and her father, Lena and Dion know they are not invisible, and that makes everything else okay. Marie's father intuitively knows what it is the girls need; he says he will not be satisfied until they are safe and have "a home" (*Lena*, 109).

Somewhat differently than in her other novels, in *Lena*, Woodson sometimes contrasts the exterior landscape with her characters' state of mind. For instance, Lena comments that "Beautiful days broke me up inside. They made me think of all the kids in the world who could just wake up in the morning and pull the curtain back from the windows and stare out at the day and smile" (*Lena*, 16). But there are also days when, like the morning after the kindly waitress feeds them a huge breakfast, and the sun is warm, and the sisters are walking toward their goal, Lena knows "what it felt like to be free" (*Lena*, 71). And the coldness of the days on the road are contrasted with the way the sun is shining bright and warm on the day Lena and Dion get on a plane to head back to Chauncey, a day when Lena "felt rich—inside, like everything about the world was falling in place and there wasn't so much empty inside me any more" (*Lena*, 106). On that day, Lena feels just like the patch of sun she sees on Miz Lily's carpet, bright and warm, in the knowledge that she is wanted, in the knowledge that she is real and visible— a knowledge made tangible by the photos Miz Lily takes of the girls to place on the mantelpiece with those of her family. And in the end, with the plane leaving the ground to carry them to Marie and her father, Lena sketches the mountain kissing the sky, as she and Dion head "home" (*Lena*, 115).

Woodson successfully accomplishes, in this set of novels, her own stated purpose; on the Random House website, she says, "I really wanted to write about friendship. I wanted to write about people crossing racial lines to be friends and people crossing class lines. I wanted to write about what it meant to be a girl in this society, in a society where self-esteem seems to go down when your reach a certain age. And the characters just started coming to me. . . . I wanted to write about freedom . . . how it's okay to feel like you need to be free of something and it's okay to have to leave sometimes. I wanted to write about when it's okay to leave and okay to stay."[11]

Writing One's Way to Home

Lonnie, in *Locomotion*, is younger than Marie and Lena, but he knows the same kind of grief and sadness as the girls have felt from the abandonment of a parent and the loss, as a result, of a sense of safety and "home." Lonnie, eleven as he narrates the story, lost his parents when their home burned on December 9, during the year he was seven, and four years later, on the anniversary of that fire, Lonnie still becomes physically ill with the memories. Since that awful day, Lonnie has been part of the foster care system, which separated him from his little sister, Lili. She was taken in by a woman who just does not care much for boys. On the other hand, Lonnie was moved about, and did a stint at a group home, before being placed with Miss Edna. Miss Edna has two sons of her own, one of whom is in the armed services, fighting in a war; the other lives upstate and does not visit very often, so Miss Edna has space in her simple house for Lonnie, but when the story opens, he does not *feel* at home there. Unlike Lena and Dion, who first learn that it is okay to leave, Lonnie is struggling to feel that it is okay to stay. For one thing, Miss Edna fusses at him to be quiet. He thinks that maybe eleven is just a noisy age, and he becomes befuddled by her admonitions, saying her voice makes "all the ideas in my head go out like candles,"[12] so that he never feels quite settled with her.

As the story opens, Lonnie is in fifth grade. His teacher, Ms. Marcus, introduces him and his classmates to various forms of poetry and encourages them to write. *Locomotion* is told in fragments rather than linearly as Lonnie uses the various poetic genres suggested by his teacher to explore his history, his feelings, and his world in general, while at the same time writing through his grief to a stronger sense of self and home. He responds to Ms. Marcus and her assignments for poetry writing because she listens to him and takes him seriously. At one point he notes that she tells him "*Good Lonnie, write that*/Not a whole lot of people be saying *Good Lonnie* to me" (*Locomotion*, 1).

Lonnie, like Woodson, uses the environment as a metaphor for his state of mind. When he recalls the peaceful pleasures of just sitting with his Mama while holding Lili as a baby, he evokes images of the sun, "getting bright and warm outside suddenly/like it'd been listening in" on their conversations (*Locomotion*, 5). This idyllic vision contrasts to his experiences in the group home, where the other residents refer to themselves as the "Throwaway Boys." He realizes, on a rainy afternoon holding no promise, that he is one of those boys now—his relatives no longer visit, he has lost track of his little sister, and that realization sits in his stomach "hard and heavy as Group Home food" (*Locomotion*, 16). At Miss Edna's house, which feels cramped and where he has to temper his voice and his actions, Lonnie escapes to the roof, telling us "up here the sky goes on and on like something/you could fall right up into" (*Locomotion*, 25). Up there, he can dream about Tahiti and Puerto Rico and Australia and Spain, not worrying about where he will have to live next,

> and then you can come on back
> and call the place you come back to
>
> home. (*Locomotion*, 25)

The white space works well to show, tangibly, the distance between Lonnie's dreams of home and where he actually lives.

The Poet's Craft

As a poet, Lonnie is attentive to sensory details. At one point, recalling how his mother used honeysuckle-scented talcum powder, he describes going to a cosmetics counter and asking to smell a sample. As the scent fills his nostrils, his mama comes alive for him again—even though he is nervous because he is afraid the clerk will think he is trying to steal her wares. Lonnie still has his dad's hat with "CON EDISON" printed on it in stark white letters (*Locomotion*, 19). Asked to write an epistle poem after hearing a model by Langston Hughes, Lonnie writes one to his father, recalling vivid images of eating hot dogs streaming with yellow mustard while the voice of the vendor yells at Lonnie and his dad for being Mets fans, yet giving them a discount for buying four dogs. He still has the memories of calling his mother, a receptionist, and hearing her voice turn from professional and cool to warm and nurturing, and he says "that stupid fire couldn't take away all of them/Nothing could do that" (*Locomotion*, 19).

Also as a poet, Lonnie has to experiment with the tools of his art as his own creator does. When Woodson decided to write *Locomotion* in poetry, a genre in which she has not published as an adult, she had to explore the ways poetry as a visual medium makes use of the page as a canvas for word pictures. She struggled with the line breaks, and finally, with assistance from her editor and others, got them just the way she wanted them—only to be told they would not fit that way on the page. So, she went back to the beginning and reworked them. Lonnie also thinks about line breaks and his use of space on the page, writing "line breaks help/us figure out/what matters/to the poet" (*Locomotion*, 4).

What matters to Woodson is that readers come to care about Lonnie and are able to see the world from his point of view. So she and Lonnie use line breaks to show his vulnerabilities. Asked to write a poem about Halloween, Lonnie tells us that in fifth grade students no longer make pictures of ghosts and pumpkins:

> We don't want to
> I mean we're not supposed to want to
>
> But sometimes
> I do. (*Locomotion*, 17)

It is the space between what he is supposed to do, and his longing for childhood that show us Lonnie's sensitivities. His teacher tells the class that most sonnets are about love, explains the form, and asks them to write one of their own. Lonnie begins with thoughts of his mother and father and little sister, and ends with the couplet, "If I had one wish I'd be seven years old again/living on President Street, playing with my friends" (*Locomotion*, 20). His poem isn't a love sonnet in the tradition of Shakespeare, but he definitely uses the form to show his feelings for his family and his longing for a home.

There is not much plot in *Locomotion*. Several events happen to characters in Lonnie's world, and he makes observations about them, but there is not the traditional novel's rising action, climax, and denouement. Instead, readers see Lonnie gradually coming to terms with his situation, gradually forging relationships with others, and gradually recognizing that he and Miss Edna can make a family, and that he does, in fact, have a home with her.

Some of these realizations come as a result of his reflections on the world around him. A new boy, Clyde, joins Lonnie's class; in Clyde, Lonnie recognizes a fellow outsider. Clyde is dressed all wrong for Lonnie's school—his pants are too short, his socks are light blue, he wears a white shirt buttoned up to the neck. Lonnie observes, "New boy looking like he wish he could/just melt right on outa the room" (*Locomotion*, 30). But Clyde also has a little sister, and Lonnie is filled with an ache for Lili when he watches them together. Looking on, he feels something in the back of his throat "close up and choke at me. Then slide on/down to my stomach and make itself some tears" (*Locomotion*, 41). So, while other students taunt Clyde, Lonnie finds a point of connection with him. Clyde is from Georgia, a place Lonnie once knew, and they sit on the playground, remembering Georgia peaches, "slow-pitching little stones" (*Locomotion*, 90), and enjoying a sense of togetherness.

Missing Lili so much, Lonnie decides to take action in order to see her more often. He asks Lili's foster mother if he can go to church with them some Sundays. Lili believes in God, carries her Bible with her on her visits to Lonnie, and wants Lonnie to share her certainty in the goodness of her God. He is skeptical, but some days, when he is with Lili and the sun is shining, and they are munching slowly on cookies, together, Lonnie feels God beside him (*Locomotion*, 76). Gradually, Lonnie is able to win, if not the affection, at least the tolerance, of Lili's foster mother, so he no longer fears losing Lili—and he sees God in his little sister's smile.

Lonnie is also moved to make the most of what he does have when he learns that one of his classmates, the class bully, has sickle cell anemia. Lonnie has been puzzled by Eric in the past. One time he went with Miss Edna to a different church and saw Eric, always large and mean at school, singing a solo with the choir, his voice like an angel's. So Lonnie figures that somewhere inside Eric there is a nicer, gentler person, which is what he tries to think about when he sees Eric being a bully on the playground. Eric becomes the subject one of Lonnie's poems when he returns to school from an extended hospital stay, skinnier and quieter than the old Eric. Even his closest friends do not seem to be able to look him in the eye, and he turns away from the other students like he "knows some things/we'll never know" (*Locomotion*, 91). Lonnie begins to realize he is not alone in having experienced sorrow and upheaval. He begins to read the Bible Lili gave him, trying to make sense of the phrase he often hears from grownups about God's "mysterious ways."

And then there is Lonnie's growing friendship with LaTenya. Woodson shows her own artistry in the details she gives us about Lonnie's responses to this young woman. We already know from his poetry that Lonnie has a good heart, that he is sensitive and yet is also just a typical eleven-year-old boy. But in having Lonnie describe LaTenya, Woodson rounds out the picture. When LaTenya watches him shoot baskets, miraculously, Lonnie's balls start to go through the hoop. He is attracted by the smell of her coconut hair grease. He likes to watch her jump rope. And when she shows him the bump on her hand where the extra finger with which she was born has been cut off, asking if Lonnie will now call her a freak, he just rubs the spot and smiles and whispers, "No" (*Locomotion*, 96).

On the other hand, Woodson also shows us Lonnie when he is angry and upset, as on the day his teacher asks the class to write a haiku, and Lonnie produces

> Today's a bad day.
> Is that haiku? Do I look
> Like I even care? (*Locomotion*, 14)

The Importance of Adults in the Child's Quest for Home

Lonnie's teacher has a lot to do with his growth, just as Woodson was encouraged by those teachers who valued her writing and gave her the advice to follow her passions. Ms. Marcus is not perfect, by any means. There are things about her students she just does not understand. In his journal Lonnie writes about a commercial involving a white family fixing dinner. Ms. Marcus has emphasized the importance of using lots of details, so he is confused when she asks him why he bothered to note that the family is white. Lonnie tries to tell her he included that specific detail because it is true, reflecting "If you're white you/can't see all the whiteness around you" (*Locomotion*, 12), and going on to remark that even though Ms. Marcus is his favorite teacher, she does not really understand "things like my brown, brown arm. And the white lady/and man with all that food to throw away/How if you turn on your T.V., that's what you see—people with/lots and lots of stuff not having to sit on scratchy couches" (*Locomotion*, 13). Ms. Marcus's students want to know, for instance, if Richard Wright made a lot of money as a writer, and she tells them he wrote because he loved writing, which is all she says matters—to which her students say, "Not if you're poor" (*Locomotion*, 67). When she tells the class about Eric's illness, she whispers the fact that it is common among African-Americans. But Ms. Marcus gives Lonnie an identity. She tells him, "*You have a poet's heart, Lonnie*" (*Locomotion*, 87), and he knows that is a good thing to have, and feels good about himself, knowing he has one. As he processes his experiences through his writing, he becomes more visible to himself and to others, and he is able to start relaxing into Miss Edna's house.

Lonnie realizes that Miss Edna really does want him to make his home with her one day when, after she gets her paycheck, they go to the grocery store to stock up on Twinkies. The clerk remarks to Miss Edna that her son must really like Twinkies, "And Miss Edna looks at me sideways/then she smiles and says/*Yeah, I guess he does*"—without correcting the clerk about the nature of their relationship (*Locomotion*, 37). On the anniversary of the fire, knowing Lonnie will be sick, Miss Edna calls in to say she will not be at work, and she prays to God to lessen Lonnie's burden. She introduces him to her neighbor, and Lonnie connects with Todd, who raises pigeons. With Todd, Lonnie comes to appreciate the beauty and softness of the birds, the way their sounds come together like a song that makes you "believe in everything/you ever wanted to believe in" (*Locomotion*, 35–36). When Miss Edna's son decides to move back home, Lonnie finds her dancing with a broom, because she is so happy, and she wants to include Lonnie in her joy. He writes a list poem about the food they make to celebrate Rodney's return. Food is important to Woodson's characters, and the kinds of foods they eat and share indicate a great deal about their frame of mind (*Locomotion*, 82). And then Rodney himself helps Lonnie feel at home. He calls Lonnie, "little brother" while shooting hoops with him, giving Lonnie a sense of belonging and connection.

At the end of the book, readers know Lonnie will be okay. He, like Lena and Dion, now has a home. Lili thinks everything has turned out well because Lonnie has read the Bible she gave him; he lets her think this, because she is his younger sister, and he would say anything "to keep her smiling" (*Locomotion*, 100). But it is his growing identity as a writer, and his sense of home at Miss Edna's, that have helped him find a center. On a perfect day, watching Lili smile, or when he digs into Miss Edna's sweet potato pie, he senses in himself the certainty of Ms. Marcus's words, "*One day I'll see your name in print. . . . You have a gift, Lonnie*" (*Locomotion*, 99). The poems now come to him day and night, the days make themselves into poems, with pictures of people laughing and "eating and reading and playing ball and skipping along and spinning themselves into poetry" (*Locomotion*, 100).

The novel is about, in part, Lonnie's growth as a writer. But in allowing Lonnie to tell his story through poems, Woodson also shows her own growth as a writer who now trusts herself enough to experiment with form, and to choose a narrator in some ways quite different from herself: Lonnie is young, male, heterosexual. But she gives Lonnie the gift of writing as a tool for survival, knowing firsthand the value of writing as a way of learning about oneself and the world. Lonnie tells us that writing makes him remember; when he writes, his family comes back to him, "like somebody pushed the rewind button" (*Locomotion*, 42). But Lonnie also reminds us that writing is hard work, that it takes persistence, saying "You don't just get to write a poem once/You gotta write it over and over and over" (*Locomotion*, 62). And sometimes, Lonnie knows that the writing is never going to go public. Ms. Marcus asks to see all of his poems, but Lonnie refuses, because "some things just your own" (*Locomotion*, 59).

As a young adult, Woodson's brother found her journals and blabbed about some of the contents to their grandmother, so now she, like Lonnie, struggles to give herself "permission to tell the truth and not let this fear of self-expression stunt her growth as a woman or as a writer."[13] At least to the public, it is clear that Woodson has not been stunted in her development as a writer. In *Locomotion*, Woodson's tendency toward lyrical, spare prose becomes actual poetry, and she writes an elegiac, richly detailed story through poetry of a young man's quest for self and home that works because of her ability to give us Lonnie's voice and to make us care about him.

In some ways it is unfair to return to Woodson's earlier novels of friendship after the satisfying reads of *I Hadn't Meant to Tell You This*, *Lena*, and then the beautifully written, lyrical *Locomotion*. But in other ways it is valuable to examine the Maizon and Margaret trilogy in light of what followed them. While it is true that this trio of novels cannot compare to Woodson's later books in terms of their craftsmanship, it is useful to see how the themes Woodson later develops are first explored in the earlier works, and how she experiments with the artistic elements of her writing in ways that she then shapes and controls more effectively with practice over time, which is what the next chapter explores.

Notes

1. Hazel Rochman, "Review of *Hush.*" *Booklist* 98 (January 1 and 15, 2002). Retrieved from www.ala.org/booklist/v98/ja1/61woodson.html on 10 November 2002. Keyword: Woodson, Jacqueline.

2. Samiya A. Bashir, "Tough Issues, Tender Minds," *Black Issues Book Review* 3, no. 3 (May/June 2001), 78.

3. Jacqueline Woodson, *I Hadn't Meant to Tell You This*. (New York: Bantam/Doubleday/Dell Books for Young Readers, 1994), 4. Hereafter cited as *Tell*.

4. Jacqueline Woodson, "Going to My Room and Closing the Door," in *Speaking of Journals: Children's Book Writers Talk about Their Diaries, Notebooks, and Sketchbooks*, ed. Paula W. Graham (Honesdale, PA: Boyds Mill Press, 1999), 64.

5. Woodson, "A Stolen Childhood," 2.

6. Roger Sutton, "Review of *I Hadn't Meant to Tell You This*," *Center for Children's Books* 47 (May 1994), 239.

7. Carolyn Polese, "Review of *I Hadn't Meant to Tell You This*," *School Library Journal* 40 (May 1994), 136.

8. Jacqueline Woodson, *Lena*. (New York: Delacorte, 1999).

9. Lamb.

10. Brown, "From Outsider to Insider," 2.

11. "Jacqueline Woodson," Retrieved from www.randomhouse.com/teachers/authors/wood.htm on 4 September 2001, 5.

12. Jacqueline Woodson, *Locomotion*. (New York: Putnam, 2003).

13. Woodson, "Going to My Room and Closing the Door," 61.

~

CHAPTER FOUR

On Being Friends:
The Margaret and Maizon Trilogy

Woodson began writing the manuscript that eventually became *Last Summer with Maizon* during her college days. Published in 1990, it is the first in a trilogy including *Maizon at Blue Hill*, which appeared in 1992, and *Between Madison and Palmetto*, the 1993 completion of the story of friends Maizon and Margaret. *Last Summer with Maizon* was greeted by critical acclaim for Woodson's ability to evoke a sense of place, and Karen Brailsford, in a *New York Times* review, admired Woodson's "poetic, eloquent narrative that is not simply a story of nearly adolescent children, but a mature exploration of grown-up issues: death, racism, independence, the nurturing of the gifted black child, and, most important, self-discovery."[1] Other reviewers, such as Roger Sutton and Susan Schuller, noted that there are gaps in the narrative. It is true that in this first effort Woodson prefers "dialogue over action,"[2] and that at times the reader is left wondering "just what happened and why."[3] However, looking back at this first novel from the vantage point of Woodson's artistic maturity in works such as *Locomotion* and *Hush*, it is possible to see how the writer begins to deal with the themes and issues she continues to explore in increasingly sophisticated ways, and how she develops her artistry, creating a signature style even in the very early novels.

Writing as Catharsis

In *Last Summer with Maizon*, eleven-year-old Margaret Troy is facing many changes in her life. Her father has just passed away, leaving behind Margaret, her mother, and her baby brother. Her mother now has to go to work, and Margaret is often left alone—both physically, as her mother is home far less often than she used to be, and emotionally, as her mother is also distanced from her daughter by her own grief. Added to the family tragedy, Margaret learns that her longtime best friend, Maizon Singh, has been accepted at an exclusive boarding school, one where Maizon's grandmother hopes she will be challenged, as a gifted student, in ways beyond what the public schools can offer. So, Margaret will enter sixth grade very much on her own.

Margaret is the central character in this story, told in the third person, by a semiomniscient narrator who gives us insight into both Margaret's and Maizon's emotional states. But Margaret takes center stage beginning on page one with a comment about the importance of writing as a way to make sense out of the chaos in her world, telling us, "I haven't written in a long time . . . but now with the Blue Hill thing and all I feel like I should."[4] In general, both Margaret and Maizon model Woodson's own belief in the importance of language as thinking, in the importance of putting words and names to emotions and experiences as a way of coming to terms with them, and capturing them both for future reflection and for gaining distance, in the process, from them. For example, Margaret repeats phrases similar to "My daddy died today" (*LS*, 32), and Maizon is smart enough to realize why she does so. She knows that Margaret "was trying to make sense of the words, rolling them around on her tongue until they found a place to settle in her brain, a place where they'd become real" (*LS*, 32).

Mrs. Peazle, Margaret's teacher, asks the class to describe their summer vacation. Margaret is initially distracted, unable to focus her thoughts, and Mrs. Peazle, very realistically, is not terribly sympathetic and scolds Margaret for her inattentiveness. But when she realizes what Margaret's summer has taken from her student, she asks Margaret to stay after class. At that point, the teacher gives Margaret an extra assignment, asking her to express all her feelings—about Maizon going away, about her father's death, about anything important to her. She gives Margaret the freedom to use any format that seems to work: poetry, prose, a short story, an essay. And she encourages Margaret by saying both that she expects the girl to have "something wonderful" to read to the class the next day (*LS*, 63), as well as by noting Margaret's pretty dress, the one she and Maizon had both planned to wear so they would look like twins.

Suddenly, Margaret feels both visible and capable. In responding to Mrs. Peazle's task, Margaret begins to find her voice, and discovers a talent for writing that had gone unnoticed in the past, as she often lived in the more academically gifted Maizon's shadow. Margaret produces a poem that strikes her classmates into silence and that Mrs. Peazle submits to a poetry contest, which Margaret ultimately wins. As the novel unfolds, Margaret continues to use writing as a way to organize her thoughts and make sense of her emotions; at one point, she spends three hours writing in her diary, not noticing how time has slipped by. And she writes letters to Maizon, too, sharing the details of her life, sharing her thoughts about friendship and events on Madison Street.

In Margaret as writer, Woodson gives us a slice of herself as a child, writing political protest songs and poetry as a way of venting her anger and disillusionment with the world. In Margaret, Woodson provides her young readers with a model for dealing with pain and anger and the emptiness loss of any sort creates inside the soul. It is through sharing poetry that Margaret begins to make friends with Hattie, the older daughter of another resident of the apartment house where she lives; it is through her writing that Margaret becomes visible to other students at the school she attends, moving out from behind Maizon's shadow; it is through writing that she gains confidence in herself as someone with something to say.

Dealing with Loss

Woodson tackles the theme of abandonment in various forms throughout the body of her work. Even in her picture books such as *Our Gracie Aunt* about children living in the foster care system, or *Sweet, Sweet Memory*, about a young girl and her family coming to terms with the death of her grandfather, or even *Visiting Day*, about a child coping with the fact that her father is in prison, Woodson explores this theme, which is first introduced, in multiple forms, in her first novel. Margaret, as has been noted, faces a sense of abandonment in the wake of her father's death, but she also feels abandoned by her mother and by her friend. Meanwhile, Maizon's own experiences, as she gradually comes to share them with both Margaret and the reader, show how early abandonment has shaped her personality. Maizon's mother died in childbirth; her father, unable to face the grief of losing the love of his life, unable to find the strength to parent his new daughter, leaves her with her Grandmother Singh. While Margaret often feels as though the outgoing, gifted Maizon has everything, we learn that Maizon's public persona actually masks the insecurities she feels as a result of having grown up without a mother and father.

Maizon's situation in some ways parallels Woodson's own, as she grew up under her grandmother's care in South Carolina. Even when she and her siblings moved to Brooklyn to live in their mother's house, it was their grandmother who provided the everyday security and comfort many parents provide. Woodson says that, now that she has become a mother herself, she realizes even more clearly "that my grandmother really raised us, that my grandmother was my mother . . . my mother doesn't know how to hold the baby, feed the baby, change the baby." In Woodson's work, Mrs. Singh is the first of several grandmotherly women of importance in providing guidance and safety to young girls modeled on her grandmother.

Of the other themes on which Woodson elaborates in later works that are also introduced in *Last Summer with Maizon*, perhaps the most important is that of friendship, and its role in the development and growth of the individual. Margaret and Maizon are such good friends that they want to be twins. They often try to wear the same outfits, even though this is difficult. Margaret's family is less well off than Maizon's, and Maizon's grandmother, like Woodson, enjoys sewing, so Maizon often has new clothes made to order.

When either girl is in the throes of strong emotion the other knows how to just listen, to allow the friend the space to let her feelings out. At one point, Margaret begins yelling at Maizon, shouting, "You're not so smart, Maizon Singh. . . . You think you know everything, but you don't" (*LS*, 9). Maizon is aware that Margaret's grief over her father's death is affecting her, and she does not reply; she merely follows Margaret out of the room and sits beside her. Later, Margaret is railing against the injustice of losing her dad, and again, Maizon just "held on" (LS, 37). As school starts, Margaret is surprised to find that girls who, in the past, paid little attention to her now act friendly. They tell her they like her better when she is not in Maizon's shadow, describing Maizon as "bossy and snotty" (LS, 77), and Margaret does not defend her friend—which makes her sad and lonely in the end, and prompts her to write to Maizon, and to visit Grandma Singh so they can share their memories of Maizon.

Grandma tells Margaret about the more private Maizon, the vulnerable Maizon whom the public seldom sees: "I think Maizon blames herself. She blames herself for everything [her mother's death; her father's leaving]. She covers it up, though. She tries to be brave and cool" (LS, 94). Margaret accepts this new knowledge, thinking how she used to believe Maizon knew everything but now realizing this is not true, and in some ways Margaret likes her friend the better for the realization. In *Maizon at Blue Hill*, it is knowing that Margaret will take her back, without questions, accepting her unconditionally as her friend, that helps Maizon make the decision to leave Blue Hill. It is interesting that Maizon thinks she can keep the anguish and loneliness she experienced at the school to herself, but Margaret recognizes the change in her friend, seeing something in her face that is "sad and faraway, even when she laughed. It was a look that said something had been broken and could never be fixed" (LS, 101).

The Importance of Neighborhood

Last Summer with Maizon foreshadows many additional topics to which Woodson will return in later works. This first novel reminds readers that being a family means taking responsibility for one another, so that, in spite of her own grief, Margaret tries to care for her brother, L'il Jay, and for her mother. It reminds us that there are many different kinds of families, all deserving of respect. It introduces issues of class. The girls and their neighbors, Ms. Dell and Hattie, recognize the implications of the building that is being constructed on neighboring Palmetto Street that will have higher rents than they are used to paying. They worry—as Woodson currently does—about whether some of their neighbors will be forced out of the homes they have long inhabited as "rich people" move into the neighborhood (*LS*, 71). In a recent NPR commentary, Woodson reflects on the fact that her Park Slope neighborhood is changing so that longtime residents and friends of hers are being forced to move as rents are hiked "and new reports of red-lining and racist realtors make the papers more often than one can care to believe."[5]

In this first novel, Woodson also introduces readers to a variety of spiritualities, another issue with which various of her later characters wrestle. Ms. Dell is clairvoyant and trusts her gift to see the future. Maizon's Grandma Singh, on the other hand, is part Native American, and both she and Ms. Dell frequently express the perspective that "The Lord works his magic in ways we don't understand. You wonder who He is and why He does what He does. But you know it's not for us to question" (*LS*, 43). She talks about rituals from her own childhood, such as when she buried a feather cape she and her father had made with her father when he died so that he would always have a part of her with him (*LS*, 43).

Introducing the Importance of Education

In *Last Summer with Maizon*, Woodson begins to explore issues related to education. Education is important to Woodson herself. She grew up hearing her grandmother say, "Nobody can take your education away from you," and she learned that education is a way out of certain circumstances, that education gives the individual tools for winning arguments. Woodson believes that education gives the individual the ability to see the world differently, as does reading all sorts of books, and education promotes questioning. As Woodson puts it, "I'm all about empowerment. Without education, we go back to slavery."

Education is important, therefore, in Woodson's books. In this first novel, Margaret's mother finds the courage to go back to school after her husband's death in order to become an architect. It is through her teacher's encouragement that Margaret begins to climb out of her despair. Maizon and her grandmother struggle to determine whether it is worth the difficulties of being an outsider, leaving the safety of home, in order to get a quality education; Maizon in particular wishes there were a place in the public school system for gifted black girls. Another minor character, Bo, faces the particular concerns of young black men trying to find a place in a society that often fears them; later in the trilogy, Bo will begin attending a public school for black males where the curriculum includes attention to anger, fear, and self-esteem issues. Of such schools, Woodson says, "There's definitely a place for schools like Baldwin Prep that give those kids who can feel like they're not valued by society a system of support. That's important. And I think the same thing about kids who are gifted and talented, but those programs can lead to segregation, and those kids then can get all the resources and all the service, instead of kids who need that more, so they make me nervous. . . . In a community where education isn't valued, those programs can give kids a place to ask questions who really want to learn. I think the public education system hasn't really figured out how to do this well, and I don't know how to fix it, but we have to try to figure out why there is still so much segregation in those classes."

In other titles, Woodson gives her readers characters who are teachers, such as Bernadette in *The Dear One*, or Lonnie's teacher in *Locomotion* who gives him the world of writing that saves him from his grief. There are teachers who also coach, such as Evie's track coach in *Hush*, who gives Evie a way to find her sense of self. Her sister's hope for a better future comes from her acceptance at an experimental college, while their mother begins to regain her sense of place in the world when she is able to be a teacher once again. Marie's father, in the books about Lena and Marie, is a professor of literature at the college level, and one of the things Lena wants most is for her sister Dion to have a good school, one where she can truly develop her talents as a lover of poetry and language.

As a mother, Woodson continues to struggle to find the kind of educational environment of most value to children, particularly those who, for whatever reason, are not part of the majority power structure. She says that she did, herself, have teachers that were far from perfect, and she notes that the teachers in her books are often flawed, failing to truly understand their students of color. But she has not yet made a poor teacher the subject of a book: "I'm not at a point where the really bad teachers have found their way into the fiction because I don't know how to work them out yet, and work out the impact they've had on me or on characters, so I don't know what that story is."

Woodson is grateful to those teachers who gave her faith in herself as a writer, and so she tries herself to give something to children and young adults. As a writer, she consistently shows characters who value education and take school seriously. And she uses her position to try to educate parents and teachers in the real world as well. For example, the school in her own increasingly affluent neighborhood asked if she would be willing to do a reading or workshop—for free. She responded by saying she does not make free visits to schools that are not in underserved communities, and she suggested that perhaps the school could arrange to invite classes from more impoverished communities to meet in the auditorium, so that the students from both places could meet, at least for a short time, and share the experience of having Woodson read for them and talk to them as an author. She wants her own daughter to go to a school that truly values diversity and that continues to "do the work" of helping students, teachers, and parents make connections across all kinds of boundaries.

Of Metaphor and Detail

Even in her first novel, Woodson's style has a poetic quality that will become increasingly pronounced over time. She uses metaphors in sketching personality, such as the fact that Margaret, who has long, thick, wavy hair, habitually keeps it rigidly tied back. Her father, in a tender scene at the opening of the novel, loosens it, showing his hope that she will herself loosen up, become freer as she gains confidence in herself. She uses the weather as a metaphor for the state of her characters' situations; on the day of Margaret's father's heart attack, rain and gloom encompass Margaret's world, and there is an empty lot on Palmetto Street that looks like a "black hole big enough to swallow whole anything that came close enough" (*LS*, 26). As that black hole begins to fill with the start of construction on a new apartment building, the weather turns milder, and Margaret's heart begins to lighten, though she knows change is inevitable. Woodson's ability to create a sense of place comes through even in this very early work. We see Madison Street, we feel the hardness of the stoop as the girls sit there, in matching black dresses, talking after the funeral, digging in the dust with sharpened Popsicle sticks. We can see with her the view Margaret has from her window, and we sense the stillness and comfort of Maizon's Grandma's house as soon as the walnut-brown door "creaks open with a whine" into a cool, dimly lit vestibule (*LS*, 41).

And Woodson shows herself able to capture the intensities of emotions and the myriad feelings of young adults. Margaret's grief is palpable throughout the beginning of the novel. As she adjusts to her father's physical absence, other emotions find expression. For instance, there is a scene in which Margaret meets Bo, someone she has known a long time, en route to school. It becomes clear that these two young people are noticing each other in new ways, however, just from the small details Woodson includes, such as the way Margaret shifts her books awkwardly, and Bo pulls his tee-shirt away from his neck and picks at invisible bits of something on his jeans, and their words come out in fits and starts, and Margaret's hands begin to sweat and her face flushes. Later, when Maizon has returned to Madison Street and the girls are together again, they are described as chasing gold leaves scattering from the trees down the street, showing their delight in being reunited.

Growing Up and Growing Apart

In *Maizon at Blue Hill*, Woodson turns the focus of the narrative to Maizon, who tells her own story of her experiences at the exclusive Blue Hill boarding school to which she has been accepted in *Last Summer with Maizon*. Perhaps Maizon's story rings so true because it "probably" comes out of Woodson's own sense of isolation at Adelphi, though Woodson also says "when I'm writing it's sooo subconscious, the things working out. But I'm sure that sense of isolation had to come from someplace that I knew."

Of the three books in the Maizon and Margaret trilogy, this second effort shows most clearly the writer Woodson is in the process of becoming. In using the first-person narrative, Woodson settles into a sense of voice that is central to the strength of this novel. Because the story is told through her eyes, Maizon—which rhymes with "raisin"—emerges in all her strengths and weaknesses. The reader often knows more about her than Maizon knows about herself as we follow her to Blue Hill and through the ups and downs of her days there. She is clearly conflicted about what she wants. On the first page of the book, she tells us, "All I wanted was to stay right on Madison Street with my best friend Margaret and go to PS 102."[6] But that is not true; the reader knows she also wants to go to Blue Hill; we know she has not been forced into accepting admission to the school. However, we do know that she has concerns about how she will fit into the school community, because when she first saw pictures of the school population during one of her admissions interviews, she asked if other black girls attended Blue Hill, and, if so, why they were not portrayed in the publicity photos. She is told that the school is working to be "more inclusive—bringing in more minority students who otherwise wouldn't be able to have a boarding school experience if it weren't for scholarships" (BH, 23). This answer provides some cause for concern. But as her grandmother points out, staying on Madison Street is "safe," and if she stays there too long, she will begin to think of the neighborhood as defining life in general. Grandma encourages her, because going to Blue Hill is "a chance for you to learn beyond the boundaries of Brooklyn. Outside of New York City. There is more than this, Maizon. There's a whole *world*. You need to see that. And the only way to do so is to leave" (BH, 5).

Maizon is most concerned about whether she and Margaret will change in ways that will make it difficult for them to be best friends once they are going to different schools, having different experiences. As a child, Woodson recalls reading the line "We grow up. We grow apart."[7] And this is a theme, echoing throughout her work, that she introduces in *Maizon at Blue Hill*. As the girls sit talking in the hours before Maizon has to leave Brooklyn, Maizon is aware of suddenly "wanting to cry. Her [Margaret's] hair was pulled back away from her face and braided down the back of her neck the way it usually was, and her skin was the same caramel brown it had always been. She was right there in front of me—not even half a foot away, but even as we sat there talking, something was already moving in between us. We were slipping away from each other. It was like we had begun to speak in different languages" (BH, 13–14). For example in the later short story "Slipping Away," Jocina and Marie, longtime summer friends, reconnect as always one June, but there is a space between them. Jocina is scared: "A fear like nothing else I've ever felt creeps slowly up my spine. Marie, my summer friend. Every summer for as long as I can remember"—but Marie goes silent during one of their conversations and Jocina feels

Marie "slipping backwards, away from me. Sitting right there but slip-ping away. And there is no way to catch her. No way to hold on."[8] Both Maizon and Margaret, like their later counterparts, are aware that, as they experience sixth grade in different ways, they inevitably *will* find more space between them.

Confronting Issues of Race and Class

One of the most significant ways the girls do, in fact, grow apart is that Maizon's life at Blue Hill causes her to reflect on issues of race and how it affects one's place in the world in ways that Margaret does not have to confront. At Blue Hill Maizon is greeted by Dana Charlesetta King, "Charli," who assumes that Maizon will want to meet the four other black girls right away, and that she will want to sit with them at dinner. Actually, Charli confides, there is a fifth black student, but the others do not have much to do with her; Maizon will not learn why this is so for some time. Meanwhile, Maizon also experiences prejudice within the small black community that exists at Blue Hill. The other girls know she is from Brooklyn, and even the way they say the word makes Maizon uneasy; it sounds, in their mouths, "like Brooklyn was a place at the end of the map that no one in her right mind would ever go to" (*BH*, 38). Sheila in particular talks about how New York is full of killings and violent crime of all sorts. Additionally, the other girls take some pains to explain to Maizon that they are not on scholarships, a fact of which they are quite proud. They are a bit leery of befriending Maizon because she is, in fact, a scholarship student, which in their minds will cause the white students to think that their stereotypes of blacks as poor are based on reality.

The other girls are older than Maizon and have already begun think-ing about continuing their education after graduation from Blue Hill. In their dialogues about their future plans, Woodson is able to show her readers some of the issues they need to consider when they themselves start to think about where to attend college. Marie, for example, is thinking about traditional Ivy League schools—Yale, Harvard, and Brown. She wants to study languages and is interested in the different ways people speak about themselves and others. On the other hand, Charli argues that black women belong at historically black institutions such as Morehouse, Spellman, or Howard, saying "They're *black* league, girl" (*BH*, 42). Sheila thinks Marie is silly to "waste her melanin" on Harvard; Marie thinks Sheila is silly to waste her straight A average on Spellman (*BH*, 43).

The girls talk about language, a topic Woodson also addresses in her essay "Who Can Tell My Story." There, Woodson tells us that at her grandmother's house, she and her family "speak a different language," one comprised of a southern dialect sprinkled with her brother's hip-hop idioms. She and her brother listen to music "that plays with language, that pushes against grammatical and linguistic walls" and as they incorporate language from their music, from their friends, from their various travels and their life experiences, their family language comes to tell the story of their history—all its people, places, and events.[9] Marie thinks the way an individual speaks says a great deal about who he or she is, and notes that people do, in fact, judge other people by their mode of speech. Charli, however, consciously uses less formal constructions and wants to be up front about her racial heritage. Asked to take sides, Maizon responds, "Language is fluid. . . . It changes—I mean the way we speak. I don't think one way is right or the other is wrong as long as you can get your point across" (*BH*, 42). Woodson's own perspective is that there is a language of the outside world, the world of power that an individual has sometimes to slip into, like "putting on a nice pants suit," for certain occasions or reasons—to apply for a fellowship or a job. But she also says that she would not choose this language for a "lazy Sunday afternoon."[10] Told she has "a lot to learn," Maizon takes the challenge, responding, "Then I'll learn it. . . . I'll learn *everything*" (*BH*, 42).

In general, Maizon feels she is just not ready to see the world in black and white terms. When she goes into the dining hall for the first time with Charli, Sheila, and Marie, she is worried about the way they present themselves as banding together against the rest of the school; Maizon is hopeful she can make friends across racial boundaries and intuitively knows that if she is branded as being part of Charli's group, that will be less likely to happen. At the same time, Maizon is annoyed and angered by another student named Susan, the tour guide assigned to show her around the campus. Susan is an example of white people at their most irritating, commenting blithely, when shown a picture of

Margaret, that she is pretty and that she thinks many black girls are pretty, with clear skin and nice teeth (BH, 64), assuming Maizon's public school is both full of violence and does not offer a good education, even saying Maizon has a small room because she is on scholarship and so is not contributing to the cost of maintaining Blue Hill.

Actually Maizon shows herself similarly to be capable of such categorical ways of thinking; she is surprised to find out that her roommate, Sandy, a white girl, is a scholarship student because she thought no white person would have trouble paying for a Blue Hill education. As she does in the later I Hadn't Meant to Tell You This and Lena, Woodson gives us characters that help us break our stereotypes based on racial and class assumptions. In Maizon, Woodson provides a positive role model for how to begin challenging our assumptions. Because she is bright and articulate, Maizon is also, at least sometimes, self-reflective, and she wonders what it is that makes white people strange to her and why, even though Charli, Marie, and Sheila are threatening in some ways, they are also "safe." She hears Ms. Dell's voice in her head, reminding her that she has never been in a situation before attending Blue Hill in which she had to ask herself such questions, and she comes to believe Ms. Dell's words, when, speaking for the author, the older woman says, "Racism doesn't know color, death doesn't know age, and pain doesn't know night" (BH, 76). Lena's "We all just people here" echoes Ms. Dell's comment.

On the other hand, Maizon learns something about how to protect herself when challenged. Another student named Sybol asks, "What's it like for you?"—meaning, "What is it like to be black?" (BH, 89)— Maizon counters by saying she would like to know what it is like for Sybol. She stares into Sybol's eyes; there she sees a fear of herself that makes her angry: "She had no right to have such a fear" (BH, 90). But she also senses in Sybol and in the other girls watching this interaction a desire to be the "special one." Because of these insights, Maizon begins to distance herself from the other black girls. They want to protect her, saying they tried, too, to reach out across racial barriers, but were hurt in the end. Maizon maintains that they did not try hard enough and resolves to figure things out for herself.

As Woodson thinks about the challenges her own daughter faces, one of the tools she hopes to give Toshi, as she gives Maizon, is the ability to stand her ground, but to be sensitive and perceptive about others and their fears and needs at the same time. But the author also shows how wearing it is to walk this delicate line. In the end, Maizon cannot respond to her roommate's offer of friendship; she likes Sandy and appreciates her willingness to look beyond race, but she senses a distance between them that has nothing to do with miles, but that has to do with "knowledge, experience, and pain" (BH, 103). She grows incredibly weary of worrying about where to sit in the cafeteria, about being in the minority in many, many ways, and of being alone.

Issues related to interracial relationships, which Woodson explores more fully in later books, such as *The House You Pass on the Way* and *From the Notebooks of Melanin Sun,* or *If You Come Softly,* are introduced very gently in *Maizon at Blue Hill.* There is a teacher, Mrs. Bender, who is white. She tells the girls that she was married to a black man who "woke up one day and realized he was married to a white woman. I guess the revolution he was fighting wasn't ready for interracial marriage. He got out of bed and ran down to city hall—changed his name to some back-to-Africa something and filed for divorce" (BH, 35), an act the girls all agree is "stupid." Also, it turns out that the fifth black girl, Pauli, is, in fact, the product of an interracial relationship. Charli, Sheila, and Marie, in spite of the differences of opinion over language and college choices, all think of Pauli as an "oreo," saying, snidely, "She's assimilated" (BH, 56).

Woodson, like Pauli, had friendships with white students, and in college she had a romantic relationship with a white woman in spite of joining an all-black, heterosexual sorority,[11] and through Pauli, Woodson gives voice to the importance of finding one's own way. Pauli tells Maizon that her mom is black and her dad is white, and that she went through periods of denying both parts of herself, but ultimately decided she cannot choose between the two—she IS both. When she came to Blue Hill, she wanted to be on the math team, an all-white group; she did not want to be limited to friendships with only three other girls, but in choosing to make her own way, she admits she alienated Charli, Sheila, and Marie. And so Maizon finally decides to join the field hockey team, realizing that nobody seems to notice she is the only black face on the field. What is important is team spirit and playing the game, an experience Woodson shared through her time on the track team. But that sense of belonging on the field is, ultimately, not enough to keep Maizon at Blue Hill.

Being Grounded, Being Home

So Maizon calls Margaret and asks her to tell Grandma that she wants to come home. Interestingly, however, Maizon lies to Margaret about why she is leaving Blue Hill. She tells her friend that the other girls hate her, that no one speaks to her. Upset with herself, Maizon realizes that the truth is harder to tell—that she in fact is the one who isolated herself, "closing myself off from everyone and everything because I didn't belong to any of it" (BH, 128). It is for this reason that Maizon does not write to Margaret, though Margaret writes her several letters. Maizon is jealous both of Margaret's success in writing and the poetry contest prize and is afraid to be seen as a failure; she does not want Margaret to know who she is at Blue Hill, about how alone she is. She realizes that some parts of growing up have to be experienced alone. She knows, for instance, that she will not tell Margaret about walks and talks she had with Sandy. Maizon recognizes that her time at Blue Hill has given her insights that Margaret is not experienced enough to share.

Maizon is afraid of Grandma's disappointment, but to her surprise, Grandma welcomes her back. Maizon is clear that she wants to find a place where she can be both black and smart, and Grandma accepts that perhaps it was too soon for Maizon to be on her own. Maizon learns that "I know what's right for me sometimes. Home is. Home's where I should be for now" (BH, 129). She also shows her character in the ending paragraph, where she reflects, "I'd make something of it all . . . something strong and solid. And somewhere inside that strong, solid thing, I'd find a place where smart black girls from Brooklyn could feel like they belonged" (BH, 131).

Woodson is concerned about providing such places for our students. While she was not always happy in school, in many of her books, as in her life, she shows school to be important as a place where, in spite of flawed teachers, students can explore themselves and their world. In these early novels, she begins to work out her own philosophy of education. For example, Maizon wonders why she cannot just skip a grade, rather than go to Blue Hill. Grandma understands peer pressure, knowing that if Maizon went into a higher grade she would want to keep the same hours and have the same privileges as the students with whom she would be surrounded, and Grandma does not want her to grow up too fast (*BH*, 7).

But Maizon *is* different from her peers. She actually does not like television, and so to fill the time others her age spend watching TV, Maizon creates a contest for herself. She resolves to read all the fiction in the library of which she can pronounce the name. And she does not just read; she comprehends, so that she is able to tell her teacher that she likes *Grendel* better than *Beowulf*, or the Green Knight better than Sir Gawain, and why. Thus, after she returns to Brooklyn from Blue Hill, she and her grandmother know she cannot return to PS 102. Margaret has learned about a new school, a magnet school, free to everyone in the city, called Pace Academy, and both girls think that they could benefit from being in such an environment. In *Between Madison and Palmetto*, the girls attend this school and begin to mature in its environment, which is both nurturing and demanding.

The Writer's Craft—Sustaining a Story

One of the difficulties in writing books in a series is the problem of how to connect them to each other, while making each one able to stand alone. Woodson handles this problem in several ways. She includes the same dialogue in the second work to show how it is building upon the first. When Maizon is heading off to Blue Hill by train in *Maizon at Blue Hill*, we have the same dialogue, with Maizon as narrator, which takes place in *Last Summer with Maizon*, focused on Margaret. Margaret's contest-winning poem appears in both—and so we see the reaction to Margaret's status as writer from both her own perspective and Maizon's.

And, the books are also connected by Woodson's style, one full of attention to the details of action and dialogue that create vivid portraits of her characters. Woodson realistically portrays the thinking and habits of young adults. For instance, as the time approaches for Maizon to leave Madison Street, the girls break the number of days into hours, then minutes, then seconds. Margaret, as is true for several later Woodson characters, shows her nervousness by picking at cuticles, and they have an extended conversation at one point about how to make clicking sounds when chewing gum. As is true of many girls entering sixth

grade, one topic that both attracts and repels them is that of their developing bodies, and they are aware of their breast size—or lack
thereof—and worry about what it will be like when their periods begin.
Maizon is not in any hurry for this event to take place.

Woodson's use of poetic language to create a sense of place is consistent across the books. Also, she contrasts Blue Hill with Madison
Street as a way of connecting the novels just as she contrasts Margaret's
and Maizon's thoughts and reactions to their new experiences. While
Margaret, on her own in *Last Summer with Maizon*, begins to do the
awkward dance of girl-boy attraction with Bo, Woodson contrasts
Maizon's feelings to those of Margaret. Boys "bore the heck" out of
Maizon (*BH*, 37), and she does not enjoy hanging around with the
other black girls who spend a great deal of time "drooling over" pictures
of their boyfriends. Maizon notes that even smart girls seem "dumber
than tree stumps" (*BH*, 57) when they get around boys or start talking
about them.

Maizon's character is developed through her conversations with others, which is how readers learn she can be a bit of a know-it-all. Sheila
taunts her at one point, saying, "Don't you read the papers? They're only
written at a third grade level!" (*BH*, 39), to which Maizon responds that,
in fact, the tabloids are written at that level. But, Maison continues, the
New York Times is written at the seventh grade level and has more information than the tabloids, but no comics. The other girls just stare at her;
it is clear they, in fact, do not read the *Times*, but that Maizon does.
Woodson's artistry is evident in the way she can make Maizon well-
rounded, believable in her less than ideal characteristics, and yet vulnerable as well, so that readers care about her. At one point, Maizon looks
out at the cobblestone paths of Blue Hill, thinking about how rich the
whole school looks, how beautiful her surroundings are. But, there is an
"empty place at the center of my stomach. . . . It made my legs weak, even
made me aware of how my toes felt inside my loafers" (*BH*, 46). At another point Maizon is overcome with the beauty of the sunset and longs
to share it with someone, but she thinks she does not know Charli and
the others well enough to show them how she responds to the world's
natural beauty, which intensifies her loneliness (*BH*, 53).

Woodson recalls that when *Maizon at Blue Hill* was first published,
readers were angry with the ending. "They were like, she's a black girl,

she should've stayed, and what kind of message are you sending by having her leave? But I'm like, 'She was not HAPPY there!' Should she stay just so she can be part of the talented tenth and set an example? Do you forsake yourself for someone else in that situation? I don't think so." In fact, Maizon, in choosing to leave Blue Hill shows a sense of strength and self-knowledge that make her a very positive role model for readers of all races. She recognizes that she has to go home in order to finish becoming herself. As Woodson also notes, "There is no doubt she is going to become something amazing in the world." Having the grit to say, "This is not working for me" is something all of us need to learn how to do. In the next book in the trilogy, we see Margaret and Maizon continuing their journey into selfhood, supporting each other, but also cognizant of the fact that such journeys are, in the end, individual ones.

When Woodson began working on *Last Summer with Maizon*, she knew there would be a second book. She thinks, in retrospect, that it was Wendy Lamb, her editor at Delacorte, who suggested writing a third story about Maizon and Margaret. Lamb concurs, remembering eating lunch with Woodson and her agent at that time, Liza Voges, and suggesting that the story of Maizon and Margaret continue after Maizon's return home, and Lamb offered the author a contract based on the idea rather than on an actual manuscript.[12] Woodson says, "By the time I got to *Between Madison and Palmetto*, I was so sick of those characters. I just thought, 'I can't do this anymore.'" In some ways the third part of the trilogy reads with less energy than its earlier counterparts have. But, all three books, especially taken together, document Woodson's desire to write for girls in particular because she says she "learned early on that the world isn't a girl friendly place. Girls are desperate for identity and love. . . . Society says if you can go out and do A, B, and C, this is how you can get it. And the girls do A, B, and C, and they realize they were lied to. I want to show young people that there are other ways."[13]

Juggling Voices

In the third novel, Woodson begins with Maizon and Margaret at a New Year's Eve party hosted by Ms. Dell, Margaret's neighbor. They are dressed alike, in black crushed velvet dresses, with black tights. We learn that Ms. Dell's daughter, now 21, is studying to be a nurse, that Margaret's mother is progressing in her art skills, and as a result of going back to school, now has a good job as a designer and illustrator with an architectural firm, and that Bo and Margaret have "hung out together a lot."[14] There is a stumbling block for readers of the first two books in that the narrative clearly states, "Then in seventh grade Maizon had gone off to Blue Hill" (*MP*, 8), whereas the first two books have Margaret facing sixth grade alone while Maizon starts sixth grade at Blue Hill. At any rate, the girls are now in eighth grade together at Pace Academy, which is described in this novel as a *private* school, although when it was introduced at the end of *Maizon at Blue Hill*, Margaret said it was free to everyone in New York.

The narrative is not clearly focused on one or the other of the girls, which makes it harder in some ways for the reader to feel connected to the story. Instead, it shifts about, sometimes zooming in on Margaret and at other times putting Maizon center stage. Both girls are still dealing with the absence of their fathers in their lives, both are finding their way into more mature boy-girl relationships, and both struggle with issues of race. Bo plays a more important role in this story. He is thriving at Baldwin Prep—an all black, all boy school for young men who "hadn't done well academically in the regular school system. SELF-ESTEEM, SELF-AWARENESS, SELF-LOVE was engraved in block letters on the front of the school" (*MP*, 11). As a result of his conversations there with teachers and other boys like him, Bo voices his mistrust and dislike of most white people. This is significant because, at the end of *Maizon at Blue Hill*, the girls watch a white girl named Caroline as she leans out the window of her apartment in the building that has changed the tenor of the neighborhood, bringing in more well-to-do residents, for whom the city now sweeps the streets and collects the garbage more than it used to do (*MP*, 15). Bo resents the ways the white, richer, newcomers have made the neighborhood visible to the city officials, and he is very aware that people like Caroline and her mom, confronting Bo, now almost six feet tall, on his own street at night, would run from him. In both *Hush* and *If You Come Softly* other boys like Bo are, in fact, treated quite violently just because of the color of their skin. But Caroline becomes significant in *Between Madison and Palmetto*, and her friendship with both Maizon and Margaret causes some tension in their relationship with Bo.

As a result of the loneliness Maizon felt while at Blue Hill, where she was one black face among many, many white ones, Maizon has some sympathy for Bo's position. But, also because of her experiences at Blue Hill, Maizon is more willing to cross color lines than she might have been before leaving the neighborhood. In this story, Maizon and Caroline become close, to the point that Margaret often feels excluded. Meanwhile, Margaret is frustrated by her developing body. She feels out of control as her breasts swell and her rear end becomes rounder and fuller (MP, 20). Her grief for her father has subsided. She thinks about him less and less, and "now he was just a small shadow" (MP, 23)— though at any moment she can still almost catch a glimpse of him, and then her throat constricts and tears burn her eyes. Margaret thinks perhaps she cries less for her father now because she has other things to cry about: her mother is no longer home when Margaret arrives after school, her younger brother is growing up and needs her less, everyone in the neighborhood is worried about possible rent increases, which could mean she would have to leave her home, and she misses the old Maizon, the pre-Blue Hill Maizon, who no longer calls up to Margaret's window. Ironically, Maizon's perspective is that Margaret bonded with Ms. Dell and Hattie while she was away, and so now is happier with them, or just being alone, than she is with Maizon—which is why Maizon now spends more time with Caroline.

Dealing with Puberty—Self-Esteem and Body Image

Margaret contrasts her own developing figure with Maizon's and does not like the comparison. Maizon, like Woodson as an adolescent, is tall, lanky, and flat-chested; in "Common Ground" she reports that at 15, "I was tall and thin and pretty but I didn't know this. I paid scant attention to my body and my dress and half the time didn't care."[15] In an effort to take some control of her life back, Margaret experiments with bulimic behaviors. Maizon, proving that their history of friendship is one she values, figures out what Margaret is doing and confronts her. The resulting dialogue is one of the freshest and most believable elements of the novel (MP, 41–44). Each girl wants to look like the other. Maizon is letting her very kinky hair grow out, so that she looks wild, the way Margaret does when she allows her hair out of its braid, and she longs to have some of Margaret's curves, while Margaret wants to be slender like Maizon and feels herself to be getting "fat all over" (*MP*, 41). Maizon's hair is a metaphor for her developing sense of confidence, a developing sense of self now that she has left Blue Hill behind her, but the way Margaret's body is changing has undermined the self-esteem she gained when she won the poetry contest in the earlier novel.

Eventually Margaret's mother figures out that her daughter is eating the food placed in front of her, and then making herself throw it up, or just hiding it. Mama is smart enough to realize the reasons behind Margaret's actions. In an emotionally charged scene, she also confronts Margaret, without being accusatory, though their voices do escalate, as Margaret says Mama just wants to control her diet the way she controls every other aspect of her life, while Mama yells she just wants her daughter to live. Mama suggests running as a way for Margaret to give herself some sense of control over her body, and Margaret agrees to at least try. As is true for Evie in *Hush*, running helps Margaret both physically and emotionally, and she tells Maizon, "My body feels different. It's starting to feel okay. Like it belongs to me" (*MP*, 105).

Parent–Child Conflicts

The tensions between Margaret and her mother are nothing compared to the tensions between Maizon and Cooper, the father who abandoned her on the day she was born and who has now returned to Brooklyn, wanting to have a place in her life. The girls have had an ongoing argument over who has it easier in terms of dealing with a father's absence. Maizon says, in *Maizon at Blue Hill*, that she hates her father for leaving her, and that Margaret is "lucky. She had a word for what her father was. Death was something solid—something with a name and a place to it. Something certain. But for where my father was, I didn't have anything" (*MP*, 59). She alternates through the first two books between wanting her father to come back into her life and praying that he never reappear. She reflects that "Absence isn't solid the way death is. It's fluid, like language. And it hurts so much . . . so, so much" (*MP*, 59).

The realism of the scene in which Maizon returns from school to her grandmother's house and Grandma introduces her to Cooper is painfully accurate, perhaps reflecting Woodson's own experiences when her mother reconnected with her father as Woodson turned fourteen, a man she had not known before this time. The descriptions of how Cooper acts and how Maizon feels make the novel worth reading, in spite of the fact that some reviewers have called it "flat" and the plot, "thin."[16] Cooper sits, waiting for Maizon, "swishing a cup of something between his hands" (MP, 48). He smiles at her, walks toward her, proud and stunned at how grown-up she looks, but Maizon backs away, and his eyes fill with hurt. Maizon has difficulty taking in the fact that this man is sitting in her grandmother's house, and in spite of all the times she has imagined being reunited with him, she just cannot accept his presence right away. She stings him by cutting off his attempts at conversation, saying she belongs to her grandmother: "I'm hers. I don't have anything to do with you. I don't know you. I don't want to know you" (MP, 51), yelling at him that he has missed her whole life. Then she runs out of the house, out into the cold, feeling lost and alone as she never has before.

Grandma and Margaret both try to persuade Maizon to give her father a chance. Maizon does not understand why Margaret would want her to do so, but Margaret points out that at least Maizon has a father, and says she would give anything to have her own father back again. To his credit, Cooper backtracks a bit, and tries to take things slowly with Maizon, and gradually they work toward the beginning of an understanding. They talk about the fear many white people have of black males; they talk about how seeing all-white ads on television and in magazines make Maizon feel ugly. Cooper, showing his own earned wisdom, however, says that "No hate is justified" (MP, 92), including the hatred of his daughter for him. He explains his actions without apologizing too much for them, saying he was very young when Maizon was born and, grieving for his newly-dead wife, who passed away giving birth to Maizon, he felt he lacked the strength to give her what she "would need to survive" (MP, 95). Challenged by Maizon to explain what he has been doing for so many years, years without attempting to write or call Maizon, he says, "I was walking this world trying to figure out who I was in it. . . . Sometimes . . . you have to try to forget the people you love just so you can keep on living," echoing Marie's mother in I Hadn't Meant to Tell You This (MP, 78). But it becomes evident that he is stronger now, more self-aware, and is willing to start from scratch with his daughter.

Levels of Friendship

In the end, the girls find their way to a different level of friendship through the arts. Maizon has written a monologue that has been selected for presentation at their school. Caroline is the actress delivering it; Margaret is the director. Together, they work to understand how the line "Where there once was, there isn't now" (*MP*, 85) resonates for each of them. The monologue, thinks Margaret, was "about change, how it affects this one girl" (*MP*, 87), but they realize that change affects everybody. And in their own ways, they begin to relax into the changes. Caroline relaxes into the neighborhood; Margaret and Bo relax into a more romantic kind of male/female relationship; Maizon relaxes into a kind of friendship with her father. Maizon and Margaret, on a day that is budding with the green of spring, spend an afternoon together, talking about all the changes they have experienced, but also holding on to their friendship as an anchor that will help them navigate their ways into the future. This theme of the importance of friendship that accepts change is one that Woodson returns to in many different forms throughout her essays, novels, and short stories, and it is in this early trilogy that she gives her readers models of real affection and what friendship means.

Something Different, Something New

The novel *The Book Chase* is an anomaly in many ways. It is a very different genre than Woodson's other books—both those before and after it in terms of publication—and presented challenges in terms of the restrictions placed upon the author. Writing for the television show *Ghostwriter*, Woodson had to conform to prestructured characters and a half-hour time limit for plot development. Asked how she came to take on such a project, Woodson recalls that her agent's girlfriend was the producer for the series. At the agent's suggestion, the producer approached Woodson, who agreed to try her hand at writing for the show because she appreciated its appeal on several levels. It is about a group of close friends, who have their ups and downs and jealousies and miscommunication problems—after Margaret and Maizon, Woodson knew how to write a story about friends. The characters happen to come from diverse ethnic and social backgrounds, and Woodson valued that about the show. And, most importantly, the characters communicate among themselves and with *Ghostwriter* by writing, so the show and Woodson were in sync in terms of their belief in the importance of writing as a learning tool.

What is interesting about this unusual work in Woodson's literary canon is how she is able to be herself within the confines of a very different medium. Because it was to be a book tied to a television show (although it never was used as a television script), Woodson could use her developing skill as a writer of dialogue to great advantage while also weaving into the plot-driven narrative attention to history, the value of books, the importance of collaboration, and the development of problem-solving strategies. Grandma Cole is hosting a family reunion to which two of her grandchildren, cousins Jamal and Casey, have been allowed to invite several friends. Jamal and Casey are sent to the basement to find "family treasures" suitable for display; they discover a first edition of *The Narrative of Frederick Douglass 4*, which apparently has been in the family for years, and within its pages are bits and pieces of family history, including letters of Grandma Cole's grandfather to her grandmother and Casey's mother's first spelling test.

As Jamal and Casey are investigating, Ghostwriter appears, "a glowing, sparkling ball of light"[17] who communicates with a variety of young people using different media. He appears to Jamal on Jamal's computer screen; he writes to Jamal's classmate Leni in Leni's songbook. He has also corresponded with a number of other friends of Jamal's, including Alex and Gaby Fernandez, Rob Baker, and Hector Carrero, as well as with Casey. All of these individuals appear at the reunion, which celebrates the family's African heritage: there is a spread of African foods such as groundnut stew and milk pudding, a kinte cloth print decorates the back of the sofa, and Jamal's mother is wearing an African print dress with headband. Woodson uses her story to educate her readers about African-American culture and history. The young people are charged with keeping the Frederick Douglass narrative safe, a charge they take seriously as Ghostwriter has told them, "STAY CLOSE. KEEP WATCH" (BC, 17), and so they browse through it and talk about the man and his life as other individuals wander through the party. We learn from a delivery boy that Douglass was dyslexic. He tells

Jamal and company, "He couldn't read or write without a whole lot of trouble. But look at all the stuff he did—founded a newspaper, wrote a bunch of books, *and* worked to free the slaves" (BC, 30). We learn from the fiancé of one of Jamal's cousins, who is a book collector, that the book is worth a great deal of money. We learn from Aunt Estelle about the importance Douglass placed on writing when she tells the group that Douglass felt compelled to write three accounts of his own life as a black slave because "he knew that if he didn't, people might not ever learn the truth about those terrible times. See, there wasn't anybody writing much about black folks' history, about black folks' lives, back then. Not anybody who knew what it was really like" (BC, 49).

Then the book disappears. Much more so than in her other stories, Woodson had to create a plot. This is a mystery, where the expectations of the genre include a crime, a hunt for the criminal, a climax in which the criminal is found out, and then some kind of resolution. In the *Ghost-writer* stories, Jamal and company serve as the detectives, putting together clues, with the help of fragments of advice from their *Ghostwriter* friend. They check out leads, use logical, deductive reasoning, engage in problem solving, and eventually solve the case. For example, as the group is running through a list of possible suspects, Casey says they should put Aunt Estelle on the list "because she is mean" but the others challenge her, noting that "that isn't evidence. . . . That's just what you think" (BC, 40). Thus readers learn something about the difference between proof and opinion. At one point Ghostwriter uses words in his communications that the detectives do not know, so they model using a dictionary to find a definition, and then, confronted with several possibilities, model how to sort out which definition fits with Ghostwriter's meaning. Two of the girls try to determine what Ghostwriter means in telling them "Hispaniola 300 naut. Mi." They go to a bookstore (their first choice was a public library, but it was closed), and use the reference books to learn about nautical miles (BC, 62). Later, some of the group take the A train to 125th Street in Harlem: "the neighborhood was alive. Vendors were crowded along the sidewalk, selling T-shirts, jewelry, and hats from folding tables. Others had laid out beautiful African coverings on blankets" (BC, 47). In showing readers how the detectives experience Harlem, Woodson is able to paint a vibrant, electric picture of it, challenging stereotypes readers might hold. Thinking Hispaniola might be a place, they use an atlas; not all the group members are familiar with this kind of book, so Jamal educates them, telling them it is "like an encyclopedia of the world" (*BC*, 71).

In the end, the detectives catch Milton, the book collector, in the act of trying to fence the manuscript to a dealer in antique books. They thank Ghostwriter for his help in leading them to the right culprit, and for the opportunity the adventure provided to learn more about history and the family's past in the process, noting that, no matter how much *The Narrative of Frederick Douglass* might be worth to a bookseller, to them it is "priceless." This *Ghostwriter* story is a fast read that avoids sounding didactic because Woodson is able to convey the information about Douglass, slave history, and African culture through the words of the young detectives as they learn it. Like so many of her other works, this story emphasizes the importance of friendships across racial and socioeconomic lines, the value of writing as a way of thinking, and the importance of family. Stereotypes are challenged, such as those readers might hold of Harlem, and at one point as the detectives visit with "mean" Aunt Estelle in her own home, they realize that she is not so prickly after all. She is open and warm, telling them she never married because she finds men too much to handle. When the thief turns out to be Milton, who is studying to be an attorney, and who dresses impeccably in designer suits, the young people truly learn that they cannot judge a book by its cover.

In the next chapter, the focus shifts to two books that deal with the issues surrounding being different and the importance of moving beyond stereotypes into an understanding of the individual. Woodson calls the novels discussed in this chapter her "good novels."[18] After she published her friendship stories, she was invited to speak at schools and libraries because she seemed "safe." But as she gained confidence as a writer and began pushing the boundaries of what was accepted in writing for young adults—for instance introducing characters wrestling with their sexuality—invitations to speak became less frequent. Or Woodson would show up to talk to a group of students only to find that none of her books were on the library shelves. And yet, it is in *From the Notebooks of Melanin Sun* and *The House You Pass on the Way* that her skill as a creator of character matures and her prose style moves toward an increasingly lyrical, poetic use of language. These are the works on which the next chapter centers.

Notes

1. Karen Brailsford, "Review of *Last Summer with Maizon*," *New York Times Book Review* (July 29, 1990), 121.

2. Roger Sutton, "Review of *Last Summer with Maizon*," *Bulletin for the Center for Children's Books* 44 (October 1990), 49.

3. Susan Schuller, "Review of *Last Summer with Maizon*," *School Library Journal* 36 (November 1990), 121.

4. Jacqueline Woodson, *Last Summer with Maizon*. (New York: Dell/Yearling, 1990). Hereafter cited as *LS*.

5. Jacqueline Woodson, "Commentary: Division of Race and Wealth in the Development of New Neighborhoods," *National Public Radio Commentary* (August 26, 1999). 1. Retrieved from www.npr.org on 9 September 2002. Keyword: Woodson, Jacqueline.

6. Jacqueline Woodson, *Maizon at Blue Hill*. (New York: Delacorte, 1993). Hereafter cited as *BH*.

7. Woodson, "Common Ground," 2.

8. Jacqueline Woodson, "Slipping Away," in *Am I Blue? Coming out of the Silence*, ed. Marion Dane Bauer (New York: HarperCollins, 1994), 57.

9. Woodson, "Who Can Tell My Story?" 1.

10. Woodson, "Who Can Tell My Story?" 1.

11. *Among Good Christian Peoples*.

12. Lamb.

13. Diane R. Paylor, "Bold Type: Jacqueline Woodson's 'Girl Stories,'" *Ms. Magazine* 5, no. 3 (November/December 1994), 97.

14. Jacqueline Woodson, *Between Madison and Palmetto*. (New York: Delacorte, 1993).

15. Woodson, "Common Ground," 2.

16. Marilyn Long Graham, "Review of *Between Madison and Palmetto*," *School Library Journal* 39 (November 1993), 111.

17. Jacqueline Woodson, *The Book Chase*. Illustrated by Steve Cieslawski. (New York: Bantam, 1994). (Part of The *Ghostwriter* Series, copyright by the Children's Television Network.)

18. Hayne, 378.

CHAPTER FIVE

～

On Being Different:
From the Notebooks of Melanin Sun
and *The House You Pass on the Way*

A *Horn Book* reviewer of Woodson's *From the Notebooks of Melanin Sun* writes, "The author of *I Hadn't Meant to Tell You This* has again created a sensitive adolescent faced with a difficult emotional task. . . . The first-person narrative is strong and clear; Melanin's emotions are raw and often painful, and his response to his mother is both harsh and realistic. Woodson tells a powerful and ultimately hopeful story in this concise novel."[1] In this work, Woodson really hits her stride, mastering the use of the first-person narrator both to tell a story and to develop a reader's ability to walk in the shoes of a character who perceives himself as "different." The strength of Melanin's voice and Woodson's accuracy in portraying the turmoil and perceptions of her character made this novel an award winner. *From the Notebooks of Melanin Sun* was named a Coretta Scott King Honor Book, an ALA Best Book for Young Adults and an ALA Notable Book in the Field of Social Studies, as well as a National Council of Teachers of Social Studies Notable Children's Trade Book in the Field of Social Studies.

Following the success of Melanin Sun and his story, Woodson published *The House You Pass on the Way* in 1997, in which she "crafts a more complex examination of gayness in the emerging adolescent,"[2] giving us Staggerlee and her lyrical description of growing up "different."

Both characters are sympathetic, articulate, and insightful, and they represent Woodson's affinity for the outsider in ways that are logical extensions of her novels of friendship and family life.

Creating Melanin Sun

So who is Melanin Sun and what is his story? When the novel opens, Melanin is almost fourteen; he is 5 feet 10 inches tall and still growing, with short dreadlocks and a neat, tidy way of dressing designed to attract the girls. In her characteristic way, Woodson roots this young man in his physical location. He gives us Brooklyn at the height of the hot, hot summer, with a breeze just noticeable enough "to let us know we're still alive."[3] Melanin then tell us that his mother EC (short for Encanta Cedar), named him to celebrate the richness of his skin color and the fact that she could sense sun and light at the center of his soul (*Sun*, 7). He goes on to reveal a significant aspect of his personality, saying he cannot always find words for his thoughts. He knows they are in his head, "but there's all this silence in my mouth, all this air" (*Sun*, 1).

Because of his reticence, Melanin has sometimes been mistaken for a slower learner, but in fact he is a gifted young man, insightful, perceptive, and able, with pen in hand, to catch those elusive words and create poignantly poetic descriptions of what he has experienced and felt. For example, Mel is able to paint, with words, a picture of the word "alone": "Some days I wear alone like a coat, like a hood draping from my head that first warm day of spring, like socks bunching up inside my sneakers. . . . Alone is the taste in my mouth some mornings, like morning breath, like hunger. . . . Today, alone is this . . . tiny note beside the box: Dear Melanin Sun, I miss you. Love, Ma" (*Sun*, 27–28).

Mel and his mother have always been close; he has never known his father, and his mother, single with a baby at age twenty, struggled to find a place to live with her son. She landed in a neighborhood of first generation West Indians and Puerto Ricans, "a world of akee and pastels, of salsa and calypso" (*Sun*, 9), a world full of language rich with contributions from many cultures, a world near Flatbush and Prospect Park. In this noisy neighborhood, EC has encouraged Melanin's writing talents, and has appreciated his silences, telling him it is fine to be quiet as long as he listens well.

And so Melanin has a series of notebooks in which he captures his thoughts and reflections after listening to his world. In the past, Melanin was afraid these notebooks would be found and that the finder would make all his private thoughts and feelings public. As we have seen, Woodson had that experience herself when her brother shared her own adolescent journal entries with her grandmother. In the particular summer with which the novel is concerned, Melanin's ability to listen well, to take in what is going on around him, is about to be challenged, and that is why he decides it is okay to share his notebooks. He wants to get everything that happens to him down on paper, in his voice, from his own point of view because, as he puts it "Difference matters" (*Sun*, 1).

The Writer's Craft—Foreshadowing

Melanin gets frustrated because so many people try to "force their own world onto everybody else's" (*Sun*, 14). In his own case, Melanin thinks it is silly when other people ask him what it is like not to have a father; he says, obviously, he has no way to compare his situation to something different and that "it feels the way it feels" (*Sun*, 14). But he asks his mother, this summer when he is almost fourteen and thinking warm thoughts for the first time about a girl, if EC ever thinks about his father. Woodson provides foreshadowing of what is to come; EC tells her son that she has, in fact, been thinking about his father—and all the men in her life—a lot. Mama then asks Melanin to stay home for dinner, and to refrain from asking any of his friends to join them, telling him she has somebody she wants him to meet. Melanin, who has observed that after about two dates with any given man, EC is ready to move on, makes the understandable mistake of thinking she must be considering getting married, and he tells her he just cannot imagine calling anybody "Dad." At that point, EC goes silent, and loses the teasing smile that has been on her face, leaving the reader to wonder along with Melanin what, in fact, she has been thinking about.

As he waits for the dinner, Melanin pulls out his stamps of endangered species and is sorting them when his friends show up at his apartment. Sean tells him to stop playing with his "faggot" stamps and come outside to hang out. Again foreshadowing the issues Melanin will soon face, Melanin reflects that there are, in his mind, two kinds of "faggy." One kind he admits he sort of is—he is not supermacho, he keeps his notebooks (which are definitely NOT diaries, which is what girls keep), and he likes writing and stamps. The other kind is, to Melanin, very weird; he cannot imagine wanting to be with another guy and feeling for another guy the way he feels about Angie. He tells us, "That kind made me want to puke every time I thought about it" (*Sun*, 19–20).

Melanin also reflects on racial issues. His mother belongs to a health club, and when he first tags along with her, he is aware of how dark he and his mother are in the sea of white faces surrounding them. He tells us he has never had much reason to spend time with white people and that he is a bit disturbed to know his mother is part of this other world. Mama justifies her relationships by saying she is networking now in preparation for finding a job after she completes law school. She is nonplussed by the differences in skin color that jump out at Mel.

Melanin's concerns with being perceived as "faggy," and his discomfort with white people are important to remember as the novel progresses. Melanin and EC are waiting for her date, who is late. Mel tells his mom she should not trust a guy who does not show up on time and does not call. EC responds by saying he has made an assumption, pointing out that she never said anything about a *man* coming to dinner. Then the door opens and Kristin comes into Mel's life. He first comments on the fact of her skin color: "White white. Like Breck Shampoo-girl white but with glasses. And those straight white people teeth." (*Sun*, 31). He is confused by her presence, primarily at first because of her obvious racial difference, noting that there just had not ever been white people in his house, in his neighborhood of harmony away from "all of *their* hatred and racism" (*Sun*, 32). His discomfort is intensified over dinner by his lack of understanding of the way his mother and Kristin interact, by the way they look at each other. He just wants dinner to end so he can have his mother to himself; he is longing to ask her advice about Angie and what to say when he finally gets up the courage to call her.

Later, EC asks Mel if he and his friends ever talk about gay people. Mel once again makes the false assumption that his mother is worried about him because he cares about creatures going extinct and is not a superathlete and still enjoys hanging out with her. He tries to assuage her fears, telling her he is NOT going to turn gay on her. But that is not the reason she initiated this particular conversation; she finally tells him, her voice soft, that she is in love—with Kristin. Mel cannot process this information, which hits him in two very vulnerable spots: his fear of being perceived as gay himself, particularly in light of the harshness with which Sean talks about "faggots," and his attitude toward white people, which, it turns out, is less tolerant than he first suggests and borders on active hatred.

From Tension to Explosion

How does he cope with the fact that his mother's revelations have left him feeling alone and adrift, untied from the one relationship that has kept him balanced and focused? His reaction is perfectly detailed, raw and powerful, showing Woodson's insight into the developmental needs and thinking processes of adolescents. His first thoughts are about himself, as he wonders whether the fact that his mother is gay, a "dyke," means his own gender identity can be questioned. He screams to himself, *"I'm not a faggot! I'm not a faggot! I'm not a faggot! I'm not a faggot! I'm not a faggot—not a faggot"* (*Sun*, 63). He pulls away from Mama physically and emotionally, feeling that if she touches him, her touch will burn, screaming at her never to touch him again. She pulls him to her, both of them sobbing; Mel tries to escape, tries to punch holes in the wall the way she has punched holes in him, while she cries that she has been broken by his lack of understanding (*Sun*, 65). Like his author, Melanin turns to writing, saying that the act of putting pen to paper "is my way of swimming, of trying to keep my head above water" (*Sun*, 61).

Woodson's artistry comes through in the realism with which she describes Mel's reaction. After that first scene and its attendant blowup, Mel writes in his notebooks about the fact that sometimes, when he hears his mother and Kristin on the phone, he gets "hard," going on to say, "It hurts sometimes, when I get hard, like I'm going to explode down there" (*Sun*, 67). He does not understand this unsolicited reaction from his body, and he worries that if his mother hates men, then she might hate him as well. He writes poetically, lyrically, about the sounds of silence now that there is a gulf between Mama and him, contrasting the companionable silence they used to share while sitting in the apartment, each reading a book, to the absolute and lonely silence he now feels when EC exits the house with barely a word and the door shuts behind her, leaving behind a stillness and airlessness that is oppressive.

Mel tries to fill the silence by hanging out with his friends. They hike out of their neighborhood and realize that, where they end up, every white woman they pass clutches her purse. They respond by feeling like they *should* steal a pocketbook just to prove everybody right. Mel reflects that television only shows black people in jail or committing violent crimes—which is why he only watches cartoons. Back in their own neighborhood, Sean starts taunting Mel about his mama, thus ensuring the whole neighborhood knows what Mel wants desperately to keep secret. While Mel has been feeling incredibly hurt and angered by his mother's situation, he cannot allow Sean to denigrate her, and he throws a punch, which triggers a fight in earnest. Woodson has given hints throughout the narrative that Sean is a less-than-tolerant individual, and that Melanin has long had reservations about their friendship as a result. Nevertheless, after the fight, he feels the absence, writing in his notebooks, "It ends like this between us, without apology . . . like the last blank page at the end of a book, as if the story itself had never been" (*Sun*, 123).

On the other hand, after the fight, in some ways, Mel discovers that Ralphael, who has been upstaged by Sean in their little group for years, is a real friend. And with Ralphael's help, Melanin begins to regain some balance, as he really listens to his friend say, first of all, that what his mother does has nothing to do with who Melanin is and what he does in the future, and, secondly, that EC looks calm and happy with Kristin, and that this should count for something in Mel's mind.

Limning Relationships

Woodson's skill in limning relationships in general contributes to the novel's power. In chapter 6, Mama and Mel go to the beach for a day. The bantering between them is light and believable; there is a closeness between the two that yet allows for space and privacy. At one point, Mel takes a walk, alone, armed with his notebook, returning to the blanket where EC is sunning herself, and she teases him, asking when she will be allowed to read what he has been writing in it. He tells her that his notebook is private, that it is about *his* life. Mama is sad, recalling when it used to be *"our* life" (*Sun,* 53). Mel points out that they still do things together, but he reminds her as well that she has a life apart from the one she shares with him. We learn, through Mel's reflections, about the past history of the mother and son, about the ways they show affection and how they cope with tensions, so that both the betrayal Mel feels when he learns about his mom's relationship with Kristin, and the effort Mel eventually is persuaded to make to see things from his mother's perspective are believable.

Because this mother and son are able to talk, and to say truthfully when what the other says is not making sense, they manage to communicate even in this difficult time in their relationship. EC becomes angry with Mel, who has been skulking about the apartment, not going out, for days after her revelations about Kristin. She asks him to eat dinner with her; he yells that he does not want to look at her—but they manage to get past that to the point that Mel can ask some of the questions he has had swirling through his head. He needs his mother's reassurance that she does not hate him because he is a male. He wants to know how, if EC is a lesbian, she connected with his father and had a child. He wants to know if she was attracted at all to any of the various men she has dated over the years. And he wants to know if part of Kristin's attraction is that she is white. Mama explains, "It's complicated. . . . I like the contrast of us, the differences between us—and I like the way we've found our way to each other across color lines. . . . I like *her*—everything about her, and her whiteness is a part of her" (*Sun,* 115). Mel lets his mother talk, but says he does not really follow her—and she admits she did not think he would be able to digest her words. But the fact is, they do talk and listen, and so when EC asks Melanin to spend one day trying to just see her as his mother, and to see Kristin just as Kristin, it makes sense to the reader that he agrees.

Gaining Perspective—
The Importance of Talking and Listening

His mother has promised Mel that he can walk out of that one day however he walks out of it, but she is firm: she has raised him to be tolerant and to respect others—and she deserves some of that respect herself.

One of the real strengths of this novel is that Woodson is clear in delivering the message that adults have a right to their own lives; Mama tells Mel that regardless of his feelings, Kristin is going to be a part of their world, saying, "I'm sorry if this hurts, if it's hard, but it *is*, and that's the jumping off point" (*Sun*, 112). So Mel finds himself at the beach again, this time with EC and Kristin. Ultimately it is Kristin herself who finds a way to ease the burning, raw emotions that have been damaging Mel's equilibrium. Kristin, in a lovely scene that captures her character and why EC has fallen so hard for her, helps Mel gain some perspective on what it feels like to be gay—which has the effect of helping the reader, who identifies with Mel, do the same.

Kristin's approach is delicate and personal. She first asks Mel to think about one of his friends. He says he is thinking about Ralphael. She asks Mel if he likes to hang out with Ralph and asks what they like to do together. This is easy—Mel says they talk, they shoot hoops, they go to the movies, they listen to music. Kristin then asks if he would ever consider kissing Ralph. Melanin's response is immediate and strong: "GROSS," he says. Kristin says that is exactly how she feels when she tries to kiss a guy (*Sun*, 130). Then she asks Mel if he has a girl in whom he is interested, and he thinks about Angie. Kristin asks him to remember how he feels if he is near her, or how he feels imagining kissing her—and tells him that is how she and his mom feel about each other. Kristin never belittles Melanin for his sullenness; she just continues talking and walking, sharing her own story of how she has been cut off by her family and how she has struggled to make her own kind of family.

Hearing her story, Melanin begins to consider his mother's perspective, wondering if she has been afraid that she will lose him. He even begins to wonder how Kristin feels, lacking her family structure and support, wondering if she feels at all the way he feels about not having a father. As they keep talking, Mel finds himself softening, finding that a space in his heart starts to open up to Kristin's presence, "like an eclipse—the way the moon rushes out to cover up the sun. . . . We need it all, though, the darkness and the light. The Melanin and the sun. Mama and Kristin" (*Sun*, 140). As Roger Sutton writes in *Horn Book Magazine*, while the patience with which Mama and Kristin deal with Mel's rebelliousness is a bit idealized, "his gradual rapprochement with the women is realistically paced, and his resolution with his friends and his girlfriend about the subject is left open."[4]

Woodson's handling of the relationship between Melanin and Angie is also deftly accomplished. Mel clearly is infatuated with this young woman, and there is a notebook entry in which he describes his feelings for her in a passage that echoes "Maria" from *West Side Story*, a passage in which his skill with language is beautifully evident. He thinks her name all through the first dinner at which he meets Kristin, letting the sound of it take him away from the table until he is nowhere "and everywhere. . . . Say her name slow, it's like angels crossing in front of you. . . . Say her name soft and her millions of braids are trailing behind her. . . . Make it low as a moan, deep as a holler. Angie, Angie, Angie" (*Sun*, 38–39). When Mel finally screws up his courage and calls Angie, having carried around her phone number in his pants pockets for weeks like a talisman, he surprises himself by sharing his concern for the environment, talking about endangered frog species—almost as though his fear of how Angie will react to his mother and Kristin gives him the courage to share some important part of himself with her. She responds, saying maybe they should hang out together sometime. They hang up the phone. Mel calls her back and suggests getting together right then, before he can lose the momentum.

By letting Mel describe his feelings, Woodson gives the reader a sense of immediacy. Mel is sitting on a bench with Angie beside him, and he starts "shivering from the inside out" (*Sun*, 98). He kisses her fast because he hopes that by doing it, finally, he can stop thinking about it. He kisses her so quickly that he actually bumps her lips with his teeth, and then he goes on to chastise himself: "*Stupid, stupid, stupid me*" (*Sun*, 99). But with that out of the way, the two young people start to open up; it turns out Angie and Mel are kindred spirits, because Angie, too, has trouble finding the right words to say. She tells Mel that she actually talks to herself a lot because she can have that kind of conversation without worrying about making mistakes. Mel understands her and they seem to have the potential for a relationship, but Mel worries about how Angie will react to him once she learns the truth about his mother and Kristin. The last the reader sees of Angie, she is standing on a street corner, looking small and confused, after the incident in which Sean taunts Mel in public, so that Mel's secret is revealed before he has a chance to tell Angie himself. As the novel ends, Mel has no idea what will happen with Angie. The reader hopes that, given their similarities and the way they were able to talk companionably, they may be able to reconnect, but we do not know, and like Mel, we have to live with that uncertainty.

Larger Societal Concerns— Environmental Issues as Metaphor

One of the reasons readers feel hopeful about Melanin Sun is because he is somewhat different from his peers, and his concern for the environment, for endangered species, speaks of a sensitive nature that will help him come to some kind of acceptance of all the changes in his life. In this novel, the outside world as a metaphor for internal landscapes is carried a step further in that, when Mel is considering important questions of race and sexuality, he often uses the condition of a specific species to make concrete what he is feeling. Mel is concerned about the minke whale, which is used in making cosmetics and candles; once they were protected, but Mel learns that Norway now allows hunting again. He reflects that from his point of view, nobody seems to really care about the environment. For example, while people talk about recycling and saving habitats, nobody seems to *do* much: "I don't think people even think about stuff. Not the people hunting minke whales. . . . There's a tortoise—the star-shelled tortoise. It has these beautiful raised diamond shapes on its back. Somewhere in Sri Lanka, it's dying off. Slowly, it seems, everything and everybody and every way that used to be is dying" (*Sun*, 84–85). Mel's confusion over his mother's relationship with Kristin relates to his confusion over God; he wonders how God could make something as beautiful as the perot, a bird in Galapagos, and then also make the rats that are now threatening the perot with extinction because they eat the bird's eggs. One of the reasons things soften between Mel and Kristin is because she, too, thinks about such things. She and Mel agree, talking about the last buffalo, that if they had to become extinct, they would want to disappear all at once as part of a crowd, surrounded by their species. They agree, too, that if they had to be the last of a species, they would want to run, fast and hard, in order to feel the sand and the wind and the sun one last time.

In this concern for the natural world, for the creatures humankind has threatened with its rash and egocentric use of resources, Mel is like his author. She says of *From the Notebooks of Melanin Sun*, "I had no idea what that book was going to be." But she has given Melanin a part of herself. She was disturbed by the oil spills out of the Exxon tanker several years ago, saying, "It really got to me. I couldn't look in the newspapers to see those pictures of these dead birds just floating in the water." She is upset about the disappearance of the rain forest and, as a result, tries to drink "shaded coffee," coffee grown by small farmers in ways that do not damage the rain forest ecosystem. She remembers reading about a monkey when there were only two left in the world, and being saddened that she was part of a generation witnessing its extinction, "like the dodo bird, it was here and then it was gone. And it's just wild to me that this happens, that we have this kind of impact." And, she is aware of how hard it is to live in ways that have less of an impact, noting that she uses paper, and disposable diapers, and tampons: "like there are all these ways that I have this negative impact on the environment, and I understand it's a bad thing, but I don't know how to do it differently, except being conscious and trying my best to find ways of NOT doing it."

In the end, being conscious and thoughtful is what Woodson asks of Melanin, too. On his first trip to Jones Beach with Mama, while taking a walk by himself, Mel is taunted by some white boys who talk about the "darkness" on the beach as he passes by (*Sun*, 48). Mel feels dirty, alone; he feels a sense of hatred toward white people in a way he "hadn't thought about hating them before" (*Sun*, 49). This hatred is what he and Sean and Ralphael hold onto when people get ugly with them; it helps keep them "whole" (*Sun*, 69). But in general, Mel does not often think about white people. He does not waste time imagining their daily actions or their day-to-day routines nor contemplating "what they ate or how they ate it" (*Sun*, 81–82).

Before Kristin, none of this mattered at all. Now, Melanin has to think about race in a different way; he will learn more about whites in general from getting to know Kristin in particular. He will learn more about relationships in general, about the gay community in general, from getting to know Mama and Kristin's relationship in particular. He will have to deal with issues of prejudice and stereotyping in general from coping with the way the people in his neighborhood respond to him one-on-one.

And he is up to the challenge. As the novel ends, Mel is looking at his mother and Kristin on the beach. He knows he is "groping for some sort of light on the other side of all this. Something that would guide us somewhere" (*Sun*, 140). He is painfully aware of how hard it will be, and of how uncertain the future is from his vantage point of almost-fourteen. But, he thinks, "We had each other. We would always have each other. . . . I didn't know if it would ever stop mattering what people thought. But I was sure of Mama, sure of my notebooks. And for the quickest moment, walking backwards against the sun, I was sure of me. Maybe that's all that matters" (*Sun*, 140–141).

The Story behind the Story

In terms of its publication, the history of *From the Notebooks of Melanin Sun* began in August of 1991. Woodson had met Scholastic editor Dianne Hess sometime in the fall of 1989; a mutual friend suggested Dianne might be interested in Woodson's work, and on a Sunday afternoon, while Hess was working, Woodson dropped of a partial manuscript of a story titled *Red Dirt*. Hess was impressed with the "beauty and poetry" in Woodson's writing and asked to see more.[5] Two years later, Woodson sent Hess a proposal for Melanin's story. Hess took it to her weekly editorial meeting, at which point she was "amazed and delighted at how swiftly approval came for the project."[6] Hess and her colleagues had an immediate sense that Woodson's novel would be a groundbreaking book.

Then an odd thing happened. Woodson continued working on the novel, and Hess reports, "But in the summer of 1992, I received a disturbing package of letters from a fifth-grade class. These children expressed their disapproval of Jackie's books. 'Why were they upset?' I wondered. Why were these children writing letters about a book that was not even written?"[7] It turned out that Woodson had been interviewed for a magazine article that discussed her career; in it, she had revealed that she was working on an adult novel and a book for Scholastic that would be its first to deal with gay themes, as well as racial and sexual identity issues. Scholastic "took a long hard look at the situation," but in the end they decided they would have to "wait and see what the book was going to be before passing judgment."[8]

Hess recalls that the manuscript finally arrived in June of 1993, saying, "Only an editor and a new mother can appreciate the thrill of seeing a first draft. The way a mother counts a newborn's fingers and toes, an editor hopes that the author has given birth to a well-formed story."[9] Hess immediately became entranced with Melanin and his story, responding to Woodson's draft by telling her, "This is a beautiful, honest, thought-provoking and extremely well-written novel that I know will make an impact. . . . Melanin Sun is a believable and likeable young man, his struggle to make sense of the adult world around him is beautifully drawn, and I felt with him all the way. His relationship with his mother is warm and realistic. I love that we're dealing with a functional family, albeit a functional family of two, and that their relationship is multi-dimensional—with a full range of emotions. EC is a wonderful character; like Melanin Sun, she is someone I would want to have as a friend."[10]

Although Hess told Woodson that hers was one of the strongest first drafts the editor had ever seen, and that the structure was "right on,"[11] Hess did make several suggestions for Woodson. She felt the characters of Sean and Ralphy needed to be developed and that tension had to be created that would lead more naturally to the blow-up. She suggested fleshing out Kristin and exploring her in more depth. Throughout about four rounds of editing, Hess worked with Woodson on focusing on the details within scenes that would make them stronger, such as "people's reactions to things, deepening a reason for something happening."[12] They worked on making "the journal entries more consistent in the way they were presented. They were a bit more randomly placed and timed at first."[13]

Hess was particularly impressed with an aspect of Woodson's artistry that all her editors have admired, saying, "One thing I really loved about working with Jackie was that when I made suggestions—her way of fixing things was always completely different from what I'd asked for. But it was always in response to my concerns. She would do it her own way, and most importantly, her solution would not only work, but would far exceed my expectations."[14] According to Hess, one hallmark of award-winning authors in general is this ability to "hear criticism and take a suggestion and run very far with it. . . . In this way, criticism becomes a stepping stone to excellence."[15] Also, Hess thinks that Woodson's habit of reading chapters from works in progress at public readings really helps her "tune her ear for the language."[16] As a result, notes Hess, "Her works are not only interesting and beautiful sounding—but they read smoothly out loud. Her words are polished and magnificent."[17]

Once Hess had the manuscript of *From the Notebooks of Melanin Sun* in hand, she says, "I understood something very important. This book was honest. And it was vital to have Jackie's voice heard by many people whose lives were reflected in this book—as well as for those who weren't. She writes the truth about the world *she* lives in with great depth and sensitivity. We live in a world where gay people are embraced as important, vital, high contributors to our communities. This is a world where gay people hold important jobs in every field, are contributing members of all religious organizations. . . . This is a world where gay parents are a part of the life experience of many children. . . . Should we be telling these children of exemplary parents that their lives are not okay? . . . Back in the pre-civil rights days, children's book publishers also faced having to deal with similar controversies of whether or not to publish material that dealt with civil rights. What would our world be like today had we been afraid to not stand up for basic human rights and dignity?"[18]

To Hess and her colleagues at Scholastic, the answer was clear. In spite of the potential for Melanin Sun and his story to cause some readers discomfort and to earn disapproval from others, they were determined to go to press "with our heads held high." They wanted to "create one of the few books out there that dealt with this subject matter in an honest and admirable way. This book was published for children growing up in gay households. It was for teenagers dealing with their own sexuality. And it was for anyone else living in the diverse and complex world of the present who acknowledges that life isn't just black and white."[19]

Thus Hess and Scholastic determined to give the book their best possible support. That meant that they hired Caldecott-winning artists Leon and Dianne Dillon to create the book jacket. That meant that they published the book under the Blue Sky Press imprint, which at that time was a new imprint with award-winning authors and a small list, which meant that Woodson's novel would have high visibility. And, that meant that they pulled out the "big guns," asking Virginia Hamilton to give a quote for the book jacket. In response, Hamilton wrote, "*From the Notebooks of Melanin Sun* is a very astutely written, sensitive rendition of life as a black youth knows it. In Woodson's hands, a complex story becomes a miraculous creation, a stirring, heartfelt melody tuned for our times. Melanin Sun, writing in his diaries, is one of youth's literature's wonders. We not only admire him, but grow to love him, his intelligent insights and his love of nature. We learn from him to care for the living earth, that we are intertwined with all creatures—we care for them or we despair for ourselves. After finishing this short novel, I am amazed at the poetry it delivers in so few pages. It is all like a lovely movement of sound that stays in the mind long after the musicians have left the stage."[20] It is no wonder that *From the Notebooks of Melanin Sun* went on to achieve so many awards; in addition to the Coretta Scott King Honor Award, Melanin and his author received a Jane Addams Peace Award Honor, and a Lamda Literary Award.

Difference Matters

As the incident of the letters from the fifth grade children showed Hess and Woodson, not everyone is comfortable with "the other." Mel is aware that difference will always matter to some people, and that he cannot change that; what he can control is how he himself responds to being labeled as different because of his mother's alternate lifestyle, and to how he reacts to his mother's differences. Staggerlee in *The House You Pass on the Way* will have an even harder road to hoe in dealing with difference. Melanin Sun's need to deal with difference is, in some ways, one step removed from himself. Yes, he has an unusual interest in the star-shelled tortoise and minke whale, but Angie likes that part of him. It is his mother's choices that make him an outsider. Staggerlee, on the other hand, struggles to figure out if her own outsider status, a result of her family's choices, is going to be exacerbated by her developing sense of the kind of intimate relationships she will choose for herself in the future.

Once again, in trademark fashion, Woodson positions Staggerlee in her environment at the opening of the novel. She is walking her dog,

Creek, in the depth of winter, and there is something about "the way the cold grabbed hold of her as she walked along the river"[21] that makes her remember events from the past year that she has pushed out of her mind and heart. She faces the river and wishes it were "time itself" and could take her "back to the beginning of her own time" (*House*, 2). She wants to start over—and the reader is hooked, wanting to know what this sensitive young woman is struggling to forget, why it is she wants a new beginning. Woodson does not let us into Staggerlee's world all at once. She tells us about a letter Staggerlee received, from Trout— gender unknown—"and the way her legs buckled when she got to the part about—about Trout and. . . . Yes, that had made her remember. She wanted to make sense of it all, of that summer, of what happened with Trout" (*House*, 2). But the reader still knows nothing of what those events might have been, nor who Trout is and why a letter from Trout has damaged Staggerlee's equilibrium.

Staggerlee's story is not told in Melanin's first-person narrative. Instead, as readers, we maintain a filmy sort of distance from this fourteen-year-old girl—similar to the distance Staggerlee feels from her community, a rural town called Sweet Gum, from her family, even from herself. Born Evangeline Ian Cameron, she is the third of five children. Older brother Charlie is in college; older sister Dottie is sixteen, smart and popular. School and its social aspects come easily to Dottie. Then there is a younger brother, all of two, named Battle, and a baby on the way. With her wild brown-gold ringlets, Staggerlee also carries the designation of the family's "happy child," the one who "never needed, never asked for anything, never caused any trouble" (*House*, 5).

Living in a Vacuum

And yet Staggerlee is not truly happy and content. Her father had married a white woman; "That's how Sweet Gum people talked about it" (*House*, 5). They are the only mixed race family in the entire county, and when people say to Staggerlee, "Your mama's white!" the words sound loud, ugly, accusatory, as though there is something wrong with her because of the color of her skin (*House*, 6). The family has done fairly well at hiding the sting of their neighbors' words and looks; they take refuge in music, in making music together, sitting on the front porch. Dottie sings; Charlie provides percussion; Staggerlee plays harmonica. They do not think of themselves as black, white, or interracial; they just think of themselves as a family. But the larger community has difficulty with their presence, and when Staggerlee goes to the Sweet Gum Baptist Church, looking for God, the townspeople smile in surprise and keep their distance. But Stagger takes some comfort from the stained glass windows and the portrait of Jesus there—looking neither black nor white but "both and all of it" (*House*, 7). Then the preacher starts talking about betrayal—and memories of Trout and worries Trout voiced about being betrayed by Stagger flood over her.

To get to the story of Trout, Stagger has to go back in time, back to the beginning of spring and the end of the previous school year. Stagger knows other students think she is "stuck up"; like Melanin Sun, like Feni in *The Dear One*, and the even earlier Maizon and Margaret, Stagger thinks of herself as merely quiet, a watcher, not a joiner. A younger Stagger thought it was her mixed-race heritage that made her an outsider, but she has come to realize that Charlie and Dottie are very much a part of the social hierarchy at school, and now she knows "It was something deeper—something lonely inside her, something quiet" (*House*, 12); she recognizes that she and Dottie are just very different. Dottie does not understand the river; Dottie needs to be surrounded by friends. Staggerlee is happiest by herself. And when puberty hits, Stagger goes even further inside herself. Her mama and Dottie celebrate its onset with a toast and a glass of wine, but Stagger still feels these changes in her body to be a bad thing, and she feels lost because this is not a topic she can talk about with Charlie, with whom she has always been able to discuss anything. Plus, Charlie is getting ready to go to college, and Stagger feels, even before he leaves, the space his absence will create for her.

Staggerlee's family lives in a vacuum in general. Mama, a Mount Holyoke graduate, and Daddy, who went to Columbia for two years before learning to fly planes, are not typical of Sweet Gum residents, and so are rather isolated in the town. Additionally, Mama's parents did not approve of her marriage to a black man, and Daddy's sisters have not spoken to him in the twenty years since he married a white woman. But then Daddy's sister, Hallique, dies. His other sister, Ida Mae, and her husband, Jonathon, decide that all those years of silence in the family have been wasted years, and they want to reconnect. So Ida Mae calls Daddy and asks if her adopted daughter, Tyler, can visit for the summer. Stagger is enthralled by Tyler's photo, by the way the camera captures her looking right into it, challenging it. Tyler reminds Stagger of her friend Hazel, whom she kissed in sixth grade, and she begs her mother and father to let their niece stay with them.

Hazel is no longer a part of Staggerlee's life. But her presence is still felt, and it is through Stagger's recollections of Hazel and their relationship that the reader begins to realize, even before Staggerlee herself does, that Staggerlee is struggling with her sexual identity. Hazel is a pretty girl, with long thick hair that she lets go wild at school, and she is prettily dressed by her grandmother, who makes all her clothes.

Woodson herself is a seamstress of some considerable skill, and she gives this trait to various older women in her novels; Maizon's grandmother, too, makes all her clothes. Woodson says she has no visual or musical artistic talent, but she enjoys the piecing together of materials, likes making something from nothing that is specifically designed for someone she loves; she has been known to make coats, even, for her goddaughter, and she claims that, as a writer, she pieces words and scenes together to make something whole. She gives this same quilter's mindset to Trout, who likens the process to creating a life, saying, "It's like you take all these pieces from all these parts of your life and you sew them together and then you have your life over again, only it's . . . in different form" (*House*, 60).

In Staggerlee's story, Woodson's use of the seamstress approach to writing becomes increasingly evident. The reader gets bits and pieces of Staggerlee's past and present in a nonlinear narrative that shifts back and forth in time, like a sewing machine on the zig-zag setting. Eventually the reader learns that Hazel's laugh could make Staggerlee feel "warm and safe." One day, they had kissed after school "behind a patch of blue cornflowers" (*House*, 22). And Staggerlee is in heaven. But she becomes ill and has to stay out of school for several days. Her family lives far away, outside the town—physically removed from the community that emotionally does not accept them—and when Staggerlee returns to school, wanting to be with Hazel, longing to see her hair and smile again, she is devastated to see Hazel surrounded by a group of girls. "Staggerlee touched her fingers to her lips, wanting Hazel to remember the way the cornflowers had swayed, the way the sun set down all gold and pretty that afternoon. Wanting her to remember how she had said, 'I could stay here forever—just me and you right here in all this blue'" (*House*, 23).

But while Staggerlee has been out of school with the chickenpox, Hazel has learned that Staggerlee's grandparents were important people in the town; statues in their memory adorn the town square because they were killed by a bomb while crusading for civil rights. The other students have told Hazel, who has only recently moved to the area, this piece of history, saying that because of her grandparents, Stagger thinks she is better than everyone else, and that is why she is so quiet. And, they tell Hazel that Stagger's mother is white—as well as rude and stuck up, because she, like Stagger, is quiet and unassuming. Hazel succumbs to peer pressure, and turns away from Staggerlee, leaving her all the more alone. As Staggerlee sits on the front porch on the day Hazel and her family are moving once again, hoping against hope Hazel will come say goodbye, she is filled with sorrow as "tall stalks of corn swayed slowly, and their shadows, casting out over the land, filled Staggerlee with a sadness she couldn't name" (*House*, 33).

Love at First Sight

Now Tyler, the same age as Stagger, is coming for the summer. Stagger goes with her father to the nearest town with a bus station to meet Tyler, and when she first sees this stranger, she is almost overwhelmed by her, by the fact that she has "the kind of beautiful you couldn't put a finger on" (*House*, 46), and it is love at first sight. As she stands at the Tudor bus station, "She felt something weird happening inside her stomach and all around her—like something pounding, trying to get out of her. Her mind kept running back to Hazel in the cornfields" (*House*, 47). Staggerlee and Tyler—who has renamed herself Trout—sit in the back of Daddy's truck for the ride home. The girls talk about race; Stagger admits to sometimes hating how light-skinned she is. Other kids used to call her "light bright," which she heard as a swear word. Trout tells her she should be pleased; she can pass for white. But Stagger retorts that she would not want to do that—saying, in general, that she is "me, just me," and Trout hears that, relaxes, knowing she is with a kindred spirit. Stagger tries not to look at Trout, but Trout looks hard at her, telling her to stop braiding her hair, to leave it loose and free. So Staggerlee begins playing the harmonica, surrounding them with music, but all the while she feels scared of Trout, afraid that Trout will loosen unknown parts of her, "scared that Trout had brought something deep with her, something that concerned both of them" (*House*, 54). Trout begins to sing; the girls connect through the music, talking about their favorite parts of the song "Moonlight in Vermont," and Staggerlee is in love, staring at Trout's mouth, at "the way it moves and her throat tightens up and tears form" (*House*, 55).

The girls are alike in their search for identity, in their renaming of themselves. Staggerlee adopted her name when she was nine. Watching a film of her grandparents, who were well-known entertainers, sing the old song about Staggerlee, Stagger began to recognize that the words were not really about a murder at all, but about "someone struggling to break out of all the gates life had built up around them" (*House*, 28), and she wants to be that same kind of person. Trout changed her name after watching a trout fight its way upstream because "I wanted to learn how to fight like that. I wanted to see this little fish that thought he had so much to live for. . . . You give yourself a name, you have to live up to it, though" (*House*, 56), and Trout feels like she has to fight constantly.

It turns out Ida Mae has sent Trout to Staggerlee because she does not like the person Trout "is growing up to be" (*House*, 60). In a dialogue fraught with sexual tension, as the sun glows beautiful and clear behind them, setting across the river that is Staggerlee's friend, Stagger asks Trout, "Who are you growing up to be?" (*House*, 60). Her knees are trembling, and Stagger is aware of how Trout smells, of their closeness, sitting on the bed. Staggerlee escapes, wishing—like Melanin—she had words for her feelings, words for her thoughts. She runs to the barn where she has often gone for refuge. There, she blows into her harmonica, remembering the way Trout's shoulder pressed against hers, the movement of Trout's lips, and the reader knows, as Staggerlee knows, that "there was a feeling growing inside Trout, and Staggerlee knew it because it was growing inside her too. Maybe it had always been there. . . . She knew it was secret and shameful" (*House*, 69). Aunt Hallique had understood that Trout was feeling confused about her sexual identity, had begged Ida Mae from her deathbed to give Trout some growing room, but Ida Mae had not been able to accept what Hallique had to say. In the same way, Staggerlee recalls how she had felt the afternoon after she had kissed Hazel, how she had started running home, aching to tell someone, but how she slowed down, knowing nobody at home would want to celebrate with her.

Coming Together, Growing Apart

However, while Staggerlee gives herself over to loving Trout, loving her voice, her hair, the times they spend together picking Indian paintbrush and walking with the rush of the river in their ears, Trout feels more ambiguous. Trout sometimes wants to be alone, and at those times, watching Trout "become tiny in the distance," Staggerlee "felt her heart caving in around her" (*House*, 72). Sometimes a friend from Baltimore calls Trout, and after those calls, during which Staggerlee feels her distance from Trout, Trout seems younger, less sure of herself. On the other hand, Trout eventually confesses to Staggerlee that sometimes when she is out walking in the woods, her mind is filled with thoughts of Staggerlee. They talk about their past histories, and Staggerlee, in a poignant, lyrical passage, knows "she had dreamed Trout before she came. Dreamed a girl who would be like her—liking the same things, knowing the same history. . . . She had dreamed them sitting on the porch laughing together. Dreamed the red dust rising up around them as they walked" (*House*, 72). Trout tells Staggerlee about the first time she kissed a girl. She confided to Hallique, who told her she would get crushes on lots of people, girls and boys. Worried, Trout asked her what would happen if she always wanted a girl; Hallique didn't judge, but did say that would be something best kept to herself. Staggerlee says nobody ever had to tell her she had to hide her impulses, she just has always known. She learned that from reading a book—about a woman who loved another woman and jumped off a cliff. No wonder the thought of loving women seems so scary.

Woodson recalls that she read a book called *Loving Her* by Ann Allen Shockly when she was fourteen or fifteen, remembering that she gobbled it up "hungrily,"[22] a novel about two women loving each other. But she, like Staggerlee and Trout, had nowhere to go with her responses and questions. She had a friend at school who was rumored to be gay, but they never talked about issues of sexual identity. Then, in college, Woodson met her assigned roommate, Beth, from Scarsdale, dressed in as preppy an outfit as Woodson had ever seen. Woodson remembers saying to her, "You're so preppy," to which the other woman replied, "I'm not preppy, I'm gay." And hearing those words, from another woman's mouth, made Woodson feel free to think about herself using the term. In an NPR commentary, Woodson recalls, "Up until that point . . . I never talked about being gay with anyone. I never had a language for it. And some message was there that it wasn't okay to talk about what I was feeling and what I was thinking and what I was searching for until that conversation."[23]

Trout uses the word with Staggerlee, who "felt the word settling inside her. It felt too big, somehow" (*House*, 81), but she does not run away from it, just notes that, at fourteen, it is hard to know the future. So Trout writes in the dirt with a stick, "Staggerlee and Trout were here today. Maybe they will and maybe they won't be gay" (*House*, 81). Woodson herself is somewhat ambivalent about the value of such labels: "I think in some respects it's a good thing, and in some respects it's not so good. I was talking to some friends about young children—this was about a year ago—about how we give them words, and then they have ways of talking about things—"This is the floor. That is the sky." And how without those words, they don't have a means of identifying. But then I thought that without those words, they'd have to come up with some other means of identifying, so it makes for a really creative language, and they have to experiment and really focus, "This thing has a lot of colors, and its arched and it makes me feel really good" and then someone says, "Oh, that's a rainbow," and they're like that doesn't really matter—it has colors and makes me feel good." Woodson thinks of herself as a writer as not having a large vocabulary, "so as a result, I really have to think more creatively about how to explain something, and therefore I can sometimes elicit a feeling or an emotion that I otherwise wouldn't be able to do. And I think about using the word "gay" or something else to label yourself, yeah, there's something really satisfying about being able to say, 'This is this thing that I am,' but it's more complicated than that. It's bigger than that. So when someone uses the word and attaches it to me, they're kind of underestimating who I am." The reader hopes that Staggerlee, too, will grow into an awareness of the complexities of herself, of how "gay" does not describe all of who she is and can be.

Unfortunately for Staggerlee, Trout's ambivalence about her sexuality makes her willing to explore the possibility of being heterosexual. It turns out that the girl who has been calling her all summer has been trying to set up Trout with a boy. And Trout, very much aware of the difficulties that follow from being identified as a lesbian, says to Staggerlee, "Sometimes I want that, though—to just be able to walk out into the world and *be*. I couldn't imagine going to some party with a girl as my date" (*House*, 76). Staggerlee can, saying, "If I loved someone enough, I would go anywhere in the world with them" (*House*, 76). While it is Trout who has named herself for the fish that has to fight its way upstream, it is Trout who ultimately decides she just does not have that kind of power or strength.

Staggerlee has changed as a result of her Trout-filled summer. When she returns to school in the fall, she smiles more—and people smile back. When she walks, she now keeps her head up; she looks forward, following Trout's advice, wanting to see what she is headed for. Her music teacher asks her to join the choir, recognizing in Staggerlee her grandmother's talent for singing. At home, Mama gives birth to Hope (a girl—though Woodson's older brother carries the name in her family), and Staggerlee reflects on how past people and present people and the people she will become are all inside her. In general, Staggerlee is happier, more content—until Trout's letter arrives.

It comes on a cold February day; as is often true in a Woodson novel, the outside weather reflects her main character's inner world. As she reads Trout's words on the page, Staggerlee's heart starts pounding, and with snow on the ground, last summer seems a distant dream. Trout has been seeing Matthew since her return to Baltimore in September. She has not been able to find the words to tell Staggerlee, but now is confiding that she likes being with Matthew, likes walking down the street holding his hand, likes his smile, likes how she feels sometimes like the world stops moving when she looks at him. Ida Mae likes Matthew, and he has become a fixture at their house, and Trout has even gone back to calling herself Tyler. She says, as Staggerlee has said of being both black and white, that she is both Trout and Tyler, all of it. But Staggerlee is devastated. She reads the letter over and over, "And each time, the news about Matthew sliced through her" (*House*, 99). All she can do is wait and wonder "Who would they become?" (*House*, 99).

Staggerlee may grow up to be Woodson herself. Staggerlee stares at the long dresses and high heels the other eighth grade girls are wearing for their graduation; she is clad in hiking books and a Columbia sweat-shirt, and she just does not want to wear what they are wearing, noting how precarious they look toddling about on their heels. Even after she joins the choir and develops relationships with other students so that she has the option of going to movies with someone on a weekend afternoon, Staggerlee often chooses to be alone. Woodson recalls starting to realize, at a slightly younger age, after being disenchanted with the political process, that she did not want to be part of the majority. Staggerlee may grow up and settle into gayness, as Woodson did, after experimenting with heterosexual relationships throughout high school. Interestingly, writing in 1995, Woodson said that she did not believe that, in fact, fourteen-year-old lesbians exist, but says she can write about "a fourteen-year-old girl who struggles with her identity as she watches friends with boys, sees gay couples and fears she may be seeing herself."[24]

Even more so than Staggerlee, Trout reflects Woodson's belief that "identity is fluid."[25] Therefore adults, she believes, should show adolescents "their options while giving them space to make their own decisions. Too often I have seen young girls who are labeled lesbians fiercely act out against the label, whereas if they were just allowed to be, they might become happier, better adjusted adults."[26] But the reader cannot tell how Trout/Tyler will ultimately define herself. Woodson has given both her and Staggerlee space, through their separation, to just "be." As Susan Bloom puts it, writing a review in *Horn Book*, "As Staggerlee wonders if someday there will be 'someone she could whisper her life to,' the reader feels grateful that Woodson has whispered her lyrical story to us, a story still awaiting, like all young lives, its conclusion."[27]

Woodson accurately analyzes the appeal of her work for her intended audience, saying, "I believe young people want honest. If you tell a story as you remember it, at their age, they'll read it. If you talk down to them or try to show them how much you've learned, they'll run away. When I sit down to write, I return to the places of my tenth, twelfth or fourteenth year of living. I don't explain anything because at that time I had no explanations. Life just was."[28] The power of *The*

House You Pass on the Way comes from Woodson's ability to take the reader inside Staggerlee's mind, to give us her thoughts and feelings in heartbreakingly poetic prose, and to just let her be, without giving her or the reader any definite answers.

Interestingly, Wendy Lamb, Woodson's editor at Random House notes that Staggerlee's story did not come to her author in the holistic fashion of some of her other novels. *The House You Pass on the Way* was, in terms of process, the hardest book Lamb saw Woodson tackle during her time as Woodson's editor. It went through many drafts over a two-year period. Woodson kept reworking it—and rethinking it. Lamb would edit what she had been given and would give it back to the novelist. Woodson would take it away and redraft, and it would come back to Lamb with a different plot. Says Lamb, "Jackie could have published several books from all the plots she tried out."[29] The story was always about Staggerlee, but "other characters came and went."[30] But from the very beginning, Lamb loved the character of Staggerlee and the "honesty and delicacy"[31] of the way Woodson presented teenage sexual feelings, and the richness and complexity of Staggerlee's family context.

Woodson does believe the climate is more friendly for the Staggerlees and Trouts of the world today. In an NPR commentary, she notes that while the Human Rights Watch reports that harassment may affect as many as two million teens who are struggling with their sexuality, things have changed. There are now eight hundred school-based clubs called "Gay/Straight Alliances." Some school districts have alternative proms for gay couples. More young adults now identify themselves as gay, and do so at an earlier age. As an example, Woodson says she was twenty-one before she attended her first Youth Pride rally, but she is offering commentary on a rally in 1999 when she talks to a girl who is, as Staggerlee is, just fourteen, and Woodson sees in such individuals "a defiance, a strength, a complexity."[32] A young man tells her that what is great about being gay is knowing there is a little part of you who is different from others—though Woodson also senses, still, a longing for a time in which it would not be such a big deal to be gay. She reflects, "What has changed is the way young people recognize themselves in the world, the way they have a language for who they are that is not ascribed to them by others."[33]

And yet, as Melanin and Staggerlee show so eloquently, difference does matter, and it is hard to be the outsider, hard to have to come to terms with an identity that takes the individual outside the main-stream. One of the most significant contributions Woodson makes to the world of literature for young adults is that of telling the stories of people like Staggerlee, Trout, and Melanin Sun, people who are often not given a voice. She says of herself, "I'll stay right where I am, and try to figure out how, through writing, through living, through my every-day actions, I can make this world a better place for all the kids who are coming up. I feel like, if I can do that, then I've done my work."[34]

In two of her most recent novels, *If You Come Softly* and *Miracle's Boys*, Woodson leaves behind, at least momentarily, issues of sexual identity, and focuses more explicitly on racial issues. These works, her short stories and adult novel will be at the center of the next chapter, which deals too with Woodson's current strengths as a writer for both children and young adults.

Notes

1. Maeve Visner Knoth, "Review of *From the Notebooks of Melanin Sun*," *Horn Book Magazine* 71 (July/August 1995), 468.

2. Susan P. Bloom, "Review of *The House You Pass on the Way*," *Horn Book Magazine* 73 (September/October 1997), 583.

3. Jacqueline Woodson, *From the Notebooks of Melanin Sun*. (New York: Scholastic, 1995). Hereafter cited as *Sun*.

4. Roger Sutton, "Review of *From the Notebooks of Melanin Sun*," *Center for Children's Books* 48 (July/August 1995), 401.

5. Dianne Hess, interview via e-mail correspondence with Lois Stover, December 17, 2002. Hereafter cited as Hess.

6. Hess.

7. Hess.

8. Hess.

9. Hess.

10. Hess.

11. Hess.

12. Hess.

13. Hess.

14. Hess.

15. Hess.

16. Hess.

17. Hess.

18. Hess.

19. Hess.

20. Hess.

21. Jacqueline Woodson, *The House You Pass on the Way*. (New York: Delacorte, 1997). Hereafter cited as *House*.

22. Jacqueline Woodson, "Profile: The Changing Face of America—Experience of Gay Teens," National Public Radio Commentary (May 30, 2001), 1. Retrieved from www.npr.org on 9 September 2002. Keyword: Woodson, Jacqueline.

23. Woodson, "Profile: The Changing Face of America—Experience of Gay Teens," 1.

24. Woodson, "A Sign of Having Been Here," 3.

25. Woodson, "A Sign of Having Been Here," 3.

26. Woodson, "A Sign of Having Been Here," 3.

27. Susan P. Bloom, "Review of *The House You Pass on the Way*," 583.

28. Woodson, "A Sign of Having Been Here," 3.

29. Lamb.

30. Lamb.

31. Lamb.

32. Woodson, "Profile: The Changing Face of America—Experience of Gay Teens," 3.

33. Brown, "From Outsider to Insider," 4.

34. Woodson, "Slipping Away," 61.

CHAPTER 6

~

On Maturing as a Writer: *If You Come Softly, Miracle's Boys, Autobiography of a Family Photo,* the Short Stories, and Children's Books

A recent short story, "The Rialto," published in 2001 as part of James Howe's collection *The Color of Absence: Twelve Stories about Loss and Hope,* is the product of a collaboration between Chris Lynch, known for his "boy books," and Woodson. According to the author notes at the end of the story, Woodson and Lynch are planning to transform the story into a novel. They admit the process of getting the story to the point of publication was arduous, but now feel they have a handle on how to move forward and want to finish this tale of Caryn and Ivan, a black girl and white boy who came together, and now have been taken apart, in spite of the fact that Caryn is now carrying Ivan's child. Woodson and Lynch were teaching together at Vermont College where, through sharing notes and histories, they found they were "remarkably similar people in a lot of ways. More compatible than two solitary writers tend to be."[1] Later, during a long-distance phone conversation between Brooklyn and Ireland, where Lynch was living, they decided to try writing something together, decided to try to bring their "distinctly different niches in fiction" together.[2] It was not smooth sailing. "The characters, and their creators, began a years-long tango, embracing one another, repelling one another. Months of intense interaction would be followed by months of obstinate silence. Undeniable similarities challenged by seemingly irreconcilable difference. . . . Quitting was just as hard as sticking with it, and neither option completely solved everything. In the end the story was as organic as we could make it. The characters had fought it out, played it out, and were left to confront a result that was even more challenging than what they had started out with."[3]

Tackling such a project at age thirty-nine, after winning the Coretta Scott King Award for *Miracle's Boys* and being named a National Book Award finalist for *Hush*, is typical of Woodson, who is known for pushing limits, for pushing her readers into rethinking their understanding of the world, and for pushing herself as a writer through experimentation with her craft. *Miracle's Boys*, *If You Come Softly*, her adult novel *Autobiography of a Family Photo*, her short stories, and her children's books show Woodson's maturity as an artist who can connect with readers of all ages.

Crossing Boundaries of Race and Class—Again

In the 1998, *If You Come Softly*[4] her first book with Putnam, Woodson "unerringly limns the delicate intensity and passionate innocence of first love"[5] as she tells the story of Ellie and Miah by combining Ellie's first-person voice with an omniscient portrayal of Miah's internal and external worlds. In the process, the author softly and deftly handles potentially explosive subject matter; the characters and their story make our hearts ache but also make our minds consider issues of race, class, and morality as they play out against a backdrop of family tensions. It is because we come to care so much for Ellie and Miah, because we want so much for their love to find a way through the disapproval of family and society, that the underlying messages about racism hit so hard.

If You Come Softly is not a happily-ever-after story. Woodson gives us a prelude in which we meet Elisha, called Ellie. She has had a dream about Jeremiah, Miah; her mother, whom she calls Marion, sits beside her on the bed, asking if it was a good dream. Ellie cannot remember it all; Marion advises her, while caressing her, to "remember what you can" (*If*, 2). Thus, readers know, as we move into Elisha's memories, they will lead to tragedy of some sort. But to her credit, Woodson is able to catch us up into the story of Elisha and Jeremiah to the point that we almost forget to be worried about their future. She gives us the intensity of first love, the unpredictability of it, right from page one, as Ellie tells us, "I couldn't stop looking at him, at his smile and his hair. I had never seen locks up close. His were thick and black and spiraling down over his shoulders. I wanted to touch them, to touch his face. I wanted to hear him say his name again. For a moment we stared at each other, neither of us saying anything. . . . 'Jeremiah,' I whispered to myself as I walked away from him. I could feel his name settling around me, as though I were walking in a mist of it, of him, of Jeremiah" (*If*, 1).

But the potential for tragedy is also with us. Clearly Ellie, who has never seen locks up close, is not black, and just as clearly Miah is. Woodson tells us that blackness is integral to Miah's identity: "Jeremiah was black. He could feel it. The way the sun pressed down hard and hot on his skin in the summer. Sometimes it felt like he sweated black beads of oil. He felt warm inside his skin, protected. And in Fort Greene, Brooklyn—where everyone seemed to be some shade of black—he felt good walking through the neighborhood" (*If*, 5). He lives in a world that defines its inhabitants by skin color; in the summers, in the past, he spent time in the south, like his author, with his grandmother, who would try to keep him in the shade so he would not get too black. But his father, an award-winning filmmaker, took him to see a movie about the Black Panthers shouting their famous "Black is beautiful" line, and told him that as a black man, he is a warrior, a warrior against commercials and the media and white society trying to make him feel invisible, inferior for being black. Because of his father's occupation, Miah has had the chance to travel—to India, Mauritius, Mexico—which he knows makes him different from many of his peers, both black and white. However, he feels deeply black when he is on the basketball court. He knows that, in Fort Greene, playing ball is a way of staying connected to other guys, and he has grown up playing basketball, using an empty trashcan or the rungs of ladders on a fire escape as baskets, thinking of himself as black, as a warrior. Then he meets Ellie.

Ellie is white, rich, and Jewish. She has grown up without brothers and sisters, as the twins, Ann and Reuben, were ten when she was born, and her older siblings, Marc and Susan, were already in graduate school. In many ways, Ellie has grown up without a mother, too.

Her mother, Marion, refuses to call her Ellie, so Ellie refuses to call her Mom. Marion has left the family periodically in the past, both when Ellie was little and again when she was eight, making Ellie afraid—afraid that she might say or do the wrong thing and send her mother away again.

In many ways, Ellie and Marie from *I Hadn't Meant to Tell You This* are kindred spirits, trying to understand their mothers' motivation in leaving, feeling their absence deep inside themselves. Out of fear that Marion might decide to take off once again, Ellie holds back from loving her too much, from opening up to her, from sharing herself. Like Marie's mother, Marion has found the atmosphere of her well-to-do Manhattan lifestyle oppressive, telling Ellie at one point she felt dead inside. Her husband, a successful doctor, was often unavailable, and so it fell to Marion to deal with the children—with their noise and confusion and arguments. But, unlike Marie's mother, Marion learns, after she is on her own, that she cannot live without all the things she could not live with, and so she returns, but Ellie never trusts her fully.

Miah, too, has had to cope with issues of abandonment. His parents, a high profile celebrity couple, have recently separated. He longs for siblings, for someone who can understand what he is experiencing and with whom he can share the pain his parents are inflicting on him. His beloved grandmother has died, leaving a different kind of hole inside. Miah, like Ellie, tiptoes around both parents, agreeing to go to Percy for his dad, giving up red meat and cussing for his mother. Both Miah's parents and Ellie's parents decide, in parallel ways, to send their children to Percy Academy, wanting a good education for them at a school with a high college acceptance rate. Ellie points out that if parents are rich enough, they can buy their child's way into college, but nevertheless, they both end up at Percy.

When they meet, Miah recognizes something of himself in Ellie's eyes, "that sense of loss" (*If*, 40). Both of them have wondered "where love went to, how a person could just love somebody one day and boom—the next day love somebody else" (*If*, 40). Nevertheless, they are open to the magic of love; Ellie feels "like slowly I was being wrapped inside Miah—inside his eyes, inside his voice, inside the way he talked about things" (*If*, 105). The description of the first kiss Ellie and Miah share captures with incredible delicacy the sweetness of such moments, the perfection—described as a stillness, which, the reader reflects, will have to be shattered at some point.

Revisiting Other Themes

In this product of her maturity as a writer, Woodson weaves together many subplots that serve as counterpoint to the main story, addressing themes of longtime importance to her. Most notably, Ellie's favorite sister, Anne, is gay. She calls Ellie to announce that she and her lover of four years are having a commitment ceremony. Marion had not responded positively to Anne's coming out; however, as Ann was already grown and living in San Francisco, far from Marion's Manhattan apartment, there was not much Marion could do. Ellie has felt the loss of Ann since her sister left home; now, she wants Anne to be there, so she can talk about Miah and her feelings. Anne can tell, even via long-distance phone conversations, that Ellie has met a boy, and she is excited for her younger sibling—until Ellie confides that Miah is black. Then, Ellie can "feel the air between us getting weird" (*If*, 55). Ellie feels abandoned yet again. She had hoped her sister would be supportive, would appreciate the magic of what Ellie and Miah share, but the racial divide keeps Anne and Ellie apart. Nevertheless, it is Anne's words Ellie recalls when she thinks about love, remembering Anne describing investment love, binge love, too-fast and now just holding on love, and plain love, "No reason for it, no need to explain" (*If*, 127). And, some mornings, when Ellie and Miah's fingers are entwined, that is how she feels—perfect love, no explanations needed, filling up the moment, creating a forever out of it.

In other works, such as *The Dear One*, the gay couple provided a center of gravity, modeling not only what a committed relationship could and should look like, but also how tolerance for others should come out of a couple's own experiences with prejudice. In *The House You Pass on the Way*, however, Woodson showed the difficulties inherent in interracial relationships. Having watched her parents deal with the ostracism resulting from their marriage, Staggerlee knows that, if she is gay, she too will have to face a similar lack of understanding from many people, possibly even from her family. Woodson characters are all individuals. They confront their own differences, but, realistically, they are not always able to generalize their desire for tolerance into acceptance of those whose differences are outside their own sphere of knowledge.

In Jeremiah, Woodson returns to issues of race and how race shapes identity that she introduced very early in her career when Maizon faced choices about creating a niche at Blue Hill, and developed later in *From the Notebooks of Melanin Sun*. Miah, at basketball practice, surrounded by white faces, white bodies, thinks about the difference between his two black teammates Kennedy and Rayshon. Kennedy has been at Percy for several years; on the court, he is at ease; off court, he is popular. Rayshon, however, is also new to the school and he always leaves for home right after practice. Miah learns Ray is putting himself through Percy, working two jobs to do so, and he hates the fact that Ray is working so hard and that other boys just got to sit around "talking junk" (*If*, 64). In spite of their economic differences, racial similarities pull them together, and Ray calls the three of them "The three black musketeers. . . . It was a joke, but there was something deeper to it, too. Something he and Rayshon and Kennedy understood" (*If*, 60).

As the relationship between Miah and Ellie deepens, both young people have to confront their prejudices. Ellie recalls walking with Anne through Central Park; as a young black man came running toward them, Anne panicked, assuming the worst—that they were about to be mugged. That young man turned out to be a jogger, and Ellie now wonders if her sister would have had that same reaction if he had been white. She finds her mother's comments on racial equality increasingly naïve. Marion has always told her that all peoples have suffered, that nobody has the right to feel any better than anyone else. But having met Miah, Ellie now wonders why there have been no blacks in her world, why no blacks golf with her father or quilt with her mother.

Having met Ellie, beginning to think about the future, Miah starts to ask questions of his longtime friend, Carlton, whose father is black and whose mother is white, wondering what it is like for him to be part of two different worlds. Carlton admits that he really does not know any other way, so he cannot make comparisons, but he does offer that he does not feel like his mother's white family, stiff and proper, are his real people. He notes that people sometimes stare when he and his parents are together, and he hypothesizes that his older sister, Colette, moved to England to get away from the tensions attendant to being biracial. Miah and Ellie, when they are walking together, cutting class, face similar stares and reactions. Two older ladies see them and ask Ellie if she is okay, or if she needs help; Miah reflects, "If you were with a white boy, they probably would have just smiled and kept going" (*If*, 107).

At school nobody says anything; the other students just seem to turn away from the sight of Ellie and Miah holding hands or walking with their arms around each other. Even Kennedy and Rayshon turn away from Miah; their bond of blackness is strained by Miah's evident desertion of their race. But the young people persevere. Miah tells Ellie to think of the disparaging looks and comments as rain, noting that rain does not last forever. Ellie wishes for a drought, but tells Miah that even knowing, now, what they face, she will keep on coming toward him; she will not turn away. As they walk down Fifth Avenue, Ellie holds Miah's hand tighter and tells him, "Walk through the rain" (*If*, 136). Their courage is remarkable given their youth.

So is their realistic understanding of what they face. For instance, Ellie is afraid to introduce Miah to her family for fear they will not like him because of his race and, if that is possible, she reflects, "then I might have it inside me, too"—to not be open to someone because of race (*If*, 164). Miah knows what she means, saying he sometimes wonders if "it's there, someplace, ready to spring out" and admits he often hates white people, though he loves Ellie, and he cannot figure out what this mix of feelings means. Miah even talks to his father about race. His father comments that "white people don't know they're white" (*If*, 134), noting that the bombing of black churches affect black people in ways white people just cannot imagine. But, knowing Ellie, Miah tells his father that there are white people who can and do say, "I'm white, so what am I gonna do with this—how am I going to use it to change the world?" (*If*, 136).

Moving beyond Abandonment

The theme of abandonment is evident as both Ellie and Miah share their stories of loss. As is true of Woodson's earlier main characters, both young people arrive at some form of acceptance, even forgiveness, of their parents. Miah asks his father how his mother, Miah's grandmother, would feel about the divorce. His father uses this opportunity to explain that he himself does not really know what happened except that at some point he and Miah's mother outgrew each other, he fell for Lois Ann, and that he thinks his mother would understand and would want him to be happy. Father and son come together around their shared missing of Miah's grandmother, around conversations about life after death and how they both feel her presence sometimes when they need to be comforted. Anne has told Marion about Ellie and Miah, and Marion practically begs Ellie to talk to her, sharing her own first love story in an effort to prime the pump of conversation with her daughter. Ellie, at first, thinks it is too late—the lack of trust she has in her mother runs too deep. But, as she watches Marion turn to the sink and begin to wash the dishes, "She touched one foot behind the other in a way that made my eyes fill up. She looked broken. Defeated. Lonely" (*If*, 122). Later, Ellie is able to rely on her mother for comfort in the face of Miah's death; Marion grips her hand at Miah's funeral; her father tells her to let the tears come.

Ironically, it is through Miah's death that Ellie begins to overcome her fears of abandonment. The moments leading up to his tragic end are sketched in vivid colors and vibrant words. Ellie tells Miah she wants him to come meet her family, and she gives him her Star of David necklace as an amulet. As she walks away from him, ready, finally, to share him with her parents, Miah is grinning. The words "My Ellie" (*If*, 169) roll over and over in his mind. Too excited to get on a subway home, he bounces his basketball, then starts running with it, "feeling as though he could lift up, fly" (*If*, 169). But of course he cannot fly. Instead, he is caught in the neck by a bullet fired out of fear of a tall black man running in a white neighborhood. But their shared love of Miah forges a connection between Ellie and Nelia, Miah's mother. In his death, Ellie's intensity of feeling for Miah bring him to life for Ellie's parents.

When the book ends, it is two and a half years after the tragedy. As Ellie is graduating from Percy, getting accepted into good colleges, she and her parents are closer, and she is even hoping she can look forward to talking, deeply and openly, with Anne. Meanwhile, she knows that she had something incredibly special, and she is glad she did not blink or turn away from the chance to have the kind of connection she and Miah shared. She knows that "Time comes to us softly, slowly. It sits beside us for a while. Then, long before we are ready, it moves on" (*If*, 181).

Woodson compares Ellie and Marie from *I Hadn't Meant to Tell You This*. Marie finally realizes she is not responsible for her mother's in-ability to breathe, "so she takes all her mother's letters, puts them in a shoe box, and says, 'I'm letting you go, I'm letting this go.' And with Ellie and her mom, there's a movement towards her a tiny bit because she's like 'I'm letting go of the fear of you leaving, and I'm living, I'm starting to live in this moment of you living here' because . . . you know in the course of this relationship it IS about this moment, that you might not have the next moment, and yeah, tomorrow her mother's bags might be gone again, but right now she's here."

Intersections of Narrative Voice and Theme

The concept of alternating voices that Woodson tried in *Between Madison and Palmetto* works beautifully in this later novel. The writing in *If You Come Softly* is exquisite; Ellie's first-person narration captures the intensity of her feelings as she comes of age both as an individual and in love, and the omniscient point of view Woodson uses to describe Miah and the world in which he lives works to give the reader a broader perspective. The details used to bring the characters to life are chosen with care to give the most insight with the fewest words. We know that Ellie has moments of anxiety and relies on herself when they hit because she periodically sucks on her Star of David necklace, which calms her; the fact that she then gives it to Jeremiah shows both her growing confidence in herself and the depth of her feelings for him. We learn how caring and sensitive Miah is with a few deftly drawn scenes—such as that in which he teaches a much younger boy, Little Ray, to shoot hoops, or that in which he reflects on the way the light hits in his mother's kitchen. Smells are important in this novel; Miah smells to Ellie like a mix of musk and autumn, of maleness and the out-doors (*If*, 75). Just as Ellie watches Miah, Miah watches her "when she wasn't looking. Watching the way she used her hand to move her hair out of her face, slowly, wrapping her finger around it and pulling it back behind her ear. The way she leaned over her notebook to write, a tiny frown between her eyebrows" (*If*, 78–79).

Without being heavy-handed, the author foreshadows the tragic ending of the story. At one point, Ellie and Miah are talking about dreams, about what they want to be, what they want from the future. Miah says he cannot see the future, cannot see anything, "just a big black space where I should be" (*If*, 166). And that is the same black space into which he tumbles, into nothingness, as he passes out of this world in the ending pages of the book. Woodson talks about her own experience with reading literature and loving language, saying she has come to love revisiting works by authors as varied as Pound and James as much as she loves having Sunday dinner sitting around her grandmother's table because, "Each event is buttered thick with experience and language,"[6] and in her most recent works, Woodson gives her readers a similarly thickly buttered, rich reading experience in her own use of language and attention to detail.

The Writer and Her Process

Additionally, through the character of Nelia, Miah's mother and a successful novelist, Woodson gives us some insight into her own processes as an artist. When Miah brings Ellie to meet his mother, his mother has been in a dry period, focused on the grief she has felt in the face of her husband's abandonment. But she is coming out of it. She says to Ellie and Miah, "This book has been knocking in my head for a couple of weeks. I've been resisting, but now I'm seeing what it's got to say to me" (*If*, 160). In a similar way, Woodson finds she has to be open to her characters and to what they want her to say, though she also notes that "I don't understand the process. I understand bits and pieces, and I know how the characters get to me, and I know that mood and light are important to me . . . but I can't put it all together."

As Woodson wrote about Miah, she thought, "This is the kid I'd like to have." And because of one of her current writing projects, which involves "actually trying to work on a book that's about that, that's about how the characters start trying to tell me their stories," Ellie and Miah have stayed with her. "There was this character, Jeremiah, who was with me first, and who's still with me, and in thinking about this book I'm trying to write now, there's a person who on the page is dead but in my head who isn't. What happens to that character? It's all so convoluted and complicated. But, it does start with a voice, the voice of someone I don't know until I start putting it down on the page."

Woodson was not comfortable, at first, with the fact that she was writing from the point of view of a fairly affluent, fairly protected Jewish girl. "As I sat down to write this novel, I asked myself over and over why I needed to write it. Why did I need to go inside the life of a Jewish girl? More than the need, what gave me the right? Whose story was this?"[7] Eventually she realized that she herself has been a girl, is not male—but is black, has been a long time resident of New York, and, "most of all, like the characters in my story, I have felt a sense of powerlessness in my lifetime. And this is a room into which I can walk and join them. This sense of being on the outside of things, of feeling misunderstood and invisible, is the experience I bring to the story."[8]

Nancy Paulsen, Woodson's current editor at Penguin/Putnam, recalls that when *If You Come Softly* first appeared, neither she nor her colleagues, all residents of New York, "blinked an eye" at the ending. But she later overheard librarians at the American Library Association talking about the ending, calling it unrealistic, finding the tragedy implausible given their own experiences.[9] Paulsen comments that now such perceptions have changed, saying, "Jackie has brought the reality to a lot more people of what it means to be 'the other'. . . . You get into the heads of her characters so well that you imagine being that person."[10]

Given that Woodson's partner is both white and Jewish and that they plan to raise Toshi in ways that observe and respect each partner's religious values, Woodson now feels she does, indeed, have the right and even an obligation to tell stories such as that of Ellie and Miah. She feels that she brings all her own experiences of trying to make connections across boundaries of race and class to bear on telling such stories, reflecting that "When I write of people who are of different races or religions than myself, I must bring myself to that experience, ask what it is that I, as a black woman, have to offer or say about it. Why did I as a black woman, need to tell this story?"[11] and she adds that she does not respect white writers who do not examine their own positions of power in the world, and who do not "sit down at the table" of their characters to understand their language, what makes them laugh deeply and fully, what makes them cry "the tears they hide from the outside world."[12]

When Woodson finds letters in her mail from young people touched by her stories, she is reinforced in her belief that she does, in fact, have a mandate to tell such stories, and knows, too, that she is successful in doing so. Recently, she received a note from a young girl who had just read *If You Come Softly* who told her, "Interracial dating. I didn't understand that phrase until I read your book *If You Come Softly*. After reading your book I learned the technical term for 'I don't think it looks good if a colored person and a white person are going out together.' . . . That's a phrase I've heard from one of my friend's mothers time and time again. . . . At the first dance of this year at my middle school, I danced with one of my close black friends. My mom and step-dad found out and they said I was never allowed to do that again, how it may cause me to have a bad reputation. This was somewhat like the reaction Ellie got from her sister on the phone. Thank you for writing this book. It is a great, great story about the true meaning of love. . . . Your book has really touched my life. I will always remember it." It is comments such as these that give Woodson the drive to continue offering young people stories that can challenge their perceptions and give them a sense of alternative possibilities for their lives.

Focus on Family

In *Miracle's Boys*,[13] Woodson writes a memorable novel about three young men adept at hiding their tears from the outside world but who are able, in Woodson's hands, to share their inner worlds with their readers. *Miracle's Boys* won the Coretta Scott King Award in 2001. In her acceptance speech, Woodson remarks on the importance of the award itself, saying "Like black people, it has survived and flourished and gained honor and recognition and status. . . . Because one of the purposes of this award is to counteract the inability of publishers, judges, and readers to recognize the universality of a black protagonist."[14] She argues that the award helps get books into the hands of young people of color, and if librarians and teachers and publishers would like to remove the need of the award, then they—we—need to "democratize" other awards. Meanwhile, in response to those who believe the Coretta Scott King Award and others that specifically honor nonwhites are somehow "less worthy," less desirable awards, she declares, "Here is where the real miracle comes in—that we as a people can hear this and go on to be amazing in the world, that like birches, we bend without breaking, creating our own pies when the mainstream is not sharing."[15] The brothers of *Miracle's Boy* show that ability to "bend without breaking," and, in the process, provide a model of determination and perseverance fueled by love.

In some ways, *Miracle's Boys* echoes the groundbreaking novel *The Outsiders* published by S. E. Hinton in 1967.[16] Both books tell the story of three brothers trying to maintain a sense of family and stick together after having lost their parents. Both are told by the youngest of the brothers; in both cases, the oldest of the trio has had to give up personal dreams for education and success because of the immediate pressures of keeping a roof over their heads and food on the table. But Woodson's novel is set in New York City and the gang violence into which Hinton's Ponyboy stumbles and that, eventually, leads to the death of his best friend, is more distant in Woodson's book.

Nevertheless, it is gang violence and the gang way of life that is shaping the present for Woodson's trio of young men. "NewCharlie" is the middle brother. He has recently returned to live with younger brother Lafayette—Laf—and their older brother, Ty'ree, after having spent several years at Rahway Home for Boys because he helped hold up a candy store and was caught with the gun and $250. There, he has grown hardened. Now the kids at his school think he is tough and cool, and he has a meanness that Laf never saw in him before his stay at Rahway—hence the nickname "NewCharlie." Laf is the narrator, and is starting seventh grade as the novel opens. Charlie is three years older but is repeating ninth grade. Ty'ree has graduated from high school and is employed in a publishing house, where he has worked into the position of manager of the mail room. Laf and his brothers are half Puerto Rican, have black; Milagro, which means "miracle" in Spanish, was their mother. She died as a result of her diabetes while NewCharlie was in Rahway and ever since, Charlie has hated Laf. Laf's response—which is true of so many Woodson characters—is to go silent, to try to become invisible, because, as he says, "And if I was invisible, New-Charlie couldn't hate me" (MB, 8).

Laf misses his older brother. He remembers the old Charlie, who would have cared that Laf is now catching up to him in school. He tells us that the old Charlie got teary-eyed over stray animals, and even prayed to St. Francis of Assisi; the old Charlie would tell Laf stories about Ty'ree, their mother and father, about life before he was born. Now, he only talks about gangs, and he makes fun of his younger brother, but, Laf tells us, "when he was asleep, his face spread out—all the frowns and scowls just kind of faded and he looked like Charlie again, ready to care about something, to be happy or to cry about stray animals" (MB, 5). Laf thinks about how, when he went to stay at his great-aunt's house in the summer, she would buy watermelon and scoop out its sweet red meat. Now Laf uses that image from the natural world to try to describe what has happened to Charlie: "Scooped out his heart and sent the empty bitter rind home" (MB, 6). Later Charlie will tell Laf that at Rahway, the procedures are designed to strip away the individual, to make each boy invisible in a way. He conjures up images of a world lined in cement where the young men sentenced to do time there march and march and march in line; if someone steps out of line literally or figuratively, the warden takes away something—soon there is no television, no yard time, no time in the recreation hall, "No you, no more" (MB, 12).

The story is not one of action and drama but of the internal struggle of Laf and Charlie to become visible to each other once again, and of the three boys to process their grief and guilt and arrive at a place from which they can be visible within their world. It turns out that both Charlie and Ty'ree feel a load of guilt related to the death of a parent. Laf was alone at home when his mother went into a diabetic coma. Ty'ree was with his father during a fateful outing when Ty'ree saw a woman jogging with a dog alongside a partially frozen lake; the dog took off across the ice and the woman chased it. Both went into the water and Daddy, in a moment of quiet heroism, pulled them out—but then died of hypothermia. Ty'ree has carried around guilt for years, worrying that he urged his father into an action that eventually killed him because he had always wanted a dog. He finally admits this to Laf, who says he understands exactly how Ty feels. Laf has that same sense of guilt, a sense he should have been able to *do* something for his mother—especially since Charlie makes no secret that he blames Laf for their mother's death. Ty tells Laf that their mother was gone before Laf found her, that there was nothing he could have done for her except to be there; Laf, once he understands Ty's similar pain, tries to comfort his older brother, who has held his guilt inside him for years and years.

Now Charlie thinks of his father as stupid—stupid for saving a white woman and a dog instead of watching out for himself. His time at Rahway has taught him that he *has* to look out for himself, that he cannot trust anyone else. Woodson was taught about how such environments shape those incarcerated within their walls through several visits to a juvenile detention center in Massachusetts, where she talked to the young men assigned there. They confirmed her feelings that any kind of incarceration results in a loss of sense of self. NewCharlie learned about plants at Rahway and now nurtures a spider plant and a fern in the living room window, talking to them and telling them that they have to be tough if they want to make it in the world, and that is his own philosophy, learned at Rahway, at this point. He is wrapped up in talk about gangs both because of the toughness being a gang member projects, and because belonging to a gang gives a sense of identity and purpose, it provides an automatic set of homeboys who surround and protect each other.

It turns out that Charlie's anger and pain are multifaceted. He feels helpless because he is too young to help with the bills after their mother dies. He feels left out because Ty was with their dad at his death and Laf was with his mother, but he was nowhere. He feels invisible in the family because Ty is the oldest, the smart one, the caregiver; Laf is the innocent one, the baby. But Charlie is just "the one who always messes up. . . . I ain't nothing. Nobody" (MB, 103).

Holding On

Things come to a head when Ty gets a call from the police station asking him to come collect Charlie, who has been taken in when the police apprehend a stolen car in which he is riding. When Ty'ree and Laf arrive, they find Charlie sitting on a bench, "curled up into the corner like he wanted to disappear" (MB, 98). His lip is busted open, and one eye is swollen shut; he is trembling, and one hand has swelled to the size of a bear paw. Laf is transported back in time to a moment when Charlie came to his defense. Laf had accidentally stepped on another boy's toe, and he had walloped Laf in response. Charlie kept telling Laf, "When someone hurts you, . . . you just hold on. *Hold on till the pain goes away. . . . The pain always goes away, Laf. You just hold on, you hear me?*" (MB, 99). Now, at the police station, Laf wants to hold onto Charlie. He feels something hard that has been built up in response to NewCharlie's coldness start to melt inside him. It turns out Charlie was just riding in a stolen car; he had not participated in the stealing. That evening, he had gone out with his friend Aaron, who took Charlie with him to a meeting of a gang he had recently joined and then tried to convince Charlie to join as well. But to join, initiates have to fight someone, which Charlie, in a tribute to his upbringing and true character, refuses to do, but the guy who volunteers to take Charlie home in what turns out to be a stolen vehicle decides to toughen Charlie up a bit by punching him. Although Ty'ree's first reaction is to yell at Charlie, he finally manages, as the brothers walk home in the rain, to just let Charlie talk, to tell his story, and he hears Charlie's longing to belong, to be somebody. He puts his arm around his middle brother and says to Charlie and Laf that they need to "get in out of the rain" (MB, 107). Literally, the boys seek shelter; figuratively they come to realize that if they are going to survive, they have to "get out of the rain" of their misunderstandings, of their guilts, of their fears.

But getting out of the rain is hard. In a scene that has a hint of magical realism in it, Laf is in bed, thinking about his mother and a quote from Toni Morrison of which she was fond: "The function of freedom . . . is to free someone else" (MB, 109). He is wondering how he can help Charlie be free, and in that moment, as has happened before, he feels his mother's presence. In this instance, she is sitting at the bottom of Laf's bed, massaging his feet, as she did while alive many times whe Laf was having difficulty sleeping. Similarly, in a later scene, Laf is returning from the park; to get into the house, he would have to step over Charlie, who is sitting in the middle of the front stoop. So Laf decides to just pass by, to keep walking. But he sees Mama sitting on the stoop as well. She is watching, waiting to see if Laf can figure out how to bridge the gap between himself and Charlie. Laf still is not quite sure how to proceed, but he also recalls a long ago time when he had promised his mother not to fight with Charlie, and so he reaches inside himself to make the effort, even in the face of his brother's stubborn silence. He tells Charlie he dreamed about a time when Charlie had tried to save a dog, and he tells Charlie a secret nobody else knows: when the paramedics were using electric paddles on Mama, she had, in fact, awakened briefly, and her lips had moved as though she were trying to tell him something.

Charlie begins to sob; so does Laf. Charlie wants to know why Laf is telling this story now. Laf says because he has been carrying around that secret fact like a "monkey on my back" because Charlie had not been there for him to share it with. Extending the peace offering, he hands Charlie a plastic bag of pictures, a precious few photos of the family that had not been burned up by Charlie in a rage several years earlier. Charlie softens. He confesses several important things to Laf. One is that his anger has been tied up with guilt because the last time his mother had seen him, he was being led out of the house in handcuffs, and he wishes he could have been with her, and that her last image had been of him making her laugh. And he admits the reason why he robbed the candy store, the act that led him to Rahway: he had had a plan; his mother had talked often about her hometown of Bayamon in Puerto Rico, a paradise as she described it, and Charlie wanted the money to take the whole family there, to paradise. The two brothers are still sitting on the stoop talking when Ty'ree appears. He sits down and joins them; Charlie—no longer NewCharlie—puts his arm around Laf as he and Ty start talking about life and art and money, while Laf re-joices, feeling "good and safe and free" (MB, 130).

Bringing It All Together

"Miracle's boys" will be okay. Ty starts telling his younger brothers memory stories, and they sit on the stoop as the sun sets, in a cocoon of family recollections and affection for each other and commitment to keeping their home intact. In this compelling story, Woodson inter-twines themes of importance to her since she first set pen to paper: in-visibility and identity issues, abandonment and death, and related grief, the importance of family ties even beyond death (as Aunt Cecile says, dead does not have to be dead and gone) and the value of home, the need to find alternatives to violence and racism, the value of having dreams and pursuing them, the importance of asking for and accepting help. For months after Mama died, Laf was not able to sleep and he would end up curled into a ball on Ty'ree's floor. Finally, the family ad-mits Laf is wrestling with turmoil too big for him to handle, too much for them to help him handle, and he is connected with a therapist who gives him the time and space and support he needs to start to come to terms with Mama's absence. And, the story is one of poverty—about what it means to live in a marginalized way because there is just not enough money for the basics; Ty'ree makes cornbread stretched with flour and powdered vegetable soup stretched with ketchup; the boys get food stamps, and Ty has a job, "but there was always something one of us needed that seemed to cost just a little bit more than what we had" (MB, 64–65).

In *Miracle's Boys*, too, Woodson's development as an artist is apparent. The story depends on dialogue and Laf's ruminations to advance. The author who, in rereading her early works says of the dialogue that it was just "bad," manages to give each of her characters, even the supporting cast, such as Charlie's friend Aaron and Laf's psychologist, distinctive voices, and she trusts them to talk to each other, to listen to each other. Through their dialogue, Woodson reveals the personalities of her characters and, in the process, handles important topics. For instance, at one point Laf recalls that the old Charlie had been concerned about stereotyping. After seeing a Jackie Chan film, Laf tells his older brother he wishes he were Chinese so he could do karate, to which Charlie replies that of course not all Chinese do karate and that saying so is like saying all blacks are lazy (MB, 9). Therefore, the reader knows that in spite of the protective shell he has built around himself since Rahway, Charlie has a decent center, which is emphasized by his concern for a stray dog—a compassion Woodson admits to sharing. At one point, she had three dogs and two cats in her one-bedroom apartment, and her friends would advise her to stay away from certain blocks in the neighborhood because they are magnets for strays, which Woodson always wants to adopt.

Ed Sullivan, writing a review in *School Library Journal* remarks that "Woodson's characterizations and dialogue are right on. The dynamics among the brothers are beautifully rendered."[17] Hazel Rochman writes that "the fast-paced narrative is physically immediate, and the dialogue is alive with anger and heartbreak."[18] Woodson's use of metaphor—of the weather, of images from nature—to describe her characters and to give them words for describing their emotions is poetic and allows her to say a great deal with the fewest possible words. At one point, Laf describes how he once saw a TV documentary about snakes shedding their skins and he uses this image to tell us, in a short amount of space, how losing his mother has affected him: "That's how I felt—like Mama'd been my skin. But I hadn't grown a new skin underneath, like that snake had" (*MB*, 83), so we know how vulnerable, raw, and bare he feels.

However, although the boys' economic situation is not likely to improve, in spite of everything, as Janice Del Negro writes, Woodson's story is an optimistic one: "Woodson plays it very close—most of the action takes place in the small apartment and out on the front stoop, and there are few developed characters besides the brothers. The tone is intimate, as is the point of view. . . . Hope is a good thing, and Woodson hands it to her readers like a gift at the conclusion of this emotionally cathartic, gracefully constructed family story."[19]

And it is that sense of hope that Woodson conveys in living her own life, making a home, having a child, carrying on with the work of writing in spite of all the obstacles she has had to face and in spite of societal realities that can, at times, seem too harsh to be overcome. That is the miracle of her writing. Hope comes through in her one adult novel, and in her picture books, and is at the core of her work, both the novels and short stories, for young adults. Just as Charlie advised Laf, telling him if he could just hold on, and hold on some more, the pain will go away, Woodson tells her readers to hang in there, to make connections, to find support structures, to have dreams and pursue them, to use the arts for cathartic purposes in the meantime, but to have an eye on the future while appreciating all that the now has to offer.

An Alternative Vision

Woodson's range as a writer for a variety of audiences is impressive. In the first third of her career, she wrote a novel for adults titled *Autobiography of a Family Photo*.[20] Because of the themes and age of the main character, the book works as a novel for young adults. It is only one 113 pages long; however, in those pages, Woodson crams an enormous amount of "complicated emotion and nuanced social commentary."[21] Set against the backdrop of the Vietnam era, Woodson contrasts the picture-perfect Brady Bunch family of television fame with that of her heroine/narrator; her oldest brother is a drag queen, and her little brother is half white, a constant reminder to their father of the mother's infidelity. There is another older brother, and an older sister. The unnamed narrator gives us a series of vignettes that capture her search, throughout her childhood and adolescence, for identity and for some sense of community in the midst of a neighborhood and family that are both dysfunctional. Parts of the novel first appeared as short stories in the fall, 1992 *Kenyon Review*; there, the four vignettes are identified as coming from a novel in progress to be called *Stab Wounds*.

The language is powerfully raw as well as lyrical. On the opening page, the narrator announces, drawing us immediately into her world, into a desire to know what she means, "I died once. And then I died again. And then death had no hold on me. . . . The girl sitting here with her arms wrapped around her legs is not a girl but a woman. And in that woman there are a million girls bottled, muted. A million half-lives, some skirted but bare-chested, others naked. Some with dark arms reaching upward, others stooped into bending, still as glass. A million girls. Dark. Bellowing. Multiplying. Chaos. Hari-kari. War" (*Auto*, 1). We learn that the narrator's first death happened in fifth grade. The children in the narrator's class are fascinated when a white teacher, the father of classmate Franklin Thomas, marries the black mother of another classmate, Sandra. The narrator had never imagined "it could be like this . . . a white man smiling into the eyes of his beautiful black wife" (*Auto*, 2). But the husband later shoots the wife in a fit of jealous rage, and that causes the narrator's first death, a death of dreams, for she has been in love with Franklin.

The narrator's father drives a cab. She longs to go to work with him, but he only takes her older brother Carlos, since the oldest, Troy, "is gonna be that way" (*Auto*, 13), and the baby is half white. While the narrator loves the baby, thinking his partial whiteness gives her family a tie to the white world, the father hates it. Cory, the baby, who grows up into a pale amber shade, is the "proof a black man can't leave his woman for one minute without her making a fool out of him" (*Auto*, 17). The narrator lives in fear that, eventually, their father will abandon them, unable to feel himself a man with one son who is gay and another who is half white. Whenever she looks into her father's eyes, she sees fear and wonders if he is afraid she and her sister will somehow hurt him. And this is a definite possibility. By age eight, the narrator is filled with desire—for a white boy with blond dreadlocks who makes her stomach tighten and churn, who makes her feel a heat like that of a "trash can fire, blowing a hot breeze." When she is fifteen she allows him to take her, in her mother's bed, and the description of the scene in which she learns about sex, moving from trepidation to pain to full-blown desire and response, is detailed and real, filled with the smells, the background sounds, the physical tensions as the two find a rhythm together (*Auto*, 27).

Throughout the novel the narrator aches for physical intimacy, and her longing is contrasted with other realities. Her father indeed abandons the family after Troy, the gay son, is drafted and then killed in Vietnam. Her mother goes through a succession of boyfriends, one of whom sexually abuses Angel, the narrator's older sister. Carlos, the narrator's other older brother, has a mean streak and sexual desires he has difficulty controlling. So, when the narrator is eight, he uses his knife to let himself into the bathroom while she is taking a bath, his male member hanging down, forcing her—naked, vulnerable, eight—to let him rub himself between her legs. She engages in "tripping," sending her mind a million miles away. When she tries to tell her friends, they act as though such behavior is commonplace. Every girl has a helpful hint on how to endure it; one advises her not to breathe because if she does not breathe, she will not smell and that makes it easier to imagine being in another place. Several girls talk about the rewards they get when they comply with their father/uncle/brother. At eight and nine and ten, they are no longer little girls: "It ends this way. Without words or phrases or power. Without rage. It ends sorrowfully, full of hollow spaces, guilt, doubt. It ends swallowed, forgotten until someone wakes up one morning, half-whole, their arms wrapped around their knees, bound up in the weight of moving on, to the next place" (*Auto*, 38).

The narrator also experiences desire for another girl, which makes her scared—scared that the other girl will not let her kiss her, and scared that "I will always want this, no matter who's watching" (*Auto*, 46). She is confused by the range of feelings she experiences. Her friend, Marianne, who is Puerto Rican, has a baby at fifteen. Sometimes the narrator, too, wants a baby, "something to love," but knows this is not a good idea. She does have a serious boyfriend, but will not let anything happen—and she continues to feel attractions for women. She is confused by Vietnam. She has lost her brother, and the other boys "begin to come home crazy. Tall black boys with broken blood-shot eyes, yellow-skinned, nappy-headed, hurting boys, their Afros cut down to impotent nubs, hands reaching out at the darkness, moving on their own, following the path of flailing arms, heavenward. Disconnected . . . running in circles around us, bewildered, begging, nodding off" (*Auto*, 55). She is confused by her mama, who stops speaking, withdrawing into silence after she walks in on her boyfriend with her daughter Angel in bed; Mama attacks the man with a knife until the police come and rescue him and lead him off, and Mama feels powerless and guilty for not having protected her daughter.

Angel grows up and marries a Jehovah's Witness. The baby, Cory, who has a history of eating paint off the walls, which turns out to be filled with lead, fades into nothingness as a heroine addict. Carlos, from whom the narrator protects herself by keeping a knife with her in the bedroom and bathroom, grows up to have daughters who fear him. And the narrator? "I grow up hollow, misdirected, fractured, move from place to place, job to job" (*Auto*, 100). In the end, "there is an aloneness taking hold now, slowly, like something thick and hot filling me up, piecing me together. I am told I am too skinny, too dark, too angry" and she starts walking out of the neighborhood, "walking to save my life, as if I'm walking to get out of some bad story where I'm the pitiful one. As if I'm walking right off of somebody's dumb, otherwise blank, page" (*Auto*, 13).

Autobiography of a Family Photo is not a book teachers would be able to use in a classroom; the sexual explicitness, the honesty of the portrayal of sexual and other emotional violence, the realism with which issues of race and politics are addressed ensured that the novel was published and marketed as an adult book. However, Woodson describes the novel as being emotionally true for young adults: "I would say that emotionally, it was *completely* autobiographical, . . . like that's who I was at that age, the sense of being on the outside, the sense of watching the world, of bearing witness from a powerless position." Because the narrator is a young adult, and because her observations and reflections capture so well the emotional intensity of coming of age, made more traumatic by the circumstances in which she was living, the book is an important one for high school students to read.

Also because the narrator is a nameless young girl, who feels herself to be too skinny, too black, too different—because she has boyfriends but thinks about other girls, it is easy to think that the book is, truly, autobiographical. But Woodson cautions us: "From an event standpoint, a lot of it I made up. Some of them were moments I could remember that I built fiction around, but emotionally I could point to any given moment in that book and say, 'Yes, that was me.'" For example, there is a very graphic scene in which four black girls, including the narrator, gang up on a white young man who is carrying a McDonald's bag. Asked if she witnessed such a scene, Woodson recalls, "I remember being ten or so and I was with my three girlfriends and we were walking behind this little kid and talking about that [ganging up on him], and it was one of those right/wrong times, and I remember saying, 'Jehovah's Witnesses don't do that' and stopped the moment. But in the book it became the moment; in real life it never actually happened." In general, Woodson did not fight because of her religious upbringing; her older brother was not drafted to Vietnam because Jehovah's Witnesses "don't do war," although similarly to Angel in the novel, Woodson's older sister did stay in the Witnesses long after Woodson herself dropped out, in part because she liked a boy in a different congregation.

The descriptions of the friendship between the narrator and Marianne echo that between Maizon and Margaret; the narrator and Marianne imagine growing old together, sitting in rocking chairs side by side and rocking away the days, determined to be "two old ladies together" (*Auto*, 62). The sense of affection the narrator has for her oldest brother is reminiscent of that which Staggerlee has for Charlie, or of that Lonny feels for his younger sister. The feelings of abandonment the narrator feels when her father deserts the family and then her mother goes silent are akin to what Marie and Ellie feel. And, although the ending is not as tidily hopeful as one of her books for younger audiences, there are similarities between the narrator, walking out of the neighborhood, walking for her life, and Lena, who leads her younger sister away from their abusive father, and then back to Marie's home and security. The narrator has survived a great deal and there is hope that she will find her way out of misdirection and into connection, into a story of her own making rather than staying on somebody else's blank page.

Writing on a Smaller Scale

In her short stories, Woodson also focuses on characters who are survivors. Often loners, often outsiders, they wrestle with issues explored more deeply in the novels. The stories are powerful because of their focus, because of the way Woodson shines a light on one defining segment of time in each character's life. As of this writing, there are ten short stories, including eight written specifically for young adults, as well as the four from the *Kenyon Review*, which became *Autobiography of a Family Photo*. All of the stories were published in response to invitations by editors doing a collection of pieces around a given theme. Woodson says of her writing process that she never sits down on her own, during her normal working hours, thinking she will produce a short story. In general, she says, "When I'm sitting down and this stuff is coming from an organic place and the characters start talking to me. . . . I don't think of short stories." Stories come to her a different way. She mulls over the theme for awhile, and then, "The characters come to me differently. I mean I feel like it's almost a flash flood. Like I just get this image and it's gone and the characters are there and they get resolved in the end." In a way, writing short stories for themed anthologies is similar to writing papers in response to an English professor's assignments. Still, the products of this somewhat different process resonate after the book is closed.

Woodson's earliest short story for young adults, "Slipping Away," appeared in Marion Dane Bauer's *Am I Blue? Coming out of the Silence*, in 1994. In some ways, the story of Jocina who is waiting for her friend Marie to arrive at their summer beach community resembles that of Margaret and Maizon, their immediate predecessors. It involves the moment in time when, walking along the beach, the girls start to realize that though they are longtime, forever summer friends, the future may lead them down different paths. Jocina has sexual feelings toward Marie that are not returned; Marie also expresses antigay sentiments that create a distance and "a silence between us that is cold and wet as fog."[22] In this way, the girls foreshadow something of Staggerlee and Trout.

In 1995, "Tuesday, August Third" appeared in *Afrekete: An Anthology of Black Lesbian Writing*. Like *Autobiography of a Family Photo*, "Tuesday August Third" was not aimed specifically at a young adult audience. However, the main character is Wilma, a ten-year-old girl who is waiting for her brother to return from Vietnam. Using a third-person narrator, but focusing on Wilma, Woodson evokes a neighborhood similar to that in *Autobiography of a Family Photo*, a community shaken by the return of young men from Vietnam who are now "crazy and half-dead."[23] The summer, waiting for Ray, has felt heavy and "thick like a thunder shower coming,"[24] portending the tragedy that Wilma will experience. Later, she hears a song, in Spanish—the neighborhood is racially mixed—and it makes her sad, "like the world was moving away from her, out of reach, and she was stuck here, inside, sitting cross-legged on the carpeted floor. Waiting."[25] The neighborhood includes a Cory (the same name as the half white youngest brother in *Autobiography*), but he, like Troy, the oldest brother in *Autobiography*, is "on his way to becoming the block sissy."[26] The adults, as do adults in other Woodson books, sometimes caution the young people against spending too much time in the sun for fear of how black they'll turn. And food is an important part of community ritual—the characters eat an ethnically balanced blend of dishes from fried chicken to arroz con gandules. Finally Roy arrives, seemingly himself, but Wilma makes a ten-year-old's mistake, asking honestly about what it was like in Vietnam, and whether he killed anyone, whether he has any "gook ears" in his bag.[27] With that Roy goes up to his room and hangs himself, leaving Wilma to make her way alone through the grief that chokes the house from that point on.

"What Has Been Done to Me" was published in the 1996 *Go the Way Your Blood Beats: An Anthology of Lesbian and Gay Fiction by African Americans*. The narrator is describing a very painful vacation she is taking with her mother, her mother's birthday present to celebrate the fact that, on the same day, the mother is turning fifty and the daughter, twenty-five. They sit sipping drinks, her mother nervously tasting her vodka tonic, telling her daughter that she, too, will blow up like a balloon, that pockets of fat will collect at the nape of her neck. "In the quiet restaurant, our conversation is filled with too much silence. We were, and always have been, strangers," thinks the narrator.[28] The narrator has worked hard to create a world in which she feels comfortable, and she has not wanted to come to New Orleans; she misses the close group of friends who know she is gay, misses her apartment mate, and couples evenings. She has refused to brush her teeth "for fear that the taste of her [new lover] might leave my mouth, the tips of my fingers."[29] As the narrator recalls her childhood, her family sounds very similar to that of the narrator in *Autobiography*. There is a mean-spirited brother who has spent time in the state penitentiary and who, like Cory, eats plaster with lead paint; there is a sister who moves to Hawaii to grow her own pot, and there is another brother, much older, who marries a woman with five daughters. But the situation with the mother is the most similar. Mama had been going out with Joe, who wanted to marry her and move to Long Island, where the children could have a swimming pool. The narrator, like the girl in *Autobiography*, had been excited about the possibility of having a father and of being "like the Brady Bunch, but smaller."[30] But Mama dumps Joe, and soon William is spending time in their house. And shortly thereafter, one night as the narrator leaves the bathroom after taking her bath, she finds William sitting on her bed, "stroking his crotch and smiling."[31]

The narrator in the story points out that Mama maintains that she actually asked William to leave, in response to her neighbors who were telling her she should not have two teenage daughters in the house with a man who was not her husband. But the narrator challenges her mother, saying all the children remember a huge fight, in which William was hurting her, yelling at her, calling her names—and yet she begged him not to go. Seeing the mother afterwards, the narrator resolves never to beg for anything, never to let herself be broken. Thinking about her life in the context of Mardi Gras taking place outside their hotel, which, says the narrator, is a time during which people let themselves do everything they have always wanted to do but did not because of societal constraints, the narrator wonders what she would do if she could. Her answer is, ultimately, nothing different: "You spend your life waiting for the moment when you are free of the history your life makes for you—the moment you can step outside of who you once were and into the body of the person you have always been becoming. Then, from that point on, the things that have been done to you no longer matter. They become a part of a past . . . a past that you are no longer part of . . . a past that never existed."[32] Lena, Staggerlee, Marie, Ellie, Charlie and Laf and Ty'ree, Lonny—a host of Woodson characters find a similar point of freedom from the past as they become themselves, survivors of the present and the future.

Themes familiar to Woodson readers from her novels permeate the other stories and children's books as well. In the short story genre, however, the writer explores just one aspect of a theme; taken together the stories provide a multifaceted, in-depth presentation of her theme, each facet sharpened and polished into brilliance. When combined together, they make a whole that is larger than the individual parts. In the 1998 "Thirteen," Woodson continues to explore the theme of sexual awakening. The narrator in adolescence sounds once again like Woodson herself, "tall and thin that summer with knobby knees and only the barest beginnings of breasts."[33] The narrator contrasts herself as she moves into adolescence with her younger self. As children, she and her girlfriends would count each other's newly grown pubic hairs, but now, after they have begun to develop, they have grown "silent and secretive,"[34] which frustrates the narrator, who is aware that she has a developing appreciation for the female body not shared by her friends. The narrator's mother somehow senses her desires and does not give her permission to do things such as attend a play with a female friend.

The importance of role models is evident in this story. Seventeen-year-old Alma, who is gay, promises the younger girls that when they are older, they will be allowed to make their own decisions. Meanwhile, the mother has a whole list of clothes and behaviors that she considers "mannish," such as pumas, Kangol hats, tailor-made no-side-seam carpenter pants, hands in the pockets, and playing sports. The girls manage to trade and borrow to outfit themselves as they wish to look, and they hide in the closet to watch Alma and her girlfriend kiss. Woodson, as she does with Marie and Lena or Maizon and Margaret, attends to the intimate details of girls' friendship, such as the way they "split our fingers and mixed our blood, we took the tunes of popular songs and changed them to words about our friendship. We bought pizza and split the pieces down the middle so we could share them and have room left over for Italian ice. And every Saturday we shopped for matching outfits until our wardrobes were so alike we no longer needed to borrow one another's clothes."[35] She contrasts the concreteness of these actions with the nebulousness of their feelings of being "in-between," having the narrator reflect, recalling Staggerlee, "We knew something was going to get easier, but we didn't know what. We knew 'someday' was coming, but we didn't know when."[36] At thirteen, the narrator flip-flops between practicing kissing and building forts in the backyard with her little brother, feeling both a fear of growing up, and "just the tiniest bit, free."[37] In some ways the ending is reminiscent of the final paragraph in

Autobiography of a Family Photo, in that the narrator is last pictured walking away, leaving the neighborhood behind. Woodson comments that in her own life, it was often her older sister who had to walk away in order to find herself.

A devastating fire is a crucial aspect of the 1999 "July Saturday," in which, once again, themes of sexual awakening, of friendship, and trying to make sense of the grown-up world are central. The adults, recalling the almost fatalistic middle-aged women of the trilogy, respond to the fire with comments such as "He's [the Lord's] got plans for all of us . . . from the cradle to the grave."[38] Woodson's attention to capturing a sense of place, so much a part of her novels, works in her short stories to make them read almost like photographs of a particular time and place. Here, the neighborhood has gathered for a barbeque. The neighborhood has "pretty much settled into itself"; it's not changing, is not upwardly mobile or on a downward track, but the narrator has the itch to be gone. She is aware, like so many of Woodson's other characters, that things change and she has an "itch this summer, something deep inside me burning. Some nights I wake up all sweaty and just sit there waiting for whatever is coming on to just get to starting."[39] Woodson acknowledges that she is, herself, very attentive to her environment and is affected by it. She has a house in the Catskill Mountains as well as her home in the city, and she watches the light and the weather and watches how other people respond to the details of their environments.

Strong Girls

The identity theme is explored with heartbreaking poignancy in "The Other Half of Me" published in *Tomorrowland: Stories About the Future* in 1999; editor Michael Cart invited authors to "create their own very individual visions of times to come."[40] For Woodson, responding to the invitation, "it is not the past but the present, with its vexing problems—problems like alienation, dehumanizing change, environmental ruin, and the meaning of family—that will define a future no further away than tomorrow."[41] Like Melanin's mother, this narrator's mother has chosen a different view of family, one that involves just the mother and daughter, whose name is Reverie. The entire story is a reverie, the story of their quest for "home," and like Lena and Dion, they are sure that someday they will find "someplace that feels as though it's wrapping us in its arms."[42] Reverie continues, sounding like Maizon's father or Marie's mother, "We were not running away, we were walking home. It was a long walk, one that would take years. But we'd get there. We knew we would."[43] Like Maizon's father, and unlike Marie's mother, the two women do, finally, find a place. But for Reverie the place is not enough. She was born without a father; her mother, getting old and wanting a child, used a sperm bank and chose a doner who opted to give no personal information about himself, except to offer one message to his unknown child—a message Woodson sends out clearly to her readers through all her books: "Let the world know where you stand. Don't ever be a coward."[44] And she longs to know her father, saying, "I know I've always been turning corners and looking over my shoulder, and staring men down. Looking for my father. Looking for the other half of me."[45]

At some point, as Marie finally learns, Reverie will have to let go of that quest and grow into herself. Woodson, writing in the author's notes at the end of the story, says, "Growing up in a single-mom household, I was intrigued as a child by the idea of 'father.' I didn't actually meet my biological dad until I was fifteen, at which point he and my mom decided they wanted to be a couple again."[46] Until then, like Reverie, she too had looked everywhere for her father. But, as an adult, she recognized that her mom had been "both mother and father to me, and that I had gotten all the tools I needed to be whole in the world from her."[47] Woodson wrote this story for two reasons. She had read that in 2000, those children who were products of the first known doners would turn eighteen and at that point could, if the doner allowed it, seek out their fathers. And she and her own partner were trying to determine how they should establish their own family. Using the story as a way to work out some of the issues they were facing, Woodson writes, "I have learned in my time on earth that there are so many ways to be a family. As I write, until I write the last line, I don't know where my characters will end up or who they'll be when they get there. But some part of me knows that, in the end, Reverie will be all right."[48]

Creating characters who are searching, questioning, exploring, but who have the kind of grit and determination to persevere and who are able to find a community to support them, is one way Woodson gives courage to her readers. In the short story "Beanie" published in 2001, the narrator is looking back at herself at age thirteen from the lofty vantage point of seventeen. She is remembering her prowess as a pitcher in stickball; in her neighborhood, she pitched "the first over-hand no-hitter, tall as a broomstick with a chest just starting to grow out of nowhere."[49] She is dubbed "Jelly Bean" by the boys because of the tiny size of her breasts, which shortened to Bean, and that "settled in on me in a way I kind of liked, especially when people said look out for strike outs from Bean."[50] Names and nicknames are frequently given by either the neighborhood or adopted by an individual, such as Stag-gerlee and Trout, as a way of asserting identity. As in several other sto-ries and in *Autobiography of a Family Photo*, Woodson alludes to the ways in which war haunts a neighborhood; in Bean's case, there was Carmichael, who joined the Marines at eighteen and was killed a year later, and now nobody talks about him or the war.

As is true in several of the novels, Woodson gives Bean physical, athletic skill as a way of being in the world, similar to the ways in which running track gave her, as a young adult, a sense of confidence and con-trol. With a poetic attention to detail, Bean makes the reader, too, feel what it is like to be out on the mound: "I loved being out on that sunny patch of park with about a dozen or so people gathered to watch us. And I loved the way the ball gave a little good-bye whistle when it left my hand. But more than anything, I loved the sound of the broomstick whipping through the air and hissing a strike while people looked on, surprised as all daylight, or cursed under their breath."[51]

Bean is the only girl on a team otherwise populated by boys four and five years her senior. She is just starting to become aware of the multi-ple kinds of sexual identities possible. Alma—perhaps a repeated char-acter from "Thirteen"—shows Bean and her friend Dee the "Butch-pride" fist, which is the same as the "Black Power" one, but it is for *patas*, "as we called her and the girls she loved."[52] And then there is the "block sissy" who dies from "a disease we didn't know or understand" and then more people start dying.[53] Bean and Dee have kissed more than once but they do not think of themselves as "true-blue patas" be-cause they have plans to marry and then, once their husbands die, to grow old together, rocking away the days in their rocking chairs, again like the characters in "Thirteen," or like the very early Maizon and Margaret. Reality strikes when Brooklyn decides to have a baseball league, with coaches and jerseys—but it is only for guys. And then Dee moves away, back to Puerto Rico. At first they write, passionate letters full of "I love yous," but that dwindles away. Alma, Dee's aunt, reports one summer that Dee has a boyfriend.

On the other hand, Bean is still waiting, waiting to become herself, living in the meantime, with her memories, which are like mercury, sometimes "solid and vivid as the color red, other times muted as a rainy day."[54] Sometimes she takes a ball to the handball courts, and she throws and throws "until my arm throbs with the power of throwing. Aches with the power and promise of some other bigger thing to come. More powerful than those moments on the pitcher's mound when the ball soared from my hand and cried, '*Freedom!*' through the air. . . . The handball court's a cement wall. Some evenings I believe I can send that ball screaming right on through its stone. And me not far behind."[55]

The reader does not know what Bean will become, or where she will land, but as she does at the end of *Miracle's Boys*, Woodson is able to convey a sense of hope, a sense of forward motion for her characters from which her readers can take heart. Woodson herself still plays pick-up basketball, watches pro games—rooting for the New York Knicks, the Miami Heat, and the New York Liberty in the WNBA, and she says this story was inspired by having grown up herself in the days before Title IX, "when young girls didn't really have much choice about where we could go with our athletic talents."[56]

One of Woodson's favorite short stories is another she wrote in response to a request for stories, this one on the theme of religion. "On Earth," published in 2000, is narrated by Carlene, who, with her three brothers and sisters, is shipped off to Anderson, South Carolina, to spend the summer with their grandmother. In Carolina, Carlene feels the city part of her slipping away, "the cracks in the sidewalk in front of our building are fading. The double Dutch games and running to the corner store for potato chips and cream soda are almost gone."[57] Grandmother is a fervent Jehovah's Witness. Carlene herself believes in Jehovah, saying, "I look up at the sky. It is blue and nearly cloudless. Jehovah is up in that blue. Sitting on a throne looking down at us. Looking straight through to our marrow."[58] She believes in Armageddon, in "fire falling from the sky, floods, famine and plague. If you try to hide in the water, poisonous snakes will be there to bite you. If you hide beneath your bed, God's hand will pull you from your hiding place and strike you dead. There is no place on Earth you can go and be saved. No place but into the heart of God. I stand up straight inside His heart, say my prayers, don't curse or disrespect anyone."[59]

But, like her author, Carlene grows away from her early faith. Her mother is ex-communicated for dating a man "not in the Truth." When Carlene and her siblings return home after their summer with their grandmother, technically they are not supposed to talk to their mama. But Carlene begins to wonder. How is it she is not supposed to talk to her mother, but the Ten Commandments tell her to honor her mother? Her mother is rather calm about this situation, telling Carlene her own belief, which is that Jehovah has a place in his heart for everyone. Her older sister wants to go to college; the Jehovah's Witnesses do not allow college; it is expected that young adults move into the ministry after they graduate from high school. Carlene does not understand all the rules, from no college, to no hand gestures for her schoolyard games like "Miss Mary Mack." She continues to observe and grow more puzzled. Her grandfather, now dead, smoked a pipe, but none of the church elders ever knew, which means her grandmother can continue to be proud of her holiness. Carlene comes to observe, "There is no room on the narrow road for smoking or worldly men. There is so much room at its edges for hypocrisy."[60] Moving back and forth in time as Woodson does in *If You Come Softly* and even *Hush*, Carlene, like her author, finally arrives at her own faith, knowing, "And somewhere inside of me, Jehovah will settle, become a part of my blood and bones. But my fear of Armageddon and my belief in life everlasting will grow as faint as my mother's voice, as far away as the promise of her. Familiar and foreign as a stranger's face."[61]

Images of fire and its destruction appear again in "Lorena," Woodson's most recent short story, about a young girl and her first foray into lesbian physical intimacy, and again in *Locomotion*. Asked about the repeated use of fire in her more recent work, Woodson says it comes from both those childhood experiences of listening to stories of Armageddon and from the reality of the Bushwick, the neighborhood of her youth, which was called "The Matchbox" because there were so many fires. She notes that now, as an adult, she is both "fascinated but repelled by it."

Growing as a Writer by Writing for Children

Woodson's childhood memories and her adult beliefs permeate her children's picture books as well as her novels and short stories. In both *We Had Picnic This Sunday Past* and *Sweet, Sweet Memory*, the comfort and security that comes from sharing food and story in community are celebrated. While Woodson was not totally happy with the illustrations for *We Had a Picnic*, they are bright and bold and full of action, pulling the reader into the joy of the Sunday picnic, a scene like so many others in Woodson's world that comes alive because of the specificity of the details. We see Little Astrid, two front teeth missing, carrying a pail of fresh peaches. We see Aunt Martha carrying a big pink box of store-bought cake—to everyone's delight as her homemade pies leave something to be desired. We see Teeka looking beautiful in the new dress her Grandma sewed for her, one of several Woodson characters who share her love of piecing things together, making clothes with care for others as a sign of their love. We see the plastic flies one child puts on the corn on the cob, making Aunt Sadie scream, and by the time the book ends with "We had a picnic this Sunday past. You should have been there,"[62] we wish we had been a part of the festivities and fun.

In *Sweet, Sweet Memory*, Woodson elaborates on the sentiment expressed by Laf's great-aunt Cecile in *Miracle's Boys*: "Just because you're dead doesn't mean you're dead and gone" (MB, 19). This picture book reads rather like a prelude to Laf's story. In it, a little girl sits on the porch, combing her own hair, watching her grandmother cook up a storm in preparation for her grandpa's funeral. Corn, lettuce, collards, tomatoes, cabbage, and squash are coming to fruition in the fields around her, and the girl hears Grandpa's voice: "'The earth changes,' Grandpa said, as he planted this garden. 'Like us it lives, it grows. . . . Like us . . . a part of it never dies. Everything and everyone goes on and on.'"[63] After the funeral, everyone eats and shares their stories of Grandpa. But Sarah cannot speak without all the tears flowing out of her. Uncle Mitchell "hunkering down beside" her, tells her it will pass, "A little bit at a time. Everything and everyone goes on and on" (SSM, n.p.), and Sarah whispers,

"That's my story" (SSM, n.p.). All the relatives chime in; Grandpa has told everyone the same thing, while planting his garden, year after year. And surrounded by the rest of her family, sharing the same words, the same memories, Sarah starts to smile. Later, when the vegetables are ready to be harvested, the family gathers again to share Grandpa's "sweet, sweet memory" and Sarah tells her grandma that she is also listening to the world, listening to the way "life goes on and on," as she hears the crickets and katydids, the owl hoo-hooing, the field mice shuffling about. And the family shares a "supper on the porch with the sun going down. Sweet, sweet memory, and everything, and everyone, going on and on" (SSM, n.p.).

In *Our Gracie Aunt* and *Visting Day*, Woodson gives us children who have had experiences that could easily sour them to love and joy. Like Lena and the unnamed narrator of *Autobiography of a Family Photo*, who have been abused, like Charlie whose experiences at Rahway have hardened him, like Marie and Ellie and Evie who have parents who have abandoned them in some way, in *Our Gracie Aunt*, Johnson and his sister Beebee feel themselves to be all alone in the world. While their mother has often left them to fend for themselves, as the story opens she has gone away again, and Johnson feels that this time she may never come back. A social worker appears on the scene and takes them to stay with their Aunt Gracie. Johnson has never even heard of her, and both children are wary of giving her their trust. Gradually, carefully, never trying to step on the children's memories of their mother, Aunt Gracie, like Lonny's foster mother, finds a way into their heart, tucking them under the covers, singing them lullabies, teaching them to throw spaghetti onto the wall to test for doneness, and just letting them sit on her lap, hugging them. They come to know, as do Marie and Ellie, that their mother does in fact love them, but they realize, too, that, as their Mama says, "Even when a mama loves you, she can't always take care of you. Sometimes she has to go away."[64] Nevertheless, with their Gracie Aunt, the children feel secure, and have the support they will need to come to terms with their mother's illness.

Just as there is no finger-pointing, no sense of blame attached to Mama's actions in *Our Gracie Aunt*, in *Visiting Day*, "Woodson eschews strident messages about breaking the law and judgments or discussion of why Dad is behind bars. In fact, the word *prison* never appears in the

text, letting kids focus on the father and child's simple joy at being together. Ransome's muscular, unfussy paintings mostly radiate that joy,
but there's also a subtle undercurrent of wistfulness in the child's ex-
pressions (she knows her dad will stay behind), and the views of families chatting and laughing stand in sharp contrast to the plain, perhaps
more honest, views of the prison—barbed wire atop the outside walls
and a uniformed guard in the visiting room."[65]

According to Dianne Hess, Woodson's editor at Scholastic, this picture book came to the publisher essentially in the form it now appears.
Hess says, "The original manuscript was not changed very much. I essentially split it into pages and broke the lines so that it read more like
poetry. Also the father began as an uncle, but was changed, as it made
the story stronger and more immediate."[66] Woodson and illustrator
James Ransome have both experienced visiting a loved one in jail, and
so they focus here on a love that bonds family members together regardless of circumstances. According to Hess, "The story was, in fact,
based on Jackie's experiences with visiting an uncle in prison as a child.
She loved her uncle, and as reflected in the story, made no judgments
about the situation. It merely was. There is, in all of Jackie's books, a
strong sense of family and community."[67] Smelling fried chicken at 6
a.m., getting her hair carefully braided by Grandma, the narrator, a
young African-American girl, knows it is a visiting day. Daddy is getting
ready too; we see him putting on his white shirt, brushing his teeth.
Grandma casually tells the reader that "Daddy is doing a little time,"[68]
but Woodson never uses the words "prison" or "jail"; thus the story is really about how a child feels when separated from a loved one, and how
other caring adults and their strength can help the child remain centered and secure, how "family" is an expansive and varied concept.

Editor Hess notes that as she worked on the book and talked to
various librarians and others in the publishing community, she came
to realize just how many people from all walks of life have had family
members spend time in prison. She says, "I felt it was very important
to publish a book that reflected the lives of so many people—even if
it was a subject that seems to get pushed under the rug."[69] Already
Visting Day has received outstanding reviews, and Hess is pleased to
be receiving "grateful messages" from people who are using the book
with children, adding, "And while once again, Jackie has written a

book about something people avoid talking about, she has also given the world a positive example of a strong family who understands the meaning of unconditional love."[70]

Woodson's belief in the importance of sharing history, of learning from the past, which is perhaps most clearly evident in the *Ghostwriter* novel, centered on Frederick Douglass's *Autobiography*, is at the heart of her first children's book, *Martin Luther King, Jr., and His Birthday*. Published in 1990, it describes the life of Martin Luther King, starting with the description of an incident in Martin's early life when the mother of two of his white friends tells him "I don't want my sons playing with colored children anymore."[71] That is his introduction to racism and segregation and is when he becomes aware of the unfairness of things, and he resolves to become a preacher like his father so he can voice his opposition. Woodson carefully selects key events in King's life that show his development as a civil rights activist, focusing next on King's sermon that called on his people to boycott the public transportation system after Rosa Parks was arrested, and then showing him organizing the march on Washington. She combines imagined conversation between the great man and children in his audiences with his own stirring words to give her young readers a real sense of what Martin Luther King was trying to accomplish.

Building on Martin's dream of a better world, *The Other Side*, published in 2001, is a lovely example of how Woodson deals with complex situations in a subtle, understated way, letting her character—in this case, a young black girl named Clover—tell her story in a way that invites the reader to think about its implications and ramifications. Clover's mama has told her not to climb over the fence that separates their little yellow house and its property from that of the white family who live next door. Every day Clover stares at the little girl in the pink sweater who comes out of that other house and sits on the fence. Clover asks her mama why "everyone and everything on the other side of the fence seemed far away,"[72] Mama just says, in the frustrating way of grown-ups, that it has always been like this. But Clover wants to know the girl in the pink sweater. She thinks about how the girl sits on the fence all alone; she thinks about how she looks sad when they see her in town, walking with her mama. Then it starts to rain, and when the rain stops, and Clover goes outside again, she feels free, and brave. She walks close to the fence; the little girl asks Clover her name and says her own: Annie Paul. The girls exchange smiles. Clover touches the fence; Annie says, "A fence like this was made for sitting on" (OS, n.p.). Clover says she is not allowed to go over the fence; Annie says her mama told her, too, not to climb over, "But she never said nothing about sitting on it" (OS, n.p.). And Clover realizes that "over" is not "on," and up she goes.

Clover and Annie sit on their fence, watching the world—waiting for their mamas to tell them to get down. Interestingly, neither mama interferes. Clover's mama even remarks, eventually, on how she seems to have found a new friend, and Clover's mama smiles. Eventually, Clover's friends come round with their jump rope, and Annie joins in, and then, "When we were too tired to jump anymore, we sat up on the fence, all of us in a long line" (OS, n.p.). Annie says, "Someday somebody's going to come along and knock this old fence down," and Clover echoes, "Yeah . . . someday" (OS, n.p.).

The Importance of Dialogue

In her review of *The Other Side*, Janice Del Negro observes that "This is an emotionally intricate tale presented simply and intimately, and the open-ended conclusion unself-consciously encourages discussion, examination and inquiry. . . . Woodson does not overexplain or stack the emotional deck."[73] In general, this ability to tell a story that helps readers of all ages see the world from a different point of view, and, in the process, to make connections with people on the other sides of all kinds of fences is Woodson's strength, one that comes from her belief that, in the end, the only way to get beyond "the hatred that is keeping us whole" (*Sun*, 97), is through dialogue. She says "I think people are afraid to say certain things. I think the whole PC movement was dangerous because people, their development gets arrested because they won't say certain things because they're afraid of how they'll be seen or how it will offend, and so dialogues don't happen the way they used to because people are afraid to speak. So I think for me, my journey is not being afraid to show that there's stuff I don't know, and there are things I don't understand, and that there are questions I have, and exposing that part of me, and knowing I'll survive, knowing doing so won't be the end of me."

Her willingness to engage in such dialogues and to be as open and honest as possible in her own life runs parallel to Woodson's risk-taking in her writing. She says she really does not understand her own writing process. She was afraid, for instance, of poetry and did not see herself, as an adult, as able to write in that genre. But after reading a lot of poetry for months on end and recognizing that her work was becoming more spare and minimalistic, she decided to see what happened if she let Lonnie experiment with poetry in *Locomotion*. She likens her writing process to that of sewing, saying when she is getting started, she just has to be open to what is coming, and therefore, she often writes in sketchbooks because, "I can't write on paper that has lines; it's too confining and I'm all over the place and then it's coming and I have to move to a faster form, like write in shorthand or type it or something and then go back." She continues to struggle to "give herself permission to tell the truth and not let this fear of self-expression stunt her growth as a woman or as a writer."[74]

Woodson practices telling the truth and engaging in dialogue with herself by writing constantly in her journals, which are, typically, 11-by-14-inch leather-bound artist sketchbooks. In general, she sees ways in which these journals, her private writing, connect to her fiction, her public writing. For one, the kind of fast-paced, get-it-all-out writing she does on her sketchbook pages "frees her emotionally"[75] so that she can connect with her characters, and this kind of writing "brings her to her human foundations,"[76] which is especially important when she is dealing with characters who are less than likeable. Journal writing helps her see characters such as Lena's father, the mother in *Our Gracie Aunt*, Ellie's older sister in *If You Come Softly*, or the father in *Visiting Day* as "fully human. . . . There are more sides to them, and that's about knowing and understanding my own everyday actions when I don't behave in the best manner."[77] She writes "to calm her racing thoughts and thumping pulse,"[78] and no matter what the other demands on her time, she makes sure that she writes in this kind of stream-of-conscious way as often as possible. Although she says she is not an artist, and she jokes about her lack of musical talent, she is very aware of the way her words appear on the page, and she likens writing words on the blank pages of her sketchbooks to mixing paints on a palette.[79]

And Woodson wants children to understand the value of writing. She believes that by telling their stories, children "validate their lives."[80]

She urges children and young adults to write letters, short stories, journal entries, and essays. Of herself, the author says, "If I couldn't write, I don't think I'd be able to live."[81] Woodson says that her friends describe her laughing easily, as working too much, as disliking paying full price for a bad movie, and as listening to music all the time. Shy around new people, she sometimes still feels too tall, feels her dreadlocked hair is perceived as weird, or that her nose is too big. But in her writing, Woodson has achieved a confidence and a personal style that allows her to create characters who get into our hearts and stay there, prodding us into dialogue with ourselves and our world by giving us new perspectives and events that can challenge our existing views. And this is, ultimately, Woodson's triumph. According to Dianne Hess, when Woodson received a phone call telling her that *From the Notebooks of Melanin Sun* had been named a Coretta Scott King Honor Book, the committee member who made the call offered her some advice: "You keep writing those controversial books."[82] What is remarkable is that Woodson is able to write so gracefully about controversial topics in ways that enlarge our sense of both self and "other"—and as a result, her works have been the center of remarkably little actual controversy.

Hess puts it well when she writes about her first encounters with Woodson's work. After reading the galleys of *Last Summer with Maizon*, Hess recalls, "I loved the way she was emerging as a new and unique African-American literary voice. She gave voice to a new time and a new generation in a way that had not been done before. She took people in situations that had always been thought of in certain rigid ways and presented them in new ways that broke through the stereotypes and rigid perceptions. She wrote about African-American girls in private schools and she wrote of African-American girls who helped troubled white girls. She wrote about gay characters who were interesting professionals that were not overcome by their angst over being gay. She wrote about people who never had to apologize for who they were."[83] Woodson's works help her readers understand that they, too, should not have to apologize for who they are.

Woodson says her advice for young people wrestling with their central sexual identity, or with issues of identity in general, is, "You shouldn't just take one word, you need to let yourself be more open than that. Let yourself be fearless—I don't mean not to deal with dangers in terms of things like AIDS and STDs—but I mean don't be afraid of what society is going to say. And I know that's hard to say and do because I mean people have to have some kind of foundation, some solid sense of self, and for someone who doesn't have that, it's hard to say don't worry about what society thinks. But I think it can be damaging if you're too externally focused. And I think in the tradition of "Live every day as if it were your last day," it's important to be kind to people and let yourself love. And those kinds of thoughts are what help keep me from just staying in a place that might be safer somehow." And having internalized that attitude of living each day is, in part, what allows Woodson to take risks and continue to grow as a writer.

Woodson said, in her Coretta Scott King acceptance speech, "I am grateful for young people—young people of African descent and children of all colors. I am grateful when I walk down the street and hear a young person laughing or singing or begging their mom for just a few more minutes outside. I am grateful for little kids in the schools I visit who touch my hair and gaze up at me, eager to know something and or someone different, curious and open and eager . . . to know."[84] Woodson's grandmother wanted her to be a teacher; in fact, after she got her Coretta Scott King Award, her grandmother hoped that someone would now give her a "real job." But writing is her real work. She says, "I hope readers learn about people other than themselves through literature—mine and others—just as I once learned from writers like Virginia Hamilton, James Baldwin, Mildren Taylor and Rosa Guy—writers who didn't know they were giving a young black girl from Brooklyn the message that she, too, could do this. They were teaching me the most important lesson—that even the grandest of things starts from a dream."[85]

Woodson is working on a new picture book, tentatively titled either *Show Way* or *When Soonie was Seven*, based on some of her own family history, which conveys that message of hope as achieved through family and history and story; it is a lovely, autobiographical piece written for her daughter that speaks eloquently about the power of literature to help us dream of new possibilities. Soonie was the name of her ancestor, a creator of folk art, who drew quilting maps to the north called "show way." The book is "a sort of history of black women, and moving from slavery and making folk pieces to writing books, so it's kind of autobiographical and kind of not," but it has been inspired by the author's desire for her daughter to know not only black history but her own particular family history and to know about the strong female role models in that family. It opens with the line "When Soonie's grandma was seven she was sold from the Virginia land to a plantation in North Carolina."[86] Without her parents, but armed with a needle and some thread and a piece of muslin, a gift from her mother, Soonie's grandma settled into her new life under the care of Big Mama, who told the slave children stories of other slave children "growing up and getting themselves free" (WSS, n.p.). Soonie's grandmother sewed the maps of their freedom roads onto the muslin. She had a daughter, who also learned to sew, and then that woman, Mathis May, had Soonie, born free in 1863, and she "loved that child up" (WSS, n.p.). They stayed on the land they had always inhabited, picking cotton and planting some crops of their own. It was a hard life, but a free life. At night, Soonie cut and sewed odd designs and unusual lines and made quilts called "Trail to the North," or "Show Way." As word of her talent spread, Soonie began earning money from those quilts, and she kept making them, not just to live but "to remember." Soonie then had a daughter of her own, Georgiana, who always had a book in her hand. She had two daughters, twins, whom she in turn "loved up." The one daughter grew up writing poems and sometimes turned them into songs; the other daughter stitched those melodies and words into quilts. And both grew up walking in protest marches against segregation laws. Then Ann had Jackie, who grew up reading like her grandmother and sewing like her mother and writing "the words that became the books that told the stories of many people's Show Ways" (WSS, n.p.). And as the book closes, Jackie has Toshi, to whom she whispers a story that begins, "Now Soonie was your great-great-grandma. And when Soonie's grandma was seven . . ." (WSS, n.p.).

Now Woodson herself gives her readers, children, young adults, teachers, librarians, and other adults, her own "show ways," which convey the power of having a dream and moving toward it. As Jacqueline Woodson continues to evolve, as her writing continues to explore complex issues, and as she continues to experiment with her use of language and form, there is no question that she already is, and will be, as her teacher said of her long ago, "the real thing."

Notes

1. Jacqueline Woodson and Chris Lynch, "The Rialto," in *The Color of Absence: Twelve Stories about Loss and Hope*, ed. James Howe (New York: Atheneum, 2001), 205.

2. Woodson and Lynch, 205.

3. Woodson and Lynch, 205–206.

4. Jacqueline Woodson, *If You Come Softly* (New York: Putnam, 1998). Hereafter cited as *If*.

5. Janice M. Del Negro, "Review of *If You Come Softly*," *Bulletin of the Center for Children's Books* 52, no. 2 (October 1998), 77.

6. Woodson, "Who Can Tell My Story?" 2.

7. Woodson, "Who Can Tell My Story?" 2.

8. Woodson, "Who Can Tell My Story?" 2.

9. Paulsen.

10. Paulsen.

11. Woodson, "Who Can Tell My Story?" 3.

12. Woodson, "Who Can Tell My Story?" 4.

13. Jacqueline Woodson, *Miracle's Boys* (New York: Penguin/Putnam, 2000). Herafter cited as *MB*.

14. Jacqueline Woodson, "Acceptance Speech for the Coretta Scott King Author Award," *School Library Journal* (August 2001), 58.

15. Woodson, "Acceptance Speech for the Coretta Scott King Author Award," 58.

16. S. E. Hinton, *The Outsiders* (New York: Viking, 1967).

17. Edward Sullivan, "Review of *Miracle's Boys*," *School Library Journal* 46, no. 5 (May 2000), 178.

18. Hazel Rochman, "Review of *Miracle's Boys*," *Booklist* 96, no. 12 (February 15, 2000), 1102–1103.

19. Janice M. Del Negro, "Review of *Miracle's Boys*," *Bulletin of the Center for Children's Books* 53, no. 9 (May, 2000), 342.

20. Jacqueline Woodson, *Autobiography of a Family Photo* (New York: Dutton, 1995). Hereafter cited as *Auto*.

21. Catherine Bush, "Review of *Autobiography of a Family Photo*," *New York Times Book Review* (February 25, 1995), 14.

22. Woodson, "Slipping Away," 59.

23. Jacqueline Woodson, "Tuesday, August 3," in *Afrekete: An Anthology of Black Lesbian Writing*, ed. Catherine E. McKinley and L. Joyce DeLaney (New York: Doubleday, 1995), 63.

24. Woodson, "Tuesday, August 3," 64.

25. Woodson, "Tuesday, August 3," 68.

26. Woodson, "Tuesday, August 3," 69.

27. Woodson, "Tuesday, August 3," 74.

28. Woodson, "What Has Been Done to Me," 81.

29. Woodson, "What Has Been Done to Me," 82.
30. Woodson, "What Has Been Done to Me," 84.
31. Woodson, "What Has Been Done to Me," 84.
32. Woodson, "What Has Been Done to Me," 87.
33. Jacqueline Woodson, "Thirteen," in *Queer 13: Lesbian and Gay Writers Recall Seventh Grade,* ed. Clifford Close (New York: Rob Weisbach/William Morrow, 1998), 258.
34. Woodson, "Thirteen," 258.
35. Woodson, "Thirteen," 260.
36. Woodson, "Thirteen," 260.
37. Woodson, "Thirteen," 261.
38. Jacqueline Woodson, "July Saturday," in *Places I Never Meant to Be: Original Stories by Censored Writers,* ed. Judy Blume (New York: Simon and Schuster Books for Young Readers, 1990), 77.
39. Woodson, "July Saturday," 78.
40. Michael Cart, "Preface," in *Tomorrowland: Stories about the Future,* ed. Michael Cart (New York: Scholastic, 1999), viii.
41. Cart, "Preface," viii–ix.
42. Woodson, "The Other Half of Me," 147.
43. Woodson, "The Other Half of Me," 147
44. Woodson, "The Other Half of Me," 150.
45. Woodson, "The Other Half of Me," 153.
46. Woodson, "The Other Half of Me," 155.
47. Woodson, "The Other Half of Me," 155.
48. Woodson, "The Other Half of Me," 156.
49. Jacqueline Woodson, "Beanie," in *Girls Got Game: Sport Stories and Poems,* ed. Sue Macy (New York: Henry Holt, 2001), 82.
50. Woodson, "Beanie," 82.
51. Woodson, "Beanie," 84.
52. Woodson, "Beanie," 84.
53. Woodson, "Beanie," 84.
54. Woodson, "Beanie," 89.
55. Woodson, "Beanie," 90.
56. Woodson, "Beanie," 90.
57. Jacqueline Woodson, "On Earth," in *I Believe in Water: Twelve Brushes with Religion,* ed. Marilyn Singe (New York: HarperCollins, 2000), 105.
58. Woodson, "On Earth," 104.
59. Woodson, "On Earth," 106.
60. Woodson, "On Earth," 112.

61. Woodson, "On Earth," 114.

62. Jacqueline Woodson, *We Had a Picnic This Sunday Past* (New York: Hyperion, 1997), n.p.

63. Jacqueline Woodson, *Sweet, Sweet Memory* (New York: Jump at the Sun—imprint of Hyperion, 2000). Hereafter cited as *SSM* (n.p.).

64. Jacqueline Woodson, *Our Gracie Aunt* (New York: Jump at the Sun—imprint of Hyperion, 2002), n.p.

65. Stephanie Zvirin, "Review of *Visiting Day*," *Booklist* 99 (November 1, 2002). Retrieved from www.ala.org/booklist/v99/no1/63Woodson.html on 16 December 2002. Keyword: Woodson, Jacqueline.

66. Hess.

67. Hess.

68. Jacqueline Woodson, *Visiting Day* (New York: Scholastic, 2002), n.p.

69. Hess.

70. Hess.

71. Jacqueline Woodson, *Martin Luther King, Jr., and His Birthday* (Englewood Cliffs, NJ: Silver Press, 1990), 6.

72. Jacqueline Woodson, *The Other Side* (New York: Putnam, 2001). Hereafter cited as *OS* (n.p.).

73. Janice M. Del Negro, "Review of *The Other Side*," *Bulletin of the Center for Children's Books* 54 no. 6 (February 2001), 211.

74. Woodson, "Going to My Room and Closing the Door," 61.

75. Woodson, "Going to My Room and Closing the Door," 61.

76. Woodson, "Going to My Room and Closing the Door," 61.

77. Woodson, "Going to My Room and Closing the Door," 61.

78. Woodson, "Going to My Room and Closing the Door," 64.

79. Woodson, "Going to My Room and Closing the Door," 62.

80. Woodson, "Going to My Room and Closing the Door," 64.

81. Woodson, "Going to My Room and Closing the Door," 62.

82. Hess.

83. Hess.

84. Woodson, "Acceptance Speech for the Coretta Scott King Author Award," 57.

85. Woodson, "Acceptance Speech for the Coretta Scott King Author Award," 58.

86. Jacqueline Woodson, *Show Way* or *When Soonie Was Seven*, unpublished manuscript sent to the author by e-mail on February 17, 2003. Hereafter cited as *WSS* (p.p.).

Selected Bibliography

Primary Sources

Young Adult Novels

Between Madison and Palmetto. New York: Delacorte, 1993. (Paperback Random House, 1995; Penguin, 2002).

The Book Chase. Illustrated by Steve Cieslawski. New York: Bantam, 1994. (Part of "The Ghostwriter Series," copyright by the Children's Television Network).

The Dear One. New York: Delacorte, 1991. (Paperback Random House, 2001).

From the Notebooks of Melanin Sun. New York: Scholastic, 1995. (Reprint by Scholastic, 1997).

The House You Pass on the Way. New York: Delacorte, 1997. (Paperback Random House, 1997).

Hush. New York: Putnam, 2002.

I Hadn't Meant to Tell You This. New York: Bantam/Doubleday/Dell Books for Young Readers, 1994. (Recorded Books, 1998; paperback Random House Children's Books, 1995).

If You Come Softly. New York: Putnam, 1998. (Paperback version Penguin, 2000).

Last Summer with Maizon. New York: Delacorte, 1990. (Paperback Penguin USA, 2000 and Random House Children's Publishing, 1995; new hardcover Random House, 2002).

Locomotion. New York: Putnam, 2003.

Maizon at Blue Hill. New York: Delacorte, 1992. (Paperback Random House, 1992 and Penguin USA, 2000; new hardcover Putnam, 2002).

Lena. New York: Delacorte, 1999. (Paperback by Random House Children's Publishing, 2000; Recorded Books, 2000; Bantam/Doubleday/Dell hardcover, 1999).

Miracle's Boys. New York: Putnam, 2000. (Also Thorndike Press large print, 2001; Listening Library, 2001; Books on Tape, 2001; paperback Penguin, 2001).

Children's Picture Books

Martin Luther King, Jr., and His Birthday. Illustrated by Floyd Cooper. Englewood Cliffs, NJ: Silver Press (division of Silver Burdett), 1990. (Paperback Silver Burdett, 1996).

Our Gracie Aunt. Illustrated by Jon J. Muth. New York: Jump at the Sun, Hyperion, 2002. (Also Disney Press, 2001; paperback Disney Press, 2001).

The Other Side. Illustrated by E. B. Lewis. New York: Putnam, 2001.

Show Way or *When Soonie Was Seven.* Unpublished. Sent to author via e-mail on February 13, 2003.

Sweet, Sweet Memory. Illustrated by Floyd Cooper. New York: Jump at the Sun, Hyperion Books, 2000. (Also by Disney, 2001; paperback Disney, 2001).

Visiting Day. New York: Scholastic, 2002.

We Had a Picnic This Sunday Past. Illustrated by Diane Greenseid. New York: Hyperion, 1997.

Adult Novels

Autobiography of a Family Photo. New York: Dutton, 1995. (Paperback New York: Penguin, 1996).

Anthologies

A Way out of No Way. Ed. Jacqueline Woodson. New York: Henry Holt, 1996. (Paperback New York: Ballantine, 1997).

Short Stories

"Beanie," in *Girls Got Game: Sport Stories and Poems.* Ed. Sue Macy. New York: Henry Holt, 2001, 82–91.

"July Saturday," in *Places I Never Meant to Be: Original Stories by Censored Writers.* Ed. Judy Blume. New York: Simon and Schuster Books for Young Readers, 1990, 73–81.

"Lorena," in *One Hot Second: Stories about Desire*. Ed. Cathy Young. New York: Alfred A. Knopf, 2002, 147–160.

"On Earth," in *I Believe in Water: Twelve Brushes with Religion*. Ed. Marilyn Singer. New York: HarperCollins, 2000, 101–114.

"The Other Half of Me," in *Tomorrowland: Stories about the Future*. Ed. Michael Cart. New York: Scholastic, 1999, 143–146.

"Slipping Away," in *Am I Blue? Coming out of the Silence*. Ed. Marion Dane Bauer. New York: HarperCollins, 1994, 49–61.

"Thirteen," in *Queer 13: Lesbian and Gay Writers Recall Seventh Grade*. Ed. Clifford Close. New York: Rob Weisbach/William Morrow, 1998, 257–261.

"Tuesday, August 3," in *Afrekete: An Anthology of Black Lesbian Writing*. Eds. Catherine E. McKinley and L. Joyce DeLaney. New York: Doubleday, 1995, 63–77.

"What Has Been Done to Me," in *Go the Way Your Blood Beats: An Anthology of Lesbian and Gay Fiction by African-American Writers*. Ed. Shawn Stewart Ruff. New York: Henry Holt, 1996, 81–87.

With Chris Lynch, "The Rialto," in *The Color of Absence: Twelve Stories about Loss and Hope*. Ed. James Howe. New York: Atheneum, 2001, 185–206.

Articles, Essays, and Commentaries

"Acceptance Speech for the Coretta Scott King Author Award," *School Library Journal* (August 2001): 57–58.

"Commentary: Division of Race and Wealth in the Development of New Neighborhoods," *National Public Radio Commentary* (August 26, 1999). Retrieved from www.npr.org on 9 September 2002. Keyword: Woodson, Jacqueline.

"Common Ground," *Essence* 30:1 (May 1999): 148–152. Academic Search Premier. 8 July 2002. Keyword: Woodson, Jacqueline.

"Going to My Room and Closing the Door," in *Speaking of Journals: Children's Book Writers Talk about Their Diaries, Notebooks, and Sketchbooks*. Ed. Paula W. Graham. Honesdale, PA: Boyds Mill Press, 1999, 60–65.

"The Last Waltz: Poetry and Politics," in *Analysis: Hour One—Eight Essayists Explain What They Have Learned during the Investigation, Impeachment, and Trial of the President*. Host Robert Siegel (February 19, 1999), *National Public Radio*. Retrieved from www.npr.org on 9 September 2002. Keyword: Woodson, Jacqueline.

"Profile: The Changing Face of America—Experience of Gay Teens," *National Public Radio Commentary* (May 30, 2001). Retrieved from www.npr.org on 9 September 2002. Keyword: Woodson, Jacqueline.

"Review of *Yo! Yes!*" *Horn Book Magazine* 76:6 (November/December 2000): 777.

"A Sign of Having Been Here," *Horn Book Magazine* 71:6 (November/ December 1995): 711–715. Academic Search Premier. 8 July 2002. Keyword: Woodson, Jacqueline.

"A Stolen Childhood," *Essence* 24:1 (May 1993): 81–85. Academic Search Premier. 8 July 2002. Keyword: Woodson, Jacqueline.

"Who Can Tell My Story?" *Horn Book Magazine* 74:1 (January/February 1998): 34–39: Academic Search Premier. 8 July 2002. Keyword: Woodson, Jacqueline.

"Witnessing," *National Public Radio Commentary* (November 15, 1999). Retrieved from www.npr.org on 9 September 2002. Keyword: Woodson, Jacqueline.

Films

Woodson, Jacqueline and Catherine Gund Saalfield. *Among Good Christian Peoples.* Frameline Release, 1991. 30 minutes. Retrieved from www.frameline.org/distribution at the Enoch Pratt Free Library, Baltimore, MD, 3-4170-06276-6861.

Secondary Sources

Articles

Aronson, Marc. "What Is YA and What Is Its Future: Voice, Form and Access —A Dialogue with Jacqueline Woodson," in *Exploding the Myths: The Truth about Teenagers and Reading.* Lanham, MD: Scarecrow, 2001, 129–238.

Bashir, Samiya A. "Tough Issues, Tender Minds," *Black Issues Book Review* 3:3 (May/June 2001): 78–79.

Brown, Jennifer. "From Outsider to Insider," *Publisher's Weekly* 249:6 (February 11, 2002): 156–157. 2. Academic Search Premier. 8 July 2002. Keyword: Woodson, Jacqueline.

Cart, Michael. "Preface," in *Tomorrowland: Stories about the Future.* Ed. Michael Cart. New York: Scholastic, 1999, vii–ix.

Hayne, Judith A. "Jacqueline Woodson," in *Writers for Young Adults: Supplement.* Ed. Ted Hipple. New York: Charles Scribner's Sons, 2000, 377–386.

Paylor, Diane R. "Bold Type: Jacqueline Woodson's 'Girl Stories,'" *Ms. Magazine* 5:3 (November/December 1994): 97.

Saalfield, Catherine. "Jacqueline Woodson," in *Contemporary Gay and Lesbian Writers of the United States: A Biocritical Resource Book.* Ed. Sandra Pollack. Westport, CT: Greenwood Press, 1993, 583–586.

"Jacqueline Woodson," in *Contemporary Authors: A Bibliographical Guide to Current Writers in Fiction, General Non-fiction, Poetry, Journalism, Drama, Motion Pictures, Television, and Other Fields, New Revision Series*, Vol. 8. Ed. Scott Peacock. Boston: Gale Group, 2000, 433–437.

"Jacqueline Woodson," in *Lesbian and Gay Voices: An Annotated Bibliography and Guide to Literature for Children and Young Adults.* Ed. Francis Ann Day. Westport, CT: Greenwood Press, 2000, 232–235.

"Jacqueline Woodson," Retrieved from www.randomhouse.com/teachers/authors/wood.htm on 4 September 2001, 5.

Book Reviews (Selected)

Autobiography of a Family Photo
Bush, Catherine. "Review of *Autobiography of a Family Photo*," *New York Times Book Review* (February 25, 1995): 14.

Between Madison and Palmetto
Graham, Marilyn Long. "Review of *Between Madison and Palmetto,*" *School Library Journal* 39 (November 1993) 111.

The Dear One
Fader, Ellen. "Review of *The Dear One*," *Horn Book Magazine* 67:6 (November/December 1991): 746.

Sutton, Roger. "Review of *The Dear One*," *Bulletin for the Center for Children's Books* 45 (September 1991): 26.

From the Notebooks of Melanin Sun
Knoth, Maeve Visner. "Review of *From the Notebooks of Melanin Sun*," *Horn Book Magazine* 71 (July/August 1995): 468.

Sutton, Roger. "Review of *From the Notebooks of Melanin Sun*," *Center for Children's Books* 48 (July/August 1995): 401.

The House You Pass on the Way
Bloom, Susan P. "Review of *The House You Pass on the Way*," *Horn Book Magazine* 73 (September/October 1997): 583.

Hush
McKanic, Arlene McKanic. "Staying Strong: A Black Family Endures—Review of *Hush*," Retrieved from www.bookpage/com/0204bp/children/hush.html on 10 November 2002. Keyword: Woodson, Jacqueline.

Rochman, Hazel. "Review of *Hush*," *Booklist* 98 (January 1 and 15, 2002). Retrieved from www.ala.org/booklist/v98/ja1/61woodson.html on 10 November 2002. Keyword: Jacqueline Woodson.

If You Come Softly
Del Negro, Janice M. "Review of *If You Come Softly*, " *Bulletin of the Center for Children's Books* 52:2 (October 1998): 77.

I Hadn't Meant to Tell You This
Polese, Carolyn. "Review of *I Hadn't Meant to Tell You This*," *School Library Journal* 40 (May 1994): 136.
Sutton, Roger. "Review of *I Hadn't Meant to Tell You This*," *Center for Children's Books* 47 (May 1994): 239.

Last Summer with Maizon
Brailsford, Karen. "Review of *Last Summer with Maizon*," *New York Times Book Review* (July 29 1990): 121.
Schuller, Susan. "Review of *Last Summer with Maizon*," *School Library Journal* 36 (November 1990): 121.
Sutton, Roger. "Review of *Last Summer with Maizon*," *Bulletin for the Center for Children's Books* 44 (October 1990): 49.

Miracle's Boys
Del Negro, Janice M. "Review of *Miracle's Boys*," *Bulletin of the Center for Children's Books* 53:9 (May 2000): 342.
Sullivan, Edward. "Review of *Miracle's Boys*," *School Library Journal* 46:5 (May 2000): 178.

The Other Side
Del Negro, Janice M. "Review of *The Other Side*," *Bulletin of the Center for Children's Books* 54:6 (February 2001): 211–212.

Visiting Day
Zvirin, Stephanie. "Review of *Visiting Day*," *Booklist* 99 (November 1, 2002). Retrieved from www.ala.org/booklist/v99/no1/63Woodson.html on 16 December 2002. Keyword: Woodson, Jacqueline.

Interviews
Stover, Lois. Interview via e-mail correspondence with Diane Hess, Scholastic Books, 17 December 2002.

Stover, Lois. Telephone interview with Wendy Lamb, Wendy Lamb Imprints —Random House Books for Children, 9 December 2002.

Stover, Lois. Telephone interview with Nancy Paulsen, president, Charles Putnam's Sons Books for Children, 16 September 2002.

Stover, Lois. Interview with Jacqueline Woodson. Brooklyn, New York, and via telephone, 27 September 2002 and 10 December 2002.

Index

environmental issues, 105–6, 111, 112–13; family, 19, 31, 33, 45, 71, 79–80, 98, 99, 118–19, 134, 143, 144, 145–48, 149, 158, 163–64, 165–66, 170–71; fire, 66, 158, 161, 162; first love, xii, 70, 91, 93, 105, 111, 121–22, 123, 132, 133, 134, 138, 150–51, 162–63; food, 71, 94, 98, 155, 157, 163; foreshadowing, 105, 132; friendship, 24, 32–33, 40, 53–54, 55, 59, 78–79, 83–84, 89, 92–93, 94, 97, 99, 108, 153, 154, 157, 158, 160; gang violence, 143; gay/lesbian relationships, 25, 27, 29, 32–33, 34, 107–8, 109–10, 116, 123–24, 125, 135, 154, 155, 162–163; homelessness and home, 47, 49–71, 89, 92, 147, 159, 164; hope and optimism, 149, 164, 169–70, 171; identity, 40, 42, 43, 87, 88, 92, 96, 121, 122, 125, 126, 133, 137, 143, 144, 159, 160, 169; invisibility, 6, 23, 29, 31, 37–40, 46, 61–62, 77, 141, 143, 144; language, 33–34, 39, 52, 59, 86, 104, 122, 124, 126, 127, 138; outsiders, 6, 7, 9, 33, 38, 46–47, 50, 69, 80, 104, 117, 119, 127, 141, 145, 153; parent–child relationships, 28, 39, 43–44, 45, 53, 54, 56, 59–60, 67, 76, 78, 95–96, 104–5, 106–7, 108–9, 110, 115, 133–34, 135, 138, 139, 144, 146, 152, 155, 158, 164, 165; prejudice and racial tension, 3, 36–37, 46, 50–51, 52, 55, 70, 84, 86–87, 93, 96, 106, 108, 113–14, 120, 132, 136, 137, 166; puberty, 35, 91, 94, 107, 119, 151, 160–61;

racial/ethnic boundaries and interracial relationships, 3, 9, 29, 36, 83, 86–87, 88, 93, 94, 97, 106, 113, 118–19, 120, 131, 132, 135, 136–37, 149, 150–51, 155; religion, 2–3, 39, 43–44, 69, 70, 80, 133, 141, 152, 158, 161–62, 163; role models, 19, 26, 27, 28, 34, 57, 62, 77, 82, 84, 91–92, 97, 99, 116, 126, 135, 142, 157; sexual abuse, 54, 58, 63, 151–52, 156; sexual identity, 9, 27, 103, 105–7, 120, 122–23, 126, 127, 135, 150, 151, 154, 155, 157, 158, 160; stereotypes, xii, 16, 24, 29, 33, 34, 37, 39, 55, 62, 63, 84, 96, 99, 106, 108, 113–14, 124–25, 148; strong girls, 19, 27, 40, 44, 45, 56, 61, 65, 87–88, 89, 91–92, 125, 153, 156, 158–63, 170; survival, 45, 61, 72, 151–52, 153, 170–71; value of sports and physical activity, 8, 40, 41, 42, 95, 133, 160–61; value of writing and the arts, 19, 24, 30–31, 32, 45, 55–57, 62, 66–72, 76–77, 97, 98, 104–5, 108, 118–19, 120, 122, 163, 168–69
"Thirteen," xvi, 157–58, 160
Tomorrowland, xvi, 17, 158
"A Tribute to Martin Luther King," 4–5
tripping, 6
"Tuesday, August Third," 154

Vermont College, 131
Vietnam, 5–6, 18, 149, 151–52, 153, 154–55, 160
Villarosa, Linda, 10
Visiting Day, xvi, 77–78, 164, 168
Voges, Liza, xiv, 10, 92

~

About the Author

Lois Thomas Stover is a former middle and high school teacher of English and drama. A graduate of the College of William and Mary, she earned an M.A.T. from the University of Vermont and an Ed.D. from the University of Virginia. Currently she chairs the Educational Studies Department at St. Mary's College of Maryland, where she teaches courses in children's and young adult literature and teaching methodology and supervises student teachers. A former president of the Assembly on Literature for Adolescents of the National Council of Teachers of English, she is the author of *Young Adult Literature: The Heart of the Middle School Curriculum*; *Presenting Phyllis Reynolds Naylor*; and numerous book chapters and articles on young adult literature. She also coedited the thirteenth edition of NCTE's annotated bibliography for high school readers, *Books for You*.